THE COMPLETE IDIOT'S GUIDE™ TO

Parenting a Preschooler and Toddler, Too

by Keith Boyd, M.D. and Kevin Osborn

alpha books

A Division of Macmillan General Reference,
A Simon and Schuster Macmillan Company
1633 Broadway, New York NY 10019-6705

Dedication

To our partners in parenting, Margie Sheridan Boyd and Susan Kiley, who guide and support our childrearing practices with their wisdom and love, and to our children, Jake, Megan, Ian, Charlie, Molly, and Sam, who taught us more than they know.

Copyright© 1997 by Keith Boyd, M.D. and Kevin Osborn

International Standard Book Number: 0-02-861733-9
Library of Congress Catalog Card Number: 97-070663

99 98 97   4   3   2   1

Interpretation of the printing code: the rightmost number of the first series of numbers is the year of the book's printing; the rightmost number of the second series of numbers is the number of the book's printing. For example, a printing code of 97-1 shows that the first printing occurred in 1997.

Printed in the United States of America

Managing Editor
Michael Cunningham

Development Editor
Jennifer Perillo

Production Editor
Linda Seifert

Copy Editor
Patricia A. Solberg

Illustrator
Judd Winick

Designer
Glenn Larsen

Cover Designer
Mike Freeland

Indexer
Kevin Fulcher

Production Team
Angela Calvert
Linda Knose
Daniela Raderstorf
Susan Van Ness
Megan Wade
Maureen West

Contents at a Glance

Contents

Foreword

"You know more than you think you do," Dr. Spock told parents in 1945. And indeed that famous piece of advice is true. But few parents believe it. The recurring theme of parenting is, "Am I doing the right thing?"

Our lack of self-confidence stems from many sources. On the one hand, grandparents and other friends and relatives who used to be around to provide help and advice are no longer available. With many women working outside of their homes now it's harder to build a network of other parents to compare notes with and to validate our experience. And, as our children face a more complex and difficult world, there's plenty of lip service but not a lot of practical support given to families.

On the other hand, we are deluged with "expert advice" coming from every media source, from magazines to TV talk shows to the Internet. New research on brain development, emotional intelligence, child safety, and nutrition seem to be reported every day. It is no wonder that as we try to sift through and absorb all this information, we become even less sure about what we should be doing for and with our children. Our uncertainties are compounded by the hard-to-interpret feedback we get as parents and the fact that the final verdict on how we did our job won't be in for many years.

Given all of this, I think most of us would agree with Neil Kurshan that parenting is "at once the most overwhelmingly frustrating and exasperating task and the most joyous and rewarding experience."

These words are particularly applicable to the toddler and preschool years covered in this book. Most parents, even while they are struggling with temper tantrums or a difficult adjustment to child care, are heard to say at some point, "I wish he wouldn't get any older. He's so adorable, I want him to stay just as he is now."

Interestingly, the labels we use for these two stages describe more than just their characteristics, they also tell us how significant the shift is from one to the other. To toddle is to walk, to become mobile, to venture out independently. "While toddler refers to physical development," as Dr. Lawrence Kutner points out, "preschooler refers to a social and intellectual activity: Going to school." As our infants turn into toddlers and then to preschoolers, it becomes apparent to parents that they are indeed dealing with all four dimensions of their children's development—the physical, social, emotional, and intellectual—and that these are not separate areas, but that they interact with one another in countless ways.

The Complete Idiot's Guide to Parenting a Preschooler and Toddler, Too sets the stage for this understanding both in its organization and in its comprehensive approach. Within each age range, for example, timely information on safety, health, and nutrition is woven through the advice on handling issues such as sleep routines and language development.

Parents will appreciate this book's user-friendly format. It presents a wealth of valuable information without getting bogged down with theoretical data or relying on glib "pop psychology." The most common questions are answered clearly and concisely with down-to-earth examples and solid tips on what to do and why to do it. By looking at each situation from the perspective of the child as well as the adult, the authors have added a richness and depth of understanding not often found in parent manuals.

I like this advice from the venerable early childhood educator James Hymes Jr.: "Fortunately children do not need 'perfect' parents. They do need mothers and fathers who will think on their feet and who will be thoughtful about what they have done. They do need parents who can be flexible and who can use a variety of approaches to discipline."

Susan Ginsberg, Ed. D.

Susan Ginsberg is editor and publisher of the monthly newsletter *Work and Family Life: Balancing Job and Personal Responsibilities* and the author of *FAMILY WISDOM: The 2000 Most Important Things Ever Said About Parenting, Children, and Family Life* (Columbia University Press).

Introduction

Parents are the last people on earth who ought to have children. — Samuel Butler

Do you want to be a lawyer? You'll need a college and law degree first. Want to get a job as a truck driver? You'll need to go through a training and licensing program. Want to drive a car? First you have to pass a driving test and get a license. How about going fishing? You'll probably need a permit.

But hey, if you want to become a parent, anything goes. As many observers have commented through the years, any idiot can become a parent. Yet not every idiot knows what to do once he or she has a child.

Because you've been through the first year with your baby, you know how hard it can be. Juggling work and childcare; breastfeeding, introducing solid foods, and weaning; getting your child to sleep for more than three hours; and dealing with dirty diapers. These are just some of the challenges you have already faced. But the difficulties of parenting will become even more complicated as your child learns to walk and talk and think for herself.

So Now You Have a Toddler

No responsibility can be considered more important than properly caring for children. Yet despite its importance, parenting demands virtually no prerequisites in terms of education or experience. And unfortunately, children do not come with owner's manuals.

That's where *The Complete Idiot's Guide to Parenting a Preschooler and Toddler, Too* comes in. This book offers the essential knowledge and guidance that every parent needs. Think of it as an operator's manual for your child. Here you will find information on developmental stages from ages one to four, warnings about potential pitfalls and challenges that almost every parent faces, and discussions of thorny parenting issues. Here you also will find reassurance that whatever you and your child are going through, it is perfectly normal. Lots of parents have tackled the same problems you will encounter over the next four years. So you can do it, too.

Like most parents, of course, you want to be more than just a parent to your child; you want to be a good parent. *The Complete Idiot's Guide to Parenting a Preschooler and Toddler, Too* will help you accomplish this goal. Throughout the book you will find not only information on how your child is growing, but advice on how you can grow with your child. The book contains hundreds of easy-to-use strategies and practical tips that will help you handle the many challenges that invariably come with parenting toddlers and preschoolers. By the time you finish this book, you will be convinced that any idiot can not only parent a toddler or preschooler, but do a good job of it, too.

How This Book Is Organized

The Complete Idiot's Guide to Parenting a Preschooler and Toddler, Too aims to make parenting as fun, easy, and rewarding as possible for both you and your child. The book is divided into four parts, each addressing a different year in the life of your toddler or preschooler. In each part, you will find chapters on your child's physical, mental, and emotional development; on age-appropriate health and safety issues; and on making the most of your child's playtime.

In addition, each part has chapters that address specific challenges most often faced by parents during that year of their child's life. Of course, young children do not adhere to strict schedules of development. So your child may tackle some of these challenges a year earlier or a year later. For example, Chapter 9, which deals with toilet training, comes in Part 2 of the book because most children begin disposing of diapers between their second and third birthdays. But there's nothing to prevent you from reading ahead if your child starts earlier—or from referring back to it if he starts later.

Part 1, "The Early Toddler: 13–24 Months," covers typical development during your child's second year, answers health and safety questions, and gives advice on how to guide your child's learning through play. It also tells you how to make your home childproof and how best to set limits for your one-year-old. In addition, it offers advice on helping your child to get a good night's sleep and how to handle separations with grace, good humor, and minimal fuss.

Part 2, "The Terrific, Terrible Twos: 25–36 Months," tells you how your two-year-old will grow, but it also provides advice on toilet training, handling misbehavior, and taming tantrums. You will find chapters that help you encourage your child's development of social behavior and discourage the development of prejudice. In addition, the chapter on play has a special section on how to guide your child's television viewing.

Part 3, "A Real Person: The Three-Year-Old," will let you know what to expect in terms of your three-year-old's development. You will also find information and advice that will help you nurture good hygienic and dental habits—and break bad habits. Special chapters will help you smooth the way for your child to make friends and accept the birth of siblings.

Part 4, "A Declaration of Independence: The Four-Year-Old," offers a guide to perhaps the most difficult of the preschool and toddler years. In this part, you will find pointers on nurturing personal responsibility: on teaching your child to keep himself safe and on furthering your child's development of a sense of conscience. In addition, you will find chapters that will help you answer your child's questions about sex and death, introduce your child to the computer, and prepare her for the start of school.

Extras

In this book, you will find information and easy-to-use advice and guidance on some of the thornier issues involved in day-to-day parenting. You also will notice a generous sampling of childrearing tips, words of wisdom, and health and safety warnings—all easy to spot with the following icons:

Kid Stuff

These amusing or enlightening anecdotes about parents and children—some famous and some not-so-famous—offer concrete illustrations of specific childrearing issues.

Childproofing

These words of warning help you protect your child's health and safety. They alert you to common day-to-day hazards, offer medical information and advice, or point to situations in which you'll need to consult your pediatrician.

Q-Tip

These special tips let you know how you can stimulate your child's development, make things easier on yourself and your child, save time or money, and have fun with your child.

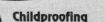

Fairy Tales

Here you will find entertaining bits of folklore and superstitions regarding young children or childrearing.

Baby Talk

Here you will find witty and/or wise observations on toddlers, pre-schoolers, and parents.

Special Thanks from the Publisher to the Technical Reviewer

The Complete Idiot's Guide to Parenting a Preschooler and Toddler, Too was reviewed by a pediatrician who not only checked the technical accuracy of what you'll learn in this book, but also provided valuable insight to help ensure that this book tells you everything you need to know to raise a happy, healthy preschooler.

Our special thanks are extended to Dr. Beth Volin. Dr. Volin is a 1979 graduate of Northwestern University Medical School and an Assistant Professor of Pediatrics at Rush Medical College in Chicago. She spent ten years in private practice before assuming her current position as Medical Director of the Pediatric Care Group at Rush. She is the mother of two school-aged children.

Trademarks

All terms mentioned in this book that are known to be or are suspected of being trademarks or service marks have been appropriately capitalized. Alpha Books and Macmillan General Reference cannot attest to the accuracy of this information. Use of a term in this book should not be regarded as affecting the validity of any trademark or service mark. Q-TIPS is a registered trademark of Chesebrough-Ponds, Inc.

Acknowledgments

Special thanks are in order. This book would never have come together without Richard Parks, who first recognized the merit in the idea; Barbara Osborn, who helped us appreciate the impact of television on our children; and Jennifer Perillo, Nancy Mikhail, and Linda Seifert, who provided keen editorial guidance that helped shape the final manuscript. Our partners in parenting, Susan Kiley and Margie Sheridan Boyd, deserve our undying gratitude, appreciation, and love. Finally, we'd like to thank those who made perhaps the greatest contribution to this book, our children: Jake, Megan, Ian, Charlie, Molly, and Sam. Thanks, kids.

Part 1
The Early Toddler: 13–24 Months

Now that you've made it through the first year with your baby, the fun really begins. Not that the first year wasn't fun, but now you can look forward to such joys as your child's first steps (and first falls) and your child's first words (unintelligible though they may be).

Up until now, your child has been fairly well-contained. Even as a crawler, your baby probably didn't get into too much mischief. Now your baby will be into everything. So take care, have fun, and don't forget to try to get a good night's sleep at least once every six months.

Chapter 1

Walk the Walk and Talk the Talk

In This Chapter

➤ Your toddler's development, from first steps to walking and running

➤ Your toddler's first words and language development

➤ How to talk to your toddler

➤ Handling your toddler's new independence

The amount of physical and mental development your child will undergo during his second year is truly astonishing. On his first birthday, your baby was still a baby, but over the next twelve months, your baby will undergo an incredible metamorphosis. He will emerge a fully formed child. Your child will go where he wants to go, speak his own mind, and soak up information faster than your computer's hard drive.

The most exciting and momentous developments of the second year center around walking and talking. Oh, sure, your baby may have begun walking and talking a little before his first birthday. But in no time at all, those few tentative steps will give way to nonstop walking, running, and climbing. And the trickle of intelligible words that your baby may have mastered at one will surge into a tidal wave by the time he is two.

Going Mobile

By your baby's first birthday, she had no doubt acquired some degree of mobility. At nine or ten months, your baby probably started to crawl (although some babies skip crawling altogether). A month or two later, she may have started to cruise: to stand and inch along the edge of a piece of furniture or other support. Your baby may have even taken her first few steps. Most children, however, do not take their first steps before their first birthday.

Standing Up for Herself

Your child's first steps are actually the final stage of a progression that started when she was about six months old. That's when the muscles in your baby's lower body began a period of rapid development. As your baby's strength and balance improved, she picked up new skills that paved the way for walking. To walk, your baby first needed to develop the following abilities:

➤ standing with support (5–8 months);

➤ cruising (9–13 months); and

➤ standing on her own (9–14 months).

Childproofing
A baby who can pull himself to standing often does so first by using the railing on the side of his crib. If you don't want your baby to make a headfirst dive to the floor, this is a good time to lower the mattress in his crib.

Only after mastering these skills can your baby begin to walk (usually around 10 to 16 months).

Keep in mind that all the ages listed here—and elsewhere in discussing child development—are approximate. Just because your child doesn't walk until 16 months while your best friend's baby walked at 10 months does not mean that your baby is in any way backward. Every baby— yours included—develops at his or her own individual pace. The age at which your child begins walking does not have any known correlation with intelligence, talent, or future abilities.

Cruising

Because some babies don't begin to cruise until after their first birthday, let's start there. Soon after learning how to use a chair, table, or couch to pull himself up to a standing position, your baby will start using these supports to increase his mobility. Your baby will move along the chair or table edge, using sideways shuffling steps. First he will slide both hands forward, then move his lead leg, and finally catch up by sliding the trailing leg.

At this point, your baby still cannot balance well when standing. He still feels insecure and will not remove either hand from the support for any reason.

Even though your baby still clings to the support with both hands, it won't be long before he lifts that trail leg. This is a huge developmental step. If only for a moment, your baby will be supporting himself on one foot—something he must learn to do before he can walk.

As your baby gains confidence in cruising, he'll take another big step. Your baby will actually let go of his precious support with one hand. He will begin moving hand over hand along the edge. As his coordination of hands and feet grows, your baby will sometimes support all of his weight with just one hand and one foot.

Now your baby is really on the move. With increasing confidence, your baby will actually reach out for another piece of furniture for support. Your baby does know his limits. He will not release the supporting hand unless he can grasp the second support. But given enough low, solid furniture placed close enough together so that he can hold on to two supports at the same time, your baby will quickly be able to remain on his feet while moving from couch to table to chair all the way around a room.

> **Q-Tip**
> To accommodate and encourage your child's ability to cruise, you may want to move some of your low, solid furniture closer together.

After one or two months of cruising, your baby will need just one hand for support. He'll use the other hand, not just to move to another piece of furniture, but to reach for a toy as well. When particularly absorbed, your baby may even let go with both hands and, without realizing it, balance without support. A great trick—but unfortunately not one that he can sustain or repeat on demand. After just a few seconds, he will sink down to his bottom or clutch at the support again.

After this accidental discovery that he can stand on his own two feet, your baby will become increasingly bold. He can now cross gaps between furniture that slightly exceed his arm span. You can encourage this development by repositioning the furniture to create larger gaps for your baby to cross. You don't want to create a chasm as imposing as the Grand Canyon—

> **Q-Tip**
> After your baby has begun crossing small gaps between furniture, it's time to start playing Come to Mommy or Come to Daddy. When he's standing and holding on to a support, sit one or two steps out of his reach. Then call him or entice him with a toy. Be ready to catch him when he walks or stumbles toward you. As soon as your child reaches you—or even almost reaches you—give him a big hug and heap on the praise.

just a few inches will do at first. Your child will get as close to the second support as possible, then release the first support and pitch toward the second.

First Steps

At this stage, your baby is almost ready to stand (on purpose) and start taking her first wobbly steps. For some time, your baby will still depend on furniture—or your legs—for support while standing. But if she sees something she wants or needs, your baby will soon take two or three steps to get it.

Be patient. Your baby may not be as focused on walking by herself as you are. Remember, during this same period, she's also learning language, exploring properties of her world, and embarking on dozens of new discoveries. Don't rush your baby through these important developmental steps by constantly pressing her to walk. Let her have fun with her new cruising abilities and enjoy the other aspects of her development as well.

She needs to dictate her own pace. As long as she can stand, she will walk in her own sweet time. And for many babies, these first steps won't take place until around 14 to 16 months.

When your baby does take her first steps, you will witness a miraculous transformation. No longer a baby, your child is now a toddler. Early walkers truly do toddle. They keep their feet wide apart. They tend to walk bowlegged. They spread their arms out wide and hold them high to maintain their balance. They stick their stomachs out so that their belly buttons always lead the way. It is truly a sight to behold.

Watch out now! Your toddler's on the move.

Q-Tip
You can help your toddler get the feel of walking by holding both her hands and walking behind her. Although you will find this hard on your back if you do it a lot—and it really won't help develop your child's ability to walk on her own—your toddler will love it.

Childproofing
Don't worry if your baby's walking or pre-walking abilities appear to regress. Especially after an illness that keeps her in bed or in your arms for several days—or perhaps after the birth of a sibling—your baby may forget some of what she has learned. Such regression is perfectly normal and only temporary. Within a few days, she will relearn any skills she may have forgotten.

Walking and Running

For several more months, your child will probably crawl more than he walks. Crawling is much more efficient to get from place to place than early toddling. Because he's had months of experience, crawling is easier and much, much faster than toddling. And crawling—unlike walking—allows your child to bring a favorite toy, book, or spoon along with him.

You no doubt find it easier to carry something when you're standing rather than on your hands and knees, but your baby doesn't. He can drag almost anything along with him while crawling. But when your early toddler is walking, he can't do anything else. Look at the strain (mixed with joy) in your child's face. He needs to pour every ounce of his concentration into taking those few steps.

Yet progress comes fast not long after those first toddling steps. Within a few months, your child may be able to get from sitting to standing without using a support. Around the same time—17 or 18 months—he will learn to climb and to stop, stoop, and pick up some treasure from the floor. By around 21 months, your child will tuck in his wings; he no longer needs to spread out his arms for balance while walking. By his second birthday, your baby will have become quite skilled at walking. Most of the time, he can go in the direction he wants and can now usually stop without pitching forward onto the floor. He may even have learned to walk backward!

In the months just before or after his second birthday, your toddler will start to run. Your toddler on the run is like a person plummeting from a skyscraper who shouts, "The fall is easy. It's the landing I'm worried about." For a toddler, taking off is no problem. In fact, as soon as you sit down, he may dart off. But he will probably have trouble making turns or stopping suddenly. Because you can't prevent every fall, do what you can to soften the landing. Carpets, rugs, and grass are all fine surfaces for children to practice running. Hardwood or linoleum floors and sidewalks pose a greater danger of bumps, bruises, and scrapes. (See, there's a good reason why your mother never let you run on the sidewalk!)

Q-Tip
Don't feel impelled to put your child in shoes just because he's started to walk. Letting your toddler wander about the house in bare feet will help him improve his balance, develop his arches, and strengthen his ankles.

If your toddler's feet are cold, try slipper socks with nonskid soles. (Regular socks can be treacherous on a hard floor, while shoes encourage relaxation of the foot muscles and walking flatfooted.)

Childproofing
Many of the most serious accidents suffered by toddlers occur at the homes of others. You cannot expect your friends without children to have childproofed their homes as thoroughly as you have (if at all). Common hazards include open electrical outlets, accessible cleaning supplies, and medicine left on night tables. So exercise extreme caution whenever you visit someone else's home.

Where Do You Think You're Going?

One frustrating aspect of early toddlers—especially to parents who don't understand the motivation behind it—is their apparent contrariness about walking. When you want to walk, your toddler doesn't, but as soon as you stop and settle down somewhere, that's when she decides to scoot away.

Contrary to appearances, however, your toddler is not trying to give you a hard time or drive you crazy. (That won't come for another dozen years or so.) She simply needs you to be settled in one place before she feels secure enough to venture off on her own. A toddler is like a homing pigeon—and you're the rooftop that serves as home base. With you securely in place, your toddler will wander away from you and then come back. Even if her back is turned, she knows where you are and how to get back to you. (Actually, if you move, even to a place where your child can still see you, it will throw her off. She may freeze in place and break into tears.)

When you want to go, however, that's when your toddler will suddenly decide to stop walking. She'll raise her arms up toward you and plead with you, "Carry me!" Your child is not being "lazy" or "unwilling" to cooperate. She simply cannot keep up with you when you are walking—a fact that makes her feel extremely insecure.

Your toddler fears separation from you—losing you—more than anything else in the world. She *needs* to stay close to you, but she can't do it by walking next to you or by following you. That's why your toddler stops dead in her tracks and wants you to carry her whenever you take her hand and try to walk. She can't manage any other way—and won't for another two years. Don't bother wasting energy by getting angry at your child for "not cooperating." Just remember to bring a stroller with you long after your baby has started walking.

Childproofing

Your baby needs constant supervision throughout the second year. Your child is not only mobile now, but also full of curiosity and wonder. So if you leave your crawler or toddler alone in a room—even just for a minute to answer the phone or get yourself a glass of water—she can quickly get into trouble. She'll empty out your rack of CDs or videos and somehow remove each one from its case. She'll dump wastepaper baskets. She'll pull things down from tables and other surfaces. So keep an eye on the scamp.

First Words

By your baby's first birthday, he may speak a handful of intelligible words: not necessarily the words used by adults, but words that you recognize as having a specific meaning. But most "talk" at twelve months is still babbling. Your child is practicing different sounds, rhythms, and intonations of speech. During the second year, however, especially the second half of the second year, language development really picks up.

Your baby learns language by listening to you—and others—use it. And though your baby certainly doesn't understand everything you say, he no doubt picks up glimmers of meaning here and there. If you speak to your baby a lot, he will understand many words before he utters anything recognizable. Indeed, by the time your baby speaks a single word or two, he will probably understand dozens of others.

This gap between your child's understanding and his ability to verbalize will continue throughout the preschool years. Your child will understand much more than he can put into words himself. This comparatively deeper understanding paves the way for verbalization. In terms of communication, it matters little that your baby can echo the sound of a word unless he understands—and you understand—what he's saying. Although experiments with making sounds are an essential part of language development, parroting is not really language; any tape recorder can do it.

Although many children do speak their first words around the tenth or eleventh month, don't worry if your baby hasn't spoken during the first year. Some babies don't speak first words until their fourteenth or fifteenth months.

Q-Tip

Try to get in the habit of providing your baby with a narrative of her life. Whenever she's alert, tell her what you are doing. "Okay, I'm going to change your diaper now. First we have to take off your pants...." Also describe to her what she is doing. "Look at you! Standing up and holding your rattle. Can you shake it and make some music? Good!" Your talking will hold your baby's interest, help her polish her social skills, further her understanding of words, and lay the groundwork for learning to speak.

Childproofing

If you have any concerns about your toddler's speech development, be sure to discuss them with your pediatrician.

What Is Your Baby Talking About?

With your baby's first word, she will "name" an object. Babies (just in case you didn't notice this during the first year) are totally self-centered. So when your child first speaks, she will begin by naming the objects that are most important to her: the people and things that excite her, please her, or make her happy. Like a latter-day Adam, your child will set out to name the objects in her world.

The first few dozen words will refer to you and other favorite people, favorite toys or other objects, and favorite foods. Because they refer to objects that are visible and tangible, your baby's first words will consist almost entirely of common nouns and proper nouns: "Mama," "Dada," "doggie," "shoe," "diaper," "spoon," "cup," or "apple," for example.

You may have noticed that when your child babbled during her first year, she did so only when she was happy. When she was sad or angry, she cried. The same will be true of your baby's first words—at least for a while. Words will initially refer only to things your child loves, and she will use them only when she's happy. So it won't be a whining, "Mamaaaa!" (Translation: "Mama, come here right now, I need you badly.") Rather, it will be a sing-song, "Maaamaaa!" (Translation: "Mama, I'm so glad you're here.")

Unfortunately, your baby's first words will be spoken in a foreign language—at least foreign to you. A bottle may be a "pala"; a rattle may be a "gib." What will make it even more difficult is that one-year-old children do not see consistency of meaning as a virtue. The bottle that was "pala" last week may be "gama" today. The rattle may now be a "mim." Within a few weeks, however, these names will become consistent: A mim is a mim is a mim (apologies to Gertrude Stein).

It should not matter that your baby is not calling a spade a spade—or a bottle a bottle. If you can understand what your baby means by her vocal sounds, then that's language! She has communicated an idea to you using the sound of her voice alone.

You might expect a steady stream of words once your baby has spoken her first. But actually, your child will pick up new words slowly for several more months. Until around 20 months, she will learn no more than a few new words a month. This will give your child a vocabulary of perhaps 30 or 40 words. These consist primarily of nouns and such simple phrases as "hi," "bye bye," "night night," and even—bless her gracious soul—"thank you." But her vocabulary also will probably include two milestones of personality development: "no!" and "mine!"

At around 20 months, your toddler's vocabulary will begin to increase dramatically. She may pick up a new word almost every day. Naturally enough, your child's vocabulary will still be centered on the things most important to her: her body parts, her crib, her toys, and other objects in her room.

No More Baby Talk

If you want to help your one-year-old begin to master the nuances of a difficult language and learn to speak, you really have to do only two things: talk to your child and listen to him.

First, talk to your child one-on-one. He will learn much more from direct conversation than he will by trying to follow a conversation that doesn't include him.

Because your baby knows you best, he will learn language more quickly from you, his primary caretaker(s), than from anyone else. He's learned to recognize the way you speak: your tones, your inflections, and your facial expressions. So talk naturally and clearly around your child and to your child.

Your baby also will need your help as a translator. This means more than just telling others what he said; it means telling *him* what someone else is saying. Certainly you will understand his fledgling attempts to verbalize better than anyone else. But remember too, that your child will understand your speech much better than that of others. So help interpret what other people try to tell your child.

Q-Tip
Picture books and simple storybooks can also help increase your toddler's vocabulary and understanding of language.

When you talk to your one-year-old, stick to the present as much as possible. Your baby's memory is not yet his strong suit. In fact, your one-year-old has little or no ability to understand the concept of either the past or the future. Talking about what's happening right now ("Wow! An airplane. Look up in the sky, Sam. It's an airplane.") allows your child to form meaningful connections between what he's seeing, hearing, or touching and what you're saying. Making connections between words and simultaneous perceptions or actions will give your baby a deeper understanding of language.

Make a point of referring to things by their names as often as possible. Use nouns (bottle, car, mama, daddy, doll, cup, nose) and try to avoid the use of pronouns. The indefinite and continually changing meaning of a pronoun confuses infants. "It" is probably one of the most used words in the English language, but think of what must be going through your one-year-old's brain as he struggles to understand what that pronoun means: Hmmm, "it" means a ball now; but a minute ago "it" meant the spoon; and two minutes ago, "it" meant a rattle. Or "they" are the books, but I thought "they" were grandma and grandpa.

Personal pronouns may be even more confusing. To a listener, hearing "you" means me and hearing "I" means you. But "I" also means your partner, who said it just a few minutes ago. And "you" also means your partner, because your child overheard you talking to your partner by that name earlier. (This confusion may become apparent when your child actually starts using these pronouns. Many toddlers reverse the two terms, speaking of their things as "yours" and your things as "my" or "mine.")

So use nouns and names instead of pronouns. "Mama's looking for Ian's spoon" will mean much more to your child than "Where is it?" or even "Where is your spoon?"

Talk in full sentences and your child will pick out the sounds he hears again and again: "How's Mikey's diaper? Is the diaper wet?" "Oh, your diaper is smelly!" "Time to change Mikey's diaper." "Now Daddy will take off the diaper." "Here's a new diaper." "Let's put on your diaper." "Now your diaper is all clean and snug." If he hears a word often enough, your baby will associate these sounds with whatever the occasions had in common. Remember, your baby is listening carefully to you, trying to make connections.

Listen Up

Because your child is listening so carefully to you, you owe it to her to do the same. When your baby actually starts trying to say words, listening to her means trying your best to understand what she's trying to communicate. If your child says, "goola," go to the general area in which she is looking (or even more helpfully, pointing). One by one, put your hand on or pick up everything that might be a goola. Repeat the word as you touch each object. Or pick your child up and let her show you what she means. Your baby might get frustrated if you don't get it right away, but she'll definitely let you know—with smiles and more goolas—when you find it. Reward your child with the goola (assuming it's safe)—and with praise for her inventiveness and her ability to communicate.

Also listen carefully to the *way* your one-year-old says a word. Until she can put more than one word together, your child will use single words to convey multiple meanings. Depending on her inflection, the word "Dada" can mean:

➤ "Yay! Dada's here!"

➤ "Where's Dada going?"

➤ "Dada, come back!"

➤ "Naughty Dada, you spilled the juice."

When you respond to your child's single-word communiques, try filling in the blanks for her. So if your child shouts, "Poon!", try to respond by saying, "Oh, did your spoon fall on the floor? Daddy will get it for you."

Some of your child's attempts to master new words will undoubtedly lead to endearing pronunciations. She may call graham crackers "Grammarary crackers" or refer to her bottom as her "bobbin." If so, adopt it if you like. It certainly won't hurt your child's language development to have a few insider words or phrases—just so long as you don't adopt your child's entire vocabulary as your own.

But while using adult words yourself, don't bother making a point of correcting the words your baby makes up or mispronounces. Your child is communicating with you in the best way she can. If you don't understand what she means, it will be a little frustrating for you—and torture for her. But rest assured, your child will try again later, perhaps with a new "word" that's a little clearer. If, however, you do understand what your one-year-old means, then she has met the essential criterion for communication. She has used "language" to convey to you her needs, desires, or observations, so why make a point of correcting her?

Certainly you can and should model the correct pronunciation of words. Say the correct word yourself in responding to your child. But don't worry if she can't quite manage it yet. If you are constantly correcting your one-year-old's vocabulary or pronunciation, you will intimidate her from making her own attempts. Besides, corrections are boring. She said what she wanted to say; you understood her, so what's the problem?

In time, your child will develop the "right" word—that is, the same one you use. But you can't force proper pronunciation or usage of language on your baby before she's ready for it. So respond to the words you do understand and try to find out what your baby means with the words you don't understand. Your baby will be delighted if you make this effort.

> **Childproofing**
> Don't worry too much if your toddler seems to have a speech impediment. The lisping or slurring of letters is common during the first years of spoken language. They will probably disappear as your child's fluency improves. In any case, these apparent impediments are no cause for concern at this early age.

First Sentences

As your child's vocabulary increases toward the end of his second year, he will start to put two words together to form simple sentences. Some typical examples demonstrate the toddler's concise expression of meaning (as well as the difficulty of the English language):

➤ "Mama comed."

➤ "Balloon boomed."

➤ "Eated Cheerio."

➤ "Mouses runned."

➤ "You sleeped." (He's talking about himself.)

➤ "Many childs."

Try to respond in the same way you did when your baby first started saying single words. Don't overcorrect pronunciation, usage, or grammar. Your child does not need your disapproval; he needs your encouragement. Try to appreciate the courage and intelligence behind his attempts to communicate. As your toddler learns to use more than one word to convey a more complete and sophisticated idea, understanding individual words will become easier. So try to figure out what your child means and respond appropriately, using complete sentences and proper grammar to fill in any words he may have left out. As long as you continue to model good grammar and speech patterns, he will pick them up and emulate them. In the meantime, do your best to accept his vocabulary and grammar.

Kid Stuff

Recognized genius Albert Einstein apparently did not say a word until well past his first birthday. As the story goes, his first words, spoken at the dinner table, were: "This soup is too hot!" His excited parents, wondering out loud why he had never spoken before, got their answer from Albert himself: "Because up to now, everything was fine."

The Seeds of Independence

Walking and talking serve as the seeds of independence. So during the second year, you will begin to see your toddler becoming her own person. She no longer needs your help to go from place to place—though she may still want it much of the time. If she sees something she wants, she can—and all too often will—go and get it herself.

In addition, experience has allowed your one-year-old to begin developing her own likes and dislikes regarding food, toys, clothes, people, and activities. And she's probably not at all shy about expressing her preferences. At some point during this year, she will shout "No!" for the first time. Get used to hearing this word. Over the next few years, you'll hear it a lot.

Saying no is an indispensable part of your toddler's separation from you. When your child says no to you for the first time, she's declaring her independence. She no longer sees herself as an extension of you and no longer wants you to exercise control over her—at least not all the time. At that particular moment, whatever you're trying to sell, she's no longer buying it.

Yet this first stand against you is by no means a full declaration of independence. Your toddler will still often cling to your legs, ask you to carry her, and cry when you try to leave her. Your child will toddle back and forth between independence and complete dependence, between wanting to do it herself and wanting your help, between rejecting and welcoming your control.

It's very difficult for your toddler to separate from you. She won't really like it when her desires conflict with yours. Most importantly, becoming her own person doesn't feel as safe as depending on you. For this reason, your toddler will separate in stages, continually moving forward and back, forward and back, and progressing, little by little, toward a degree of independence.

Where do you fit in? Try to stick to the middle of the road. Encourage your child to strike off on her own, but don't push her to do so. Protect your toddler, but don't overprotect her. Set reasonable, consistent limits, but don't hogtie her. Allow her to venture off, but keep her under your watchful eye. Let your child try new things, but if she stumbles, try to provide a soft landing for her. If you can guard your child's safety while allowing her independence, her increasing ability to do things by herself will provide the foundation for a strong ego and encourage her to take on new challenges.

Remember, just because your child now walks and talks does not mean she is truly independent. Your toddler relies on you for judgments regarding safety—a consideration that does not yet cross her mind. Your toddler also still depends entirely on you for emotional support, and she needs the help and comfort that you offer. Indeed, without the security that you provide, your toddler would never feel safe going off on her own.

Baby Talk
"Even when freshly washed and relieved of all obvious confections, children tend to be sticky."—Fran Lebowitz

You may not need to baby your child quite as much once she becomes a talking toddler. But don't expect her to be a grown up—or even a preschooler—just yet.

The Least You Need to Know

➤ Child development is not a race. Let your child take first steps and utter first words at her own pace.

➤ Just because your toddler can walk doesn't mean she'll always want to walk. Don't expect her to keep up with you.

➤ Talking and listening to your child will do more than anything else to advance her language skills.

➤ Your toddler needs more freedom, but also more security, than she did when she was a baby.

Chapter 2

Care and Feeding of Your Toddler

In This Chapter

➤ When should you call your pediatrician?

➤ Caring for a sick toddler

➤ First aid preparations

➤ Dental care and teething

In the coming years, you will need to monitor your child's health very carefully because toddlers are particularly susceptible to illness. Why? Because your child still has a relatively immature immune system, he is more vulnerable to infectious agents than you or an older child are, and more likely to become very ill when he does get sick.

Also, because your toddler is small and still physically immature, what would otherwise be a routine illness poses a greater threat to his health. Vomiting or diarrhea, for example, can dehydrate a young child more quickly than it would an older child or an adult. And colds will lead to breathing difficulties more often than they will in an adult.

In Sickness or in Health: Pediatric Visits

Although you will probably not see quite as much of your child's doctor in the second year as you did in the first, illness and well-baby visits will probably bring you to the pediatrician's office between half a dozen and a dozen times.

Well-Baby Visits

The timing of your child's well-baby visits is determined largely by the immunization schedule, as indicated by the following list. Most pediatricians today require four visits between the first and second birthdays:

Childproofing

Because no one knows how effectively the new varicella vaccine will provide long-term immunity, it may be better in the long run to contract chicken pox as a child and develop natural immunity to it than to get immunized against it. While relatively free of complications when contracted in childhood, chicken pox can be much more damaging to adults. So discuss this with your pediatrician before agreeing to give your child this vaccine.

➤ **12 months**   At your baby's first annual check-up, she may receive her MMR—a combined vaccine against measles, mumps, and rubella (German measles)—and an immunization against varicella (chicken pox).

➤ **15 months**   If she did not receive an MMR at 12 months, your child will get this shot now. She may also be given her fourth HiB immunization—a vaccine against *Hemophilus Influenza B* (a bacterial infection that can cause meningitis and other illnesses) and her fourth DPT or DTaP immunization—a combined vaccine against diphtheria, pertussis (whooping cough), and tetanus (lockjaw).

➤ **18 months**   If your child was not given HiB and DPT or DTaP immunizations at 15 months, she will receive them now. She also may be given her third oral polio vaccine or an injection against polio, though many doctors now give this third dose as early as six months.

➤ **Two years**   Finally, around your child's second birthday, you can bring her to a well-baby visit that doesn't involve getting a shot (although she may need a finger-prick blood test for lead). In fact, your toddler can now look forward to no more routine immunizations until her fourth, fifth, or sixth birthday.

Keep in mind that the vaccination schedule presented here may change by the time you read this. Recommendations regarding the polio, pertussis, and varicella vaccines, in particular, may change in the coming years as new vaccines or vaccine combinations are introduced and new research studies completed.

When to Call the Doctor

Besides well-baby visits you also will call on your pediatrician in some cases when your child gets ill. You may still feel unsure about when to call the pediatrician. You may worry that you'll bother your doctor over "nothing." On the other hand, if it is "something," you won't want to delay calling.

Try to allay these anxieties by observing the following rule:

> If your child's appearance, behavior, or symptoms of illness concern you, then make the phone call.

A doctor's assurance that your baby is well and normal can be just as important as her confirmation that your baby is sick. So feel free to call your pediatrician whenever you are concerned because your child looks or acts differently.

Certain conditions and symptoms do demand professional attention. In general, you should call your pediatrician if you observe any of the following in your toddler or preschooler:

➤ Disruptions in feeding patterns, especially a sudden loss of appetite

➤ Ingestion of any nonfood items

➤ Vomiting that differs in force or volume from normal spitting up

➤ Diarrhea, if it smells foul, shows blood or mucus, or is accompanied by a fever

➤ Constipation, if accompanied by vomiting

➤ Signs of blood in the urine or bowel movements

➤ Unusual listlessness or inactivity

➤ Convulsions (seizures)

➤ Marked changes in color or behavior

➤ Any unfamiliar or widespread rash

➤ Any burns that result in blisters

➤ Difficulty in breathing

Childproofing
With polio all but eradicated in the U.S., most cases that occur today result from the oral polio vaccine itself—a live but disabled form of the virus. Although the risk is small (about 1 in 3 million), some pediatricians now favor a polio injection—which uses a completely dead form of the virus and thus entails no risk. Your doctor may recommend using one or the other or a combination of the two as part of the series that begins at two months. Any of these recommendations is now acceptable.

Childproofing
In case of suspected poisoning, contact your local poison control center *immediately* if you cannot get through to your doctor right away. Do not wait for your doctor to return your call. Get help and information fast.

➤ A persistent cough

➤ Redness of the eyes or the discharge of pus from the eyes

➤ Discharge from the ears or ear pain (which you can recognize even in a preverbal baby by the constant turning of his head)

➤ Swelling or sinking of the remaining fontanel (A soft spot on the top of your baby's head where the bones of the skull are not yet joined; the fontanel will disappear when the bones fuse at around 24 months.)

Of course, just because your child's symptoms are not on this list doesn't mean you shouldn't call your doctor. No list could cover every conceivable condition that might warrant a call. So if you notice any major change in your child's behavior patterns—in terms of sleeping, eating, habits, or personality—which may indicate the onset of illness, call your pediatrician. You also should feel free to call your child's doctor whenever you have developmental or health concerns that cannot wait until the next scheduled visit. (Many doctors have regular call-in hours when you can address such concerns.)

When Your Child Is Sick

Whenever you call your pediatrician for a consultation about your child's illness, she will need certain information. You will need to describe the symptom(s), when the symptoms first appeared, the order in which they appeared, and their severity. Your doctor will also want to be reminded of your child's age, weight, and medical history, and any allergies. You may also want to have your pharmacy's telephone number on hand so that the doctor can call in a prescription, if necessary. If you have any specific questions, it might be a good idea to write them down before you call so that you don't hang up and then realize you forgot to ask an important question.

Take your child's temperature before you call and let your doctor know if your child has a fever and what kind of thermometer you used to take her temperature.

You can take your child's temperature in a variety of ways:

➤ In just over a minute, rectal thermometers yield the most accurate recording of your toddler's core temperature.

➤ You also can place a rectal thermometer under your child's armpit and get an accurate axillary temperature (usually about one to two degrees lower than the rectal temperature).

➤ If your child can keep her mouth closed, you can take her temperature orally with a digital thermometer. (Using a mercury thermometer for an oral reading is *never* a good idea at this age, because your toddler might bite down on it too hard and end up with a mouthful of glass and poisonous mercury.)

➤ Or you can shell out $60–75 to buy the latest home medical gadget: a tympanic thermometer that you place in your child's ear for just one second.

In many cases, of course, your doctor will want to see your child in person before making a diagnosis or writing a prescription. During an office visit, be sure to ask any questions that occur to you when your doctor diagnoses your child. If you think of others after you get home, call and ask them over the phone. It's important that you understand what your pediatrician has told you about your child's health and any medications she may have prescribed, so don't be afraid to ask questions. (If you have questions before you go, it's a good idea to write them down so that you won't forget to ask them after you reach the office.)

If your doctor prescribes any medication for your toddler's illness, for example, ask your pediatrician or pharmacist whether it should be given on a full or empty stomach. You'll also want to know how often and how long your child should take the medicine and how soon to expect improvement. You also may find it helpful to know about any possible side effects in advance.

Yuck! Giving Your Toddler Medicine

No matter what ails your child, you should avoid giving him any medication until you have sought the advice of your pediatrician. When your child does get sick, your doctor may prescribe antibiotics (which fight disease-causing bacteria) or other drugs which will help relieve symptoms and make your child more comfortable. Always check with your doctor's office not only regarding prescription drugs, but also for recommendations on acetaminophen and other pain relievers, cough syrups, or over-the-counter medications. Also consult your doctor before giving your child any medicine (for example, cough syrup) that may be left over from a previous illness.

> **Childproofing**
> Children should never be given aspirin because it increases their risk of contracting Reye's Syndrome—a potentially life-threatening condition.

With any medication, you should take care to give it to your child according to the directions of your doctor and pharmacist. Make a point of asking your doctor whether you can fit three or four daily doses of medication into your child's waking hours (first thing in the morning, last thing at night, and one or two spaced evenly in the course of the day).

With most medications, this schedule will be fine. But with a few, your doctor may insist that you maintain a strict schedule (every six or eight hours) to keep the level of medication in his bloodstream constant. (This probably means you'll need to wake your baby in the middle of the night for one dose.)

If your pediatrician has prescribed antibiotics, you must make a point of giving all of the medicine exactly as prescribed. Don't stop or stray from the medication schedule just because your child seems better (or because he doesn't like taking it). You may have eased the symptoms without finishing off the cause of the illness. If, after two or three days, you see little or no improvement, let your doctor know at once. Your child's illness may need to be reevaluated.

Believe it or not, some toddlers don't like to take medicine. Fortunately, you can take advantage of certain tricks of the trade to help convince your child to take his medicine:

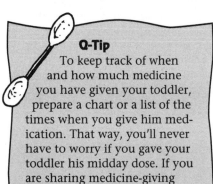

Q-Tip

To keep track of when and how much medicine you have given your toddler, prepare a chart or a list of the times when you give him medication. That way, you'll never have to worry if you gave your toddler his midday dose. If you are sharing medicine-giving duties with your partner or another caregiver, a chart can make it easier to coordinate your efforts. A chart also comes in handy if your child requires two or more medications that need to be taken on different schedules.

➤ When the time comes to give your toddler medicine, you might find it easiest if he sits in your lap. (Never give your child medicine while he's lying on his back, as this can cause him to choke.)

➤ Place the end of the syringe in a corner of your child's mouth. Aim the medicine inside the cheek, not in the front, where it can dribble out—or be spat out—and not way back in the throat, where it might cause your child to gag or choke.

➤ With older toddlers, you can try using a medicine spoon or medicine cup. However, we would recommend a syringe from the start. The calibration on syringes is much more consistent than that on medicine cups and spoons. In addition, spoons and cups make it easier for your child to spit the medicine out. Besides, most kids think it's fun to use a syringe—not just for medicine, but for juice and water, too.

➤ Don't start with apologies. Be straightforward and act as if you expect your child to take the medicine without question. If you raise doubts, you may unwittingly convince your toddler that he should resist.

➤ Have a glass of his favorite drink ready to wash away the nasty taste of the medicine.

➤ Mix the medicine with a spoonful of applesauce. Don't try to deceive your child by telling him it's just applesauce. One taste and he'll know you lied. Instead, tell him it will help make the medicine taste a little better. (Stick with just a spoonful of applesauce. The more applesauce you use, the more your child will have to eat to ensure that he takes all his medicine.)

➤ Pretend to give the medicine to a favorite stuffed animal first.

➤ Offer a reward for cooperation, something special—a favorite food, a favorite game, or a favorite book.

➤ If your child still won't open his mouth, you may have to hold his nose. Not only will this force your toddler to open his mouth, it also will minimize his ability to taste the medicine. Tell your child about this benefit.

➤ Switch to chewable pills or capsules. Many children can take these even during the first year.

Childproofing
Don't overreact to fever. Fever is actually a good thing, since it fights infections and bacterial growth. So don't feel obligated to give your child acetaminophen just because your child has a temperature of 100 degrees. Unless accompanied by discomfort (or shakes, chills, or cold sweats), a low-grade fever (under 102 degrees) does not necessarily need to be treated at all.

If your child won't take pills or capsules:

➤ Crush the pills into a powder and stir the powder into a spoonful of applesauce.

➤ Sink a pill inside a small, overripe piece of banana and ask your toddler to swallow it without chewing.

➤ Wet the capsule to make it easier for your child to slide it down his throat.

In Case of Emergency: First Aid for Toddlers

The toddler years could be called the first-aid years. Your baby's rapidly increasing mobility will give her many more chances to injure herself. So while you may have needed little more in the way of a first-aid kit than a thermometer, a medicine dropper, a bottle of acetaminophen drops, and syrup of ipecac during your baby's first year, now's the time to stock up on adhesive bandages, cotton balls, tweezers, and calamine lotion. After all, it's better to have these supplies long before you need them than not have them when your child has an accident or medical emergency.

If you have not yet done so, you'll need to put together a complete first-aid kit. Although you may not need all of these items, you will certainly need most of them as your child begins scooting around the house, looking for new and dangerous places to go and things to explore.

The following First-Aid Checklist lists the items you may need some time in the next year or two:

First-Aid Checklist

____ Acetaminophen (Tylenol or another brand), in liquid, chewable, or suppository form. (Children should not be given aspirin or anything containing aspirin and take special care to follow your pediatrician's instructions regarding dosage and frequency.)

____ Adhesive bandages of various sizes (for cuts and scrapes)

____ Adhesive tape (for holding nonstick bandages in place)

____ Antibacterial first aid cream

____ Antiseptic liquid soap (for washing your own hands before and after administering first aid)

____ Calamine lotion or other soothing lotion (for cooling the skin and reducing itching from sunburn or rashes)

____ Calibrated medicine dropper, spoon, or syringe

____ Cotton balls

____ Family medical guide (this isn't it)

____ Ice pack (to reduce aching and swelling)

____ Nonstick bandages (1-2") (for larger wounds)

____ Rectal thermometer (An expensive tympanic thermometer is far quicker and easier to use, but it may not be as accurate. So even if you decide to spring for a tympanic thermometer, you should probably get a rectal one too.)

____ Scissors (for cutting bandages, gauze, and tape)

____ Spray for relieving the pain of bee stings and insect bites

____ Sterile gauze or gauze pads

____ Syrup of ipecac (to be used only under the explicit instructions of your doctor or poison control center to induce vomiting in case of poisoning)

____ Topical pain reliever for teething (herbal or medicinal)

____ Tweezers and needles (for removing splinters)

Be Prepared: Sign Up for Infant and Child CPR

If your child chokes or stops breathing, your knowledge of cardiopulmonary resuscitation (CPR) could make the difference that saves his life. So if you haven't done so (and you really should have), consider taking a course in CPR as soon as possible. To find a course, consult your local chapter of the American Red Cross, or the American Heart Association. Local schools and hospitals, parenting organizations, or adult education programs may offer CPR courses in your community.

It would be a disservice to describe in detail, in this book, the CPR techniques used to restore breathing to an infant or child. If the occasion arises when you need to apply infant or child CPR, you'll need to know immediately what you should do. You won't have time to thumb frantically through the pages of this or any other book.

The only way for you to be truly certain that you know how to perform CPR on your child is to take a CPR course. CPR instructors will not only show you what to do, but provide you with the much needed opportunity for hands-on experience. To pass the course and get your CPR certification, you will have to practice on a dummy or doll and then demonstrate the techniques yourself. Then you will have the knowledge and the skills you need to administer CPR correctly.

Tips on Teething

By the time your baby has her first birthday, she will probably have at least eight teeth. So what's the big deal with second year teeth? After all, the first eight teeth probably didn't even seem to upset your baby all that much. Oh, sure, maybe her gums were a little red and swollen and she drooled a little bit more than usual; she may have been a little irritable when those first teeth emerged, and maybe she—and you—lost a little sleep for a few nights. But hey, you gave your baby something to chew on, maybe something cold to numb her gums, and it probably passed pretty quickly and uneventfully.

The difference in the second year lies in the type of teeth that come in. The first eight teeth that appear are almost always incisors: the relatively thin, flat, and sharp front teeth used for biting rather than chewing. They cut through the gums fairly easily and therefore, cause little pain. The second year brings two sets of molars: the bigger and broader teeth that are used for chewing. These teeth have a harder time breaking through the gums. For this reason, they tend to cause more pain than incisors.

The first set of molars is usually cut between 12 and 15 months; a second set will probably come through in the months before your child's second birthday. Unfortunately, your baby will probably find them very painful and will, quite understandably, be miserable and irritated for days.

Although cutting molars will usually cause irritability, don't assume that your baby is teething just because she seems cranky. Look for another cause, especially if her irritability is accompanied by fever, diarrhea, vomiting, or loss of appetite. Teething cannot cause any of these symptoms; only illness can.

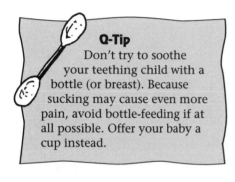

Q-Tip

Don't try to soothe your teething child with a bottle (or breast). Because sucking may cause even more pain, avoid bottle-feeding if at all possible. Offer your baby a cup instead.

Fairy Tales

Looking for a teething amulet? It was once believed that a coral necklace worn around a child's neck would ease the passage of teeth through the gums. Other popular amulets to ease teething pain have included the first tooth shed by a horse or a wolf's tooth (the latter is a little harder to come by these days).

If you suspect teething as the source of your baby's changed mood, check it out for yourself. Look for swollen and red gums and then feel with your finger. You may be able to feel the lump of a tooth underneath the gums in the days before it appears. Cutting molars also may cause redness and warmth on the cheek of the affected side.

If your baby is cutting molars, the best thing you can do to help relieve the pain is to give her something to chew on. Offer your child a teething ring, a bagel, zwieback, a frozen banana, or something else that she likes to chew. A cold teether often can offer much needed comfort. (Some teething rings feature a gel on the inside that will cool inside a refrigerator.) A small ice cube wrapped in a clean dish towel combines the best virtues of any teething aid: hardness and coldness. You also can try giving her a cold, wet washcloth or a toothbrush to chew on.

If teething toys and other chewables don't do the trick, try rubbing the tooth or gum directly with your finger. Ask your pediatrician to recommend an herbal or medicinal pain reliever that you can apply directly to the gums. Also consult your doctor about using liquid acetaminophen to ease the pain associated with teething. One way or another, you and your child will get through this painful first set of molars. And in about eight months, you can look forward to going through it all over again.

Caring for Baby Teeth

What's the point of taking good care of "baby teeth"? After all, they're only going to fall out anyway, right? True, but baby teeth do matter. They determine the placement and spacing of adult teeth and help to develop the jaw and a proper bite. So caring for your child's baby teeth is important. Early tooth decay can spread under the gums to the bone, making the bone unable to support adult teeth properly. In addition, early care of the teeth and gums will help form good habits that will last a lifetime.

One of the best things you can do to take care of your toddler's teeth is to watch his diet. Encourage your child to drink plenty of milk and eat milk products, because they are rich in both calcium and vitamin D, which will help in the formation of strong and healthy teeth (and bones).

Also, limit the eating of sugar and sweets, which contribute strongly to tooth decay. Because water has no sugar, it is better for his teeth than juice. Also water may help wash out other foods from the teeth. So although drinking juice in moderation is fine, make a point to encourage your toddler to drink water, too—especially before bedtime. The sugar you give your toddler after brushing and before bed—in juice or, even worse, in formula—will remain on his teeth until the next day's first brushing.

You don't really need to begin brushing your child's teeth until he is about 18 months old. (And you won't need to take him to a dentist until he is two.) But you do need to clean his new teeth. Check your toddler's mouth for any food stuck between his teeth and try to remove it. Then just gently rub your baby's teeth and gums with a washcloth or a small square of damp gauze to get them clean. Make sure to clean the gums as well as the teeth. If not removed, food particles and bacteria will cause plaque and decay.

Although you don't need to brush your child's teeth before 18 months, you may want to give your baby a soft toothbrush and let him watch you while you brush your teeth. Turn it into a game. See how well your baby can imitate you. Don't worry about his brushing technique at this stage. What's important is that your baby familiarizes himself with the toothbrush.

Brush Up on Toothbrushing

At around 18 months, introduce your toddler to the toothbrush for real. Choose a soft, kid-size toothbrush and brush gently at least twice a day. Make sure that one of these times falls between the evening meal and bedtime. To dislodge all food particles from between the teeth, brush up and down rather than side to side.

If your toddler seems reluctant to open her mouth for brushing or to sit still after you've started, try one of the following tricks:

➤ Ask your child to make sounds that will expose her mouth and teeth. The sillier and more fun the sounds, the greater enthusiasm you will create in your child. Both the open-mouthed "aaaah!" and the teeth-baring "eeeeee!", for example, can be achieved through a quick geography lesson of silly sounding place names: "Alaskaaaaa," "Alabamaaaaa," "Wichitaaaaa," "Tuscaloosaaaaa," "Bora boraaaaa," followed by "Tennesseeeee," "Mississippeeeee," "Hawaiiiii," "Tallahasseeeee," and "Biminiiiii."

➤ Make a silly face at your child and ask her to make a silly face at you.

➤ Name the foods you are brushing away, especially the candy or other sweets: "Did you have a cookie? I see it stuck on your teeth. There, now it's all gone."

Q-Tip

Toothbrushing becomes even more fun when you add flavors to it. Children's toothpastes not only come in traditional mint varieties, but also in fun flavors ranging from orange and strawberry to bubble gum. So offer your toddler a choice of more than one toothpaste that she likes. This will give your budding individualist a greater sense of control over the process.

Q-Tip

To encourage your toddler's future efforts as well as to demonstrate the benefits of toothbrushing, pretend that her smile after brushing is so bright that you have to shield your eyes. Your child will probably love this game so much, she'll quickly try to "blind" you again once you've "regained" your sight.

As soon as your child shows that she can rinse and spit (not like a professional ballplayer, just well enough to rinse out her mouth), you can introduce a fluoride toothpaste. Until then, you can ask your pediatrician about prescribing a liquid or chewable fluoride (and vitamin) supplement if the water in your area does not contain enough fluoride. When you do introduce toothpaste, use only a very small amount (at most the size of a pea). Too much fluoride can discolor the enamel of growing teeth.

In another nod to your child's increasing desire for independence, let her brush her teeth all by herself. Most kids want to start doing this some time during their second year. If your child wants to brush on her own, that's great. Encourage her interest. You may want to let her practice in the bathtub, where any spills or drooling will easily wash down the drain. But after your child proclaims that she is "all done," make sure that you go over her teeth again. Most children lack the dexterity to do a thorough job on their teeth until their sixth or seventh birthday.

The Least You Need to Know

➤ Call your pediatrician if anything about your baby's health or development concerns you.

➤ Learn infant CPR at the earliest opportunity.

➤ Cutting molars, which happens during the second year, hurts much more than cutting incisors.

➤ Proper dental care does matter, even with baby teeth.

Chapter 3

It's a Jungle In There: Childproofing Your Home

You can never be too safe. That's a rule that applies to every parent of a toddler. Certainly, you can't prevent your child from ever having an accident. In fact, you really shouldn't. The toddler years are all about exploring, experimenting, and experience.

In the course of your toddler's adventures, she's sure to have accidents—and eventually to learn from these experiences. But while allowing your child to explore, experiment, and grow, you'll still want to do everything you can to make sure that the accidents that do happen don't have grave consequences. By childproofing your home, you can minimize the risk of serious injury without hampering your child's exploration.

Why Childproof? Why Now?

Whether your child has just begun to walk—or soon will begin to walk—he is an intrepid and inquisitive adventurer. Remember that almost everything is still new to your child. Throughout his second year, your toddler will use all of his five senses in an attempt to examine and understand the objects in his very self-centered world.

If your child sees or hears something that interests or appeals to him, he cannot resist the urge to explore the object of his fascination. Your baby will do everything he can to get to it, grab hold of it, look at it, listen to it, and put it in his mouth.

In exploring the world, your toddler will discover the physical properties of objects. He will begin to notice similarities and differences. By the second half of his second year, your toddler will begin activities that involve sorting.

Throughout this year, your child also will begin performing experiments to find out how different objects behave. Your toddler will drop things and watch them carefully as they plummet down and crash to the floor. He will try to put one thing inside another, at first with little regard to which object is bigger. Your junior scientist will push things to see if they roll, slide, make noise, or are too heavy to move. He will tip and spill containers. All of these scientific experiments will be designed to answer the same simple question: "I wonder what would happen if I...?" Your child is discovering and exploring the concept of cause and effect.

Because your home will be your child's laboratory, you owe it to your baby to make it as safe as possible. In childproofing your home, you will create an environment where he can explore and discover as much as he can safely survey. And though he will undoubtedly still have accidents and make mistakes, he won't suffer too much harm from them.

What Are You Waiting For? An Accident?

You certainly should have started babyproofing your house as soon as your baby started crawling. If you didn't, don't delay another instant now that your baby is about to walk—or already walking. But even if you did babyproof for your little crawler, you'll need to reevaluate your safety measures and adjust them for the new skills of your toddler. Once your baby can toddle about, she'll get into everything that isn't nailed down.

The best way to ensure your toddler's safety is to get a child's-eye view of your house. Get down on your hands and knees so that you're about the same height as your one-year-old. Look around. What catches your eye? Is it that wisp of tablecloth hanging down from the dining room table? Perhaps a colorful extension cord or the cord of a lamp? Oh, look, a wastebasket—what's in there? Hey, you can see yourself in that glass coffee table! Do you think you can you pull yourself up on that folding chair?

If you already did this when your baby began crawling, do it again when your baby stands, cruises, or walks. This time, as you crawl across the floor, stop at each piece of furniture, get up on your knees, and see what you can reach. Remember that almost anything you can get your hands on, your toddler can get her hands on, too. Give everything you can reach a firm tug to see whether it moves or topples over. Repeat this procedure at an increased height when your toddler becomes a climber, too.

Watch Out!

If you really want to keep your toddler safe, you'll need to stay close to your child. Keep an alert eye on him as much as possible and maintain a constant corner-of-the-eye awareness of what he is doing. Because no matter how many hours you spend crawling about your house in search of hazards, your toddler will quickly find or invent new dangers.

You may, for example, consider your child safe and secure when he's strapped into a stroller, car seat, or high chair. This never was true, and it certainly isn't now. Now that he can toddle or scoot around on his own, he will have no patience for such confinement. So presto, change-o! He transforms himself into a miniature Houdini practicing the art of escape. And after your toddler becomes a climber, even cribs and playpens will no longer be as secure as they once were. For this reason, you'll need to remain close and alert even when your child seems securely strapped in.

For safety's sake, your toddler needs you to serve not only as his guardian angel, but also as his teacher. Even an early toddler can learn to avoid many dangers.

Remember, your child understands many more words than he can say (see Chapter 1, "Walk the Walk and Talk the Talk"). So don't hesitate to begin teaching him about safety from age one. Whenever you cook or clean or use something that poses a danger to your toddler, say, "Hot! Ow! Don't touch!" "Sharp! Don't touch!" "Icky! Poison! Don't touch!" Use dramatic gestures and pantomime to amplify your words.

Don't rely on one safety lesson to do the trick. (Your toddler has a memory like a sieve.) Even after your child seems to have gotten the message, keep a careful watch on him throughout the next two years. In the heat of the moment, your child's fascination with some forbidden object will quickly erase any memory of your warnings.

When Accidents Happen

Despite your best efforts and constant vigilance, your toddler will have accidents. Be prepared for any accidents that turn serious. In addition to maintaining a well-stocked first-aid kit, post emergency numbers and information next to every phone in your house. These emergency information sheets should include:

➤ Your name and your child's name, age, weight, and any special medical conditions or allergies that she has

➤ Your home address and phone number (most people forget this one, but grandparents and babysitters may not have this information on the tips of their tongues)

➤ Your work address and phone number

➤ Your pediatrician's name and phone number

➤ The address and phone number of the nearest hospital

➤ Names, addresses, and phone numbers of two or three neighbors, friends, or nearby relatives

➤ Phone numbers for the police and fire departments as well as the local poison control center

All Through the House: Childproofing

Your young explorer will have adventures in every room of your home. So if you want him to return safely and triumphantly from his adventures, you'll have to take child-proofing measures in every room. The child safety suggestions featured here should be implemented all over your home.

Fire Fighters

Install a smoke detector on every floor of your house and keep a fire extinguisher in the kitchen—or better yet, on every floor. Change the batteries on your smoke detectors every six months and check these and fire extinguishers regularly to make sure they work. Also, map out fire escape routes from every room in your house.

Make sure every fireplace has a secure fitting fire screen. Avoid letting your imitative toddler watch you start a fire, poke the fire, or add newspapers to improve the draw.

If you have open radiators, get a guard or cover that will keep your toddler's hands safe from burns. Avoid using portable space heaters, if possible. If you do need one, don't get the kind that has electric bars or coils that turn that attractive reddish-orange color when on. *Never* leave your child alone in a room with a space heater (or an electric fan). And, of course, store matches on high shelves out of your child's reach.

Do Not Enter: Restricted Access

If you haven't already done so, now's the time to buy safety gates that block off your stairs at both the bottom and the top. (If you put a gate only at the top, your toddler may climb all the way up the stairs and risk falling all the way down.) A pressure gate is fine for the bottom of the stairs, but never use one at the top. If your child's weight causes a pressure gate to fall at the bottom of the stairs, your child will escape serious injury. However, if the gate falls at the top of the stairs, your child will fall too. So make sure to get a gate that latches for the top of the stairs. (Pressure gates also come in handy by keeping your toddler—at least temporarily—out of certain rooms of the house.)

Locks can keep many dangers out of your toddler's reach—as long as you not only install them, but then use them. Lock all basement doors, as well as doors to the garage, tool shed, or workshop (including outside storm doors). In addition, use safety locks, rubber bands, or bungee cords to keep certain cabinets and drawers off limits to children under the age of three.

Don't lock up every cabinet or drawer, however. Your one-year-old loves to explore. Certainly you shouldn't deny your child the pleasure and growth that comes through exploration. Leave some drawers and cabinets unlocked, but make sure what's inside is safe to explore. For example, you may want to fill a low kitchen cabinet with pots and pans or plastic containers that will provide hours of safe fun for your little explorer.

Window Treatments (and Doors, Too)

Make sure that closed windows are locked to prevent your child from opening them and falling out. If they aren't frozen or painted shut, open only the top half of a window instead of the bottom. On high windows, install window grates that make falls next to impossible or install special window guards that prevent windows from being opened more than four inches. Remove the risk of strangulation by tying up the cords of window shades, blinds, and drapes.

Put stickers on plate glass windows or sliding glass doors to make them more visible to your child. You may even want to consider going to the expense of replacing them—at least temporarily—with safety glass or plexiglas.

If you're worried that your toddler might accidentally lock himself inside a bathroom or other room, tape the latch flush with the door.

Also, try adding jingle bells to your door (like those found in old-time shops). That way, you'll know whenever your child is trying to slip outside unnoticed. (You may want to consider keeping these bells on the door throughout your child's teenage years.)

> **Childproofing**
> One of the most common causes of crushed and broken fingers among toddlers is getting them caught in the crack on the hinged side of doors. So be very alert whenever your child is near an open door or a door that you're closing.

Bang, Crash, Boom!

To help prevent falls, secure any rugs in rooms where your child will spend a lot of time. During her first few months as a toddler, stay close to her. Also, get into the habit of leaving your toddler's feet bare or dressed in nonskid slipper socks when she's in the house. Slippery socks can cause falls, while shoes are neither necessary or helpful to an early walker.

Next, as you go around the floor of each room, check all furniture for sharp corners. Anything with low sharp corners should either be placed temporarily in storage or fitted with rubber or soft plastic "bumpers" that will cushion the impact. Remember to check and cushion the corners on the underside of furniture, too. In going from crawling to walking, your child is much more likely to bang her head or shoulders on the underside corner of a piece of furniture than to fall on top of a corner.

If you have glass-topped tables, you might want to replace them until your child reaches school age. Shattered glass can result in deep wounds that will not only produce significant bleeding, but may scar your child for life.

What's on the coffee table? What's on the end table? What's on the nightstand? If you don't ask these questions, your one-year-old certainly will. So before she has a chance to do it herself, remove any fragile knickknacks or other objects d'art that might get broken and/or represent a danger to your toddler. Consider temporarily putting away any table lamps, too. Make sure that any objects left on low tables (coffee or cocktail tables, bedside tables)—as well as those contained in low drawers and cabinets—are all safe for young children.

Freestanding shelves represent a significant hazard to small children. After she learns to walk, your toddler will soon teach herself to climb. To prevent your child from accidentally tipping shelves over on top of herself, secure any freestanding shelves to the wall with screws.

Make Your Home Shockproof

If your baby manages to stick something in an outlet, he may get a nasty shock. So make sure to shield every electrical outlet with a plastic outlet cover when not in use. Keep plugs for a TV or a lamp in place—and out of your toddler's hands—by fitting childproof outlet safety boxes over the plug and outlet.

Keep all electrical cords out of reach if possible. If your baby can grab a cord, he's sure to pull a lamp or clock or iron down on his head. In addition, a child who sucks or chews on an exposed electrical cord can suffer serious burns. If you need some electrical cords to remain exposed, secure them by taping them down, by using stick-on plastic sheathes specifically designed to keep cords from being exposed, or by tying up the excess length of cord with rubber bands.

Finally, make sure the electrical system is safe and up-to-date. All appliance cords should be grounded (three-pronged plugs that fit into three-holed sockets). Any frayed electrical cords should be repaired or replaced.

Reducing the Risk of Choking

To reduce the chance that your child will ingest something small enough to choke on, exercise extreme vigilance. Take care that you and your guests do not leave anything on floors or tables unless it's safe for your baby. Rid your floor and low tables of choking hazards, toxins, and anything else that might do your baby harm.

Often overlooked in the course of childproofing are wastebaskets: repositories of the unwanted and the dangerous. Unless you want to go to the trouble of monitoring everything thrown in your wastebaskets (for example, plastic bags that can smother your child, razors or other sharp objects that can cut her, or small objects that can choke her), remove wastebaskets from the rooms your child is in. Put all trash in a covered garbage pail instead.

Poison Control

Because your toddler will not recognize the smell or taste of poisons as dangerous to her health, you'll need to lock up all toxins in a place where she can't reach them. Probably because parents often overlook them, drugs and plants poison more children than any other household objects, including cosmetics and cleaning products. Common household products that can poison your child include:

➤ Alcohol, cigarettes, and other legal and illegal drugs (including vitamins)

➤ Household cleaning products

➤ Polishes (including shoe polish)

➤ Air fresheners, deodorizers, and moth balls

➤ Laundry supplies—especially bleach and spray starch

➤ Cosmetics

➤ Pesticides

➤ Kerosene or other lamp oil

➤ Household or outdoor plants and flowers, including willow, rhododendron, laurel, lily of the valley, tomato leaves, irises, daffodils, hyacinths, and buttercups.

> **Childproofing**
> If you must smoke tobacco (or other drugs)—and there's really no reason you should—please don't smoke in the house or around your child.

Keep all of these products locked up tight. Even better, remove them from child-level cabinets (especially under bathroom and kitchen sinks) and put them on a high shelf out of your child's reach—and still lock them up! In addition, keep all of these products in their original, childproof containers. When using any of these products, take what you need and recap the container and put it away immediately. Don't keep pills out, for example, to remind yourself to take them.

Because improperly administered drugs can poison your child, never give her medication without checking the label first. Make sure you've picked the right bottle and always check the expiration date. Don't "share" medicines prescribed for one child—or for an

Childproofing

If your child accidentally ingests poison, call your pediatrician or poison control center immediately. Do *not* give your child a tablespoon of syrup of ipecac (to induce vomiting) until you have talked to a doctor or poison authority.

adult—with another child. And never cut adult pills into what you consider "child-size" doses. Insist that any guests—especially grandparents, who may take a number of different medications— observe your safety rules regarding medicines.

To reinforce that medicines are not candy or toys, don't give your toddler medicine bottles—whether empty or filled with something else—to play with. Given enough practice, your child may figure out how to remove almost any "childproof" cap.

Finally, hang all tasty-looking plants from ceiling planters or place them on high shelves.

Room by Room Childproofing

Besides the general safety guidelines that apply to every room in your home, certain safety measures apply only to specific rooms.

Kitchen and Dining Room Safety

The greatest risk to your child's health in the kitchen involves burns. Here are ways you can reduce that risk:

➤ Covers that make it impossible for your child to turn stove and oven controls will help prevent fires or burns. You also can remove the knobs except when cooking.

➤ A lock for the oven door may prevent not only nasty burns, but the danger that your child will open it and then have it slam shut on his fingers.

➤ When you are cooking, use the back burners rather than front burners as much as possible.

➤ Whichever burners you use, always point all pot handles toward the rear of the stove.

➤ When you're baking or broiling, make it a practice to turn the oven light on. That way you can teach your child to stay at a safe distance whenever the light is on.

➤ Take care to remember that stoves, pots and pans, toaster ovens, irons, and some ovens remain hot long after use. Don't let your toddler go near them until you're sure they've cooled.

To avoid crushed fingers and toes, don't leave an iron or ironing board out when you aren't using them. Even if it is no longer hot, a heavy iron can do serious damage when it falls, while an ironing board can collapse on top of tiny fingers. Also remove all folding chairs, which can do the same. And put away your tablecloths for a couple of years, because they make it easy for a baby to pull the entire contents of the table down on top of himself.

Keep all small appliances unplugged and stored away from counter edges when not in use. Try to keep electrical cords tucked behind the appliances, as much out of sight as possible. You won't want your baby to turn on the blender—or pull it down on top of himself. You also won't want him turning on the microwave, so install it out of reach if possible.

Most kitchen safety rules are just a matter of common sense. For example, you probably don't need to be told to keep scissors, knives, and other sharp cooking utensils out of reach. Likewise, glasses and breakable dishes should be stored in high cabinets. Move plastic bags from lower drawers to higher ones that your child can't reach. Also keep pet food and pet bowls, which can harbor bacteria, away from your child's curious hands.

Food Safety

Some child safety rules apply to food as well. It's probably a good idea to stock child safe foods on lower shelves and in lower cabinets. Move dangerous foods (popcorn, nuts, hard candy, certain spices) to top shelves. Also, don't put cherries, plums, or other pitted fruits out in a fruit bowl that your child can reach by herself.

When your one-year-old eats in her highchair, always use safety straps. But because she may have little patience for sitting in a highchair now that she's a toddler, you may want to begin exploring alternatives. A child-size table and chairs will allow your child to sit (at least for a minute) and eat without risk of serious injury.

Some toddlers eat best when allowed to wander about a little while eating rather than being forced to eat only in their chairs. They're just too eager to get up and about again to focus on eating. If you decide to allow your child to eat while wandering about the kitchen, just make sure she doesn't eat on the run. A useful rule for eating away from the table is: Walk, don't run. We all remember how our own parents used to warn us about running with a popsicle or a lollipop in our mouths. Mama was right. In fact, it's not a good idea to let your toddler run with any kind of food in her mouth. Finally, whenever and wherever your toddler eats, stay near her in case she starts to choke.

Childproofing
Try never to drink hot coffee around your toddler and keep your cup well out of her reach if you do. A single spilled cup of coffee can give your one-year-old third-degree burns over 80 percent of her body.

Stair Safety

Crawling on stairs, especially going upstairs by himself, will be lots of fun for your toddler. You may even want to encourage your child's skill at climbing by getting a playroom set of sturdy wooden steps or a toddler slide that has three or four steps. But make sure your baby doesn't go upstairs on his own whenever he pleases. Use baby gates at the top and bottom of stairs.

When your baby does crawl or climb upstairs, stay right behind him every step of the way. When he wants to come down again, try to teach your child how to come down safely by crawling backward. Again, stay right behind your toddler at all times on the stairs.

Try not to make stairs any more difficult than they already are. Keep the stairway clear of "things to go upstairs."

Open stairways invite disaster, so if you have an open stairway, install banisters to keep your child from falling over the edge. To keep him from wedging his head between the railings (or falling through them), make sure that they are no more than four inches apart.

Finally, keep the door to the basement locked at all times. (One of the most common causes of serious injuries to toddlers is a walker crashing down the basement stairs.)

Bathroom Safety

If you haven't done so already, check the hot water temperature and reset it if necessary. To prevent scalding, water temperature should be no hotter than 130 degrees Fahrenheit. (At this temperature, your child would need to be exposed to water for more than 30 seconds to suffer a serious burn.) If hot water pipes are exposed, insulate them.

Even after you've reset the hot water heater, always check the water temperature yourself before putting your toddler in the bathtub. Keep in mind that compared to adults, young children like their bath water to be tepid. After you've put your child in the tub, don't leave your toddler alone, even "just for a second" to pick up a phone. The mere fact that your one-year-old can now sit up doesn't mean that she can't still drown. A bathtub safety seat, which attaches to the bottom of the tub with suction cups, can help your child stay upright while splashing and bathing. But even in a safety seat, she should still never be left alone in the tub.

To soften painful thuds, cover the bathtub spigot with a washcloth or a prefabricated foam "tub guard." Placing a nonskid bath mat in the tub will make it less slippery and less dangerous. Even so, set a firm rule that prohibits standing or jumping in the tub.

Believe it or not, small children have been known to drown in a toilet. A toilet-seat latch will keep your child—as well as your toothbrush, soap, washcloths, bath toys, and nearly anything else that's available—out of the toilet.

As mentioned in the section on poisons earlier in this chapter, medicines and cosmetics can be poisonous to small children. So keep these products stored in a *locked* medicine cabinet. Less toxic products that you use every day—soaps, shampoos, conditioners—can be kept out of reach in a shower caddy that hangs high from the shower nozzle.

Bedroom Safety

Bedroom safety measures apply to your room as well as your child's. To your toddler, your bedroom is a treasure-trove of small, precious, fascinating—and dangerous—objects. Take care to store coins, jewelry, sewing supplies, buttons, safety pins, hair pins, staples, thumb tacks, and paper clips on high shelves or on the tops of high dressers where they will be out of your child's sight. Make sure that your purse remains out of your child's reach as well. In your closet, hang all ties, scarves, and belts well out of your child's reach. Don't keep old dry cleaning bags; throw them away as soon as you bring them into the house.

In your child's room, store as many toys as possible in low open shelves. That way your child won't have to climb if he wants to get something for himself. If you want your child's room to have a toy chest, make sure it cannot slam shut. Most contemporary toy chests have a built-in space that guards against the crushing of fingers. Older wooden toy chests, though classic, do not have such safeguards. You can create your own finger safety zone by gluing small blocks of cork onto the two front corners of the opened chest.

Childproofing
No matter how cold it gets, never give your child an electric blanket. Layers of thermal blankets will retain plenty of heat—without the danger posed by spilled water or bedwetting on electric blankets.

At bedtime or naptime, always pull up the side rail of your baby's crib before leaving the room. And keep your child's crib—as well as any other furniture that he can climb on—away from the windows of his room.

When your toddler moves out of a crib, guard against tumbling out of bed by placing one side of his bed against the wall and using a temporary side rail on the open side. For safety's sake, you may want to consider starting your toddler off in a "big bed" simply by placing a mattress directly on the floor.

Keep diaper pails covered and, if possible, inaccessible. And try to maintain an organized changing station. After you put your toddler down on the changing table do not leave him there while you run around the room searching for a diaper pin, dash to the bathroom for a warm washcloth, or get down on your hands and knees to find the diaper cream that's slipped under the table. Even if you have secured your baby to the changing table with a strap or belt, it is unsafe to leave him alone, even for just a second.

Toy Safety

Your toddler will treat almost everything as if it were her own personal toy. Make sure that anything you give your baby to play with—pots and pans, the TV remote, laundry baskets, spoons, or even store-bought toys—is safe. This means the object:

➤ Should not be so heavy that it will hurt when she drops it (because don't worry, she will);

➤ should not be made of glass;

➤ should have no sharp edges;

➤ should not contain anything toxic; and

➤ should be too big—at least 2" in diameter—for your baby to swallow or choke on it.

These rules also should apply to anything stored or casually left low enough for your child to get her hands on.

Workshop Safety

Tools for household repairs fascinate most toddlers. Your child may even have a play tool set of his own. Tools also are very dangerous for children. So if you maintain a workshop in your basement or garage, it should be off limits to your toddler. Unless you can *fully* supervise your child's activities and explorations, it would be wise to keep him out of the workshop. Full supervision means you can't actually be doing any work in the workshop. If you're working a table saw, then the floor of your workshop is not an appropriate play area for your toddler.

Keep nails, screws, screwdrivers, hammers, and other tools well out of reach. Unplug and put away power tools (including the treacherous table saw) immediately when you are finished using them. Consider the possibility of storing folding ladders on hooks placed high on a garage or basement wall.

Yard Safety

Now that you've finished childproofing indoors, you should complete the task by making sure your yard is safe outdoors.

➤ Stair railings, railings on your porch, deck, or balcony should be no more than four inches apart to prevent your child from either falling through or getting her head stuck. If the spacing is too wide, you can solve the problem by adding screening. Railings also should have no horizontal bars that children can use to climb on—and over.

➤ How's the lay of the land? Level the ground in your yard as much as possible to eliminate ditches or holes that accumulate water. A few inches of water can represent a significant drowning hazard.

➤ Mow your lawn regularly to avoid the high grass that ticks and other insects love.

➤ Plant thick hedges or erect a fence around your yard to keep unwanted animals out (and to keep your children off the street).

➤ Whenever you and your toddler go out in the yard to play, check to see that no one has deposited litter on your lawn—or allowed a pet to do the same.

➤ Make sure all outside outlets have secure protective covers.

➤ Store all barbecue supplies, hedge clippers, scythes, fertilizers, plant food, gasoline, and any other tools or toxins on a high shelf out of reach—and if possible, behind a locked door.

➤ Do not leave industrial-size buckets unguarded anywhere in your yard. A curious toddler who peers into the bucket can fall in headfirst and get wedged upsidedown. A small amount of water, paint, or other liquid at the bottom can make a bucket a dangerous drowning hazard.

➤ If you have any playground equipment, make sure it does not have any exposed screws or bolts. Use plastic caps or duct tape to cover them. Also check regularly for rust.

➤ Several inches of sand, wood chips, or other loose material placed under swings and playground equipment will help soften your toddler's landings. If you have a sandbox, cover it whenever your child isn't using it—unless you want all the animals in the neighborhood to use it as a communal litter box.

➤ If you have a pool, fence it off. If you have a kiddie pool, empty it after every use. Never leave it full of water and unsupervised.

Childproofing

Perhaps the greatest danger to your toddler in the yard is exposure to the sun. Because your child's delicate skin has built up little protection from the sun's burning rays, avoid playing outside in the intense midday sun (11 a.m. to 3 p.m.). Make sure your yard has adequate shade, and encourage your toddler to play in the shade as much as possible. Use 15 SPF sunscreen on all exposed areas of the skin—except her hands (which may end up transferring the sunscreen to her eyes) and face. Lastly, get your child used to wearing a wide-brimmed hat (one that shadows her face) and a cotton T-shirt whenever she plays outside.

The Least You Need to Know

➤ Toddlers get into everything. So you need to make sure that everything your toddler can get into is safe.

➤ No matter how well you childproof, your child will find ways to make accidents happen, so stay alert and be prepared for emergencies.

➤ Childproof every room of your house, including closets, storage sheds, and garages. Also childproof your yard.

➤ If you cannot make a particular room safe, make it off limits to your toddler.

➤ If your child will spend any extended time in the homes of grandparents or other caretakers, make sure to take the same safety measures there.

Golden Slumbers

Toddlers and sleep: They go together about as well as oil and water. The problems toddlers have getting—and staying—asleep are many. Your one-year-old will probably suffer from separation anxiety, which makes going to sleep alone more difficult. He may get so wired from running around all day that he sometimes finds it hard to relax enough to get to sleep. Your child's need for sleep will diminish enough to make two naps too much, but one nap still too little. Finally, anxieties and tension that may beset your child, who will be trying to do so much this year, may cause an increase in nightmares and sleep disturbances. Fortunately, all of these problems can be corrected or will correct themselves given enough time.

Won't she ever go to sleep? More than one parent of an extremely active toddler has succumbed to this plaintive cry. Because toddlers, teetering between utter dependence and a desire for independence, place so many demands on their parents, parents of toddlers who sleep little may feel as if they never get a moment's peace. On the other hand, if your toddler still sleeps a lot, it may seem to you as if your baby does nothing but sleep.

How Much Sleep Does Your Child Need?

Among one-year-olds, sleep needs vary greatly from child to child. The average toddler sleeps around 12 hours a day. But the range extends from just eight hours to nearly 16. How much sleep does your toddler need?

Your baby's sleep patterns in his first year offer the best clue. Although he needs less sleep as a toddler, your child probably won't increase his up-and-about time by more than about an hour. So if your baby slept 16 hours a day, he'll probably sleep about 14 or 15 hours as a one-year-old. Unfortunately, if your child slept just 10 hours a night as a baby, he won't suddenly need more than that after his first birthday.

Your one-year-old will probably sleep around 10 to 12 hours at night—but not in a row! It's a rare toddler who sleeps more than six to eight hours at a stretch. But after half-waking at four or five a.m., your child can drift back to sleep fairly easily after some comforting. Your child will get the other two to four hours of rest he needs by napping during the day. Virtually all toddlers still take at least one nap a day and most take two. Depending on how much your child satisfies his need for sleep at night, his naps may last anywhere from 20 minutes to four hours.

How do you know how long a particular nap will last? Do you have time to do a load of laundry? Balance the checkbook? Make some business calls? Type up some letters? Or more likely, do you have time to take a nap yourself? If you stick to a pretty tight schedule regarding when and where your child goes to sleep—both at night and during the day—the length of his naps will become fairly predictable. Certainly flexibility about your child's sleep times also offers certain advantages, especially the freedom to go out during the evening. But the looser you are about your toddler's sleep schedule, the more difficult it is to predict how long he will sleep.

Getting Your Child to Sleep at Bedtime

Getting your one-year-old to go to bed is no easy task. Few self-respecting toddlers will go to bed without a fuss or a fight. Your child just has too much that she wants to do to welcome rest, no matter how reinvigorating it might prove. What's going on elsewhere around the house? Where are mommy and daddy? What am I missing? Such questions—even if not articulated—consume your toddler's feverish mind. That's why it's not at all uncommon for parents to use every trick in the book to try to get their toddler to go to sleep: rocking, cuddling, nursing, feeding, reading, singing, stories, sitting with, leaving, and punishing. And that's just in the first hour. Many parents then concede defeat, giving up until later. Of course, they'll just have to start all over then, again trying anything they can think of.

If you still nurse, bottlefeed, or even just rock your child to get her to go to sleep, you're probably desperate for a change in routine. Every time you try to put her down in her crib, your toddler probably throws a fit. What's worse, when anything wakes your baby up, even just for an instant, she cannot go back to sleep without you. At this stage, you're probably so miserably sleep-deprived—or soon will be—that you're ready to try anything to get your child to fall asleep on her own.

So steel yourself. Though you have a hard task ahead of you, the payoff—both for you and for your child—makes it will worth the effort.

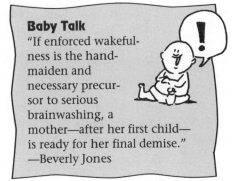

Baby Talk
"If enforced wakefulness is the handmaiden and necessary precursor to serious brainwashing, a mother—after her first child—is ready for her final demise."
—Beverly Jones

Should I Stay or Should I Go Now?

The younger you start encouraging your child to go to sleep by himself, the easier it will be. But when you finally decide that your child needs to learn how to go to sleep by himself, you may wonder about the best way to do it. Do you need to shut out your toddler entirely? Or should you stay with him every waking moment until he finally drops off to sleep?

Try to picture each of these scenarios from your toddler's point of view. Up until now, everything's been fine. Whenever he got tired, you would rock him, sing to him, feed him, and off he went. If he later woke up, you just came back to go through the same routine again. Then, suddenly—at least to your child, no matter how gradually it actually took you to come to this resolve—you decide that you've had enough of this routine. It's high time that your child learned how to go to sleep without you.

Q-Tip
Never use your child's crib or bed as a place of punishment. Nothing destroys your child's comfort at sleeptime more than seeing the bed as a prison.

So what happens? One night, out of the blue, you nurse your baby or give him his bottle, say "good night," place him in his crib, and disappear. Naturally, your child will object. He may cry and cry, but you stick in the earplugs and remain firm in your commitment to let him "cry himself to sleep," no matter how long it takes.

Is this really fair to your child? Without warning, you've abandoned your toddler totally to his own devices. Do you think that it will be easier the next night if only you can stick to your guns tonight? It won't: Sleep will come to be something dangerous and frightening for your child. From the moment that you say, "good night" and stand up to put him in his crib, your baby will start screaming and clinging desperately to you. Will you entirely abandon your child again? Or will your resolve crumble on the second night—or if not, then on the fifth or twelfth?

The alternative extreme is almost as bad. Again, everything's fine until the night when you "suddenly" decide to put your child in his crib before he's fallen asleep. Because you don't want your child to be scared, you decide to stay with him until he falls asleep. Though your toddler may not be as scared as he would be if you left, he certainly won't like it either.

For your one-year-old, it must be torture for you to stay visible but out of reach: to be able to see you, but have you refuse his pleas to pick him up. You may not have "abandoned" your child, but all the same you have "rejected" him. If you let your toddler's crying sway you, if you decide to pick him up again—or maybe even give up for now and try again later—he now knows from experience that if he cries long and hard enough, he will get the relief he wants from you. Is this helping either one of you at all?

The Sleep Solution

The ultimate solution to the problem of getting your toddler to go to sleep on her own involves a compromise between these two extremes. Leave the room, but come back periodically. You're not abandoning or rejecting your child (though she may still feel you are). You're simply leaving for a while, but are available to come back if really needed. When your baby cries (you know that she will), come back, perhaps settle her back down in her crib, say "good night" again, and then leave immediately. Keep contact short and avoid cuddling, rocking, or any of the comforts you once used to get your child to sleep.

You need to send a clear and firm message that playtime is over and rest time has begun. If your child continues to cry—as she no doubt will for at least several nights—return every few minutes just to reassure her that you're still within earshot. Or promise your toddler that you'll check on her every five (or seven or ten) minutes until she falls asleep. If you do, make sure to keep your promise. Your child needs the security of knowing that you are close by and that she can depend on you. But she really doesn't need you to pick her up to receive that reassurance. Again, just say "good night" and leave. Don't try to joke your baby out of her tears. Don't pick her up to comfort her either (unless she becomes so hysterical that she has difficulty breathing—and even then, first try to pat her back and calm her without picking her up). Be a bore: Do the same thing in the same way every time you come back into your child's room.

When you leave your toddler's room, try *not* to maintain total silence to "help" her get to sleep. This may actually do your child a disservice, making her hypersensitive to any things that go bump in the night. More important in terms of the goal at hand, if your child hears you cleaning up or walking around in a nearby room, she will be comforted by knowing exactly where you are as she drifts into unconsciousness, however unwillingly. (It may help to let your child know where you are going and what you will be doing when you leave the room.)

If you decide to try this compromise method, keep these suggested guidelines in mind:

➤ Never stay away for more than five minutes if your toddler is still crying. Indeed, if your child is very upset, visit as frequently as once a minute.

➤ Never stay for more than the minute it takes to resettle your child and repeat that quick "good night." Ignore her if she pops back up to her feet again.

➤ If your child is used to going to sleep in the dark, try to avoid turning the lights on when you go into her room. Don't do anything to disturb the monotony of your routine.

➤ Never take your child back out of the crib unless her diaper is dirty, she has vomited, or the bed is on fire.

If you maintain your resolve, bedtime should become much more peaceful for both of you within a week or two. Until this becomes the established bedtime routine, however, you can ruin it in a single night. If you leave your child to cry for too long or pick her up and then try again later, you'll have to start the "weaning" process all over again from the beginning.

It's All Routine

Though one-year-olds are great explorers and adventurers, they nonetheless tend to like routines. They prefer to know what's coming when and in what order events will unfold. For this reason, you can make bedtime proceed more smoothly by establishing pleasant and dependable routines for your child.

If you maintain consistent bedtime and naptime routines, including approximately the same bedtime every night, your child will soon adjust to a regular sleep schedule. But carrying on routines with a toddler is by no means an easy task. It requires a number of sacrifices on your part. If you are committed to upholding consistency of bedtime routines, for example, it will severely restrict your freedom to go out and do things at night (or at naptime in the morning or afternoon).

Because the slightest of changes can disrupt the entire balance, you'll need to work hard to stick to the routine almost invariably—even on vacations. So if you want to go out, say, to a movie, a concert, or a party in the evening, you'll need to first put your baby down and then get a sitter to stay with him while he sleeps. (Bedtime for a toddler can be such a headache that it almost seems unfair to turn the job over to a sitter—and it can disrupt the well-ordered schedule for days or even weeks.)

Some parents of toddlers do try to maintain the flexibility of the first year, when they could take their baby with them almost anywhere, secure in the knowledge that he would fall asleep when he got tired. It was as simple as that. However, if you do decide to take this route, be forewarned. If you keep him up for your convenience, you can't then expect your baby to drop off instantly on the nights you stay home. Chances are, your toddler will become a night owl.

In addition, any late nights—depending on how late they go—will probably disrupt your child's daytime nap schedule as well. This doesn't have to be a problem—as long as you remain flexible and enjoy having your baby stay up late with you. But if your toddler then needs to conform to the strict daytime schedule of a daycare provider, you—and he—may run into some trouble. Whether you choose routine over flexibility or vice versa is up to you. But you should consider beforehand which kind of situation you really want.

Sleeptime Soothers

In choosing the elements of a bedtime routine for your toddler, choose activities that are quiet and calming. It makes little sense to work your child into a state of excitement right before bed. Your child is no longer a baby. She won't suddenly drop off as a defense against overstimulation. Your toddler is not going to crash out of exhaustion either. Like the Energizer bunny, your child will just want to keep going and going and going and any possibility of entertainment will keep her awake.

If you've already established a bedtime routine (a song, a story, a quiet game) in your baby's first year, you can continue with that or you might want to create a new routine.

> ### Kid Stuff
> Charlie's parents gave him two blankets so that they could occasionally throw one into the wash without too much fuss. But the jig was up once Charlie found out there were two of them. After that, he demanded *both* blankets before he would go to sleep.

Whatever you choose, your bedtime routine should be a period of quiet time together. Try to make sure that everything you do in the half-hour or hour before bedtime produces calm rather than excitement and smiles rather than tears.

Your child's best soother is, of course, you. So by all means rock in a rocking chair with your toddler, sing to her, hold her while you take a stroll around the room. But these routine activities should get your child calm and ready for bed. They should not actually put your baby to sleep. If you let (or continue to let) your toddler fall asleep in your arms, it will become a hard habit to break. So stick with the practice of putting your child down in her crib *before* she falls asleep. (If you didn't do this when your child was an infant, start doing it now.) This doesn't mean putting your baby down when she's wide awake, but rather just before she falls asleep. Choose a moment when your toddler looks drowsy.

In creating your bedtime routine, choose elements that soothe both of you, quiet activities that you both enjoy. Remember: The less complicated the routine, the better. (You won't want to have to do the macarena every night.) Simplicity also leaves open the possibility that someone else can pinch hit for you and quickly master the routine, too. Whether your toddler will welcome this substitute is, of course, another story.

Q-Tip

Don't underestimate the power of a good security blanket. Sure, it will get dirty. Your child will drag it everywhere and never want you to wash it (though you may be able to get around this by having two identical blankets). But a security blanket can help your child at bedtime and in making it through the difficult transition from complete dependence to independence.

Any of the following can add richness—and hopefully relief—to your bedtime routine:

➤ A long walk together after dinner

➤ A warm bath before bed

➤ A snack before brushing, which may help fill your toddler's stomach (try to include milk or other protein)

➤ Reading together, perhaps followed by letting your child "read" a book or two on her own or following along with a book on tape

Baby Talk

"There never was child so lovely but his mother was glad to get him asleep."
—Ralph Waldo Emerson

➤ Bedtime stories (not too exciting though), which you can tell to your child: perhaps a true—or at least believable—story about you when you were a child or when she was little or a make-believe story in which your child plays the role of hero.

➤ A brief and gentle in-bed massage

➤ A game in which your toddler puts all her stuffed animals or other dolls to bed before climbing in after them (lucky child, she gets to be the last one up)

➤ Looking around the room and saying good night to various animals, dolls, and other objects (à la *Good Night, Moon*)

➤ Soothing music: either your singing or a lullaby tape

➤ Comfort items (a soft blanket, a favorite stuffed animal, anything that your child finds soothing and relaxing)

➤ Sucking a thumb or pacifier (though the latter may be more trouble than it's worth if your toddler constantly loses it)

Don't overlook any possibility if that's what it takes for your toddler to get herself asleep. After all, that's the whole idea, isn't it?

Afternoon Delight: Naptime

One-year-olds rarely get all the sleep they need at night. To supplement his nighttime sleep, your child will need to take naps. Your child won't be napping four or five times a day as he did when he was under six months old, but he'll most likely still require one to two naps a day throughout his second year.

How Many Naps Will Your Baby Need?

In the months after your baby's first birthday, he will probably still take two naps a day to meet all of his sleep needs. During these months, he will clearly reach his limit after a stretch of four to five hours of wakefulness. If he stays up longer than this, your child will become whiny, belligerent, and generally miserable. So if your toddler wakes at six, you'll probably need to put him down for his morning nap between ten and eleven.

By around 18 months, however, your toddler will probably begin to phase out one of the naps. Your child will no longer seem ready to settle down for a morning nap at, say, ten o'clock. But he certainly won't make it all the way to his usual afternoon nap at, say, three o'clock either. Nor will your toddler make it all the way from the end of his morning nap until bedtime.

By your child's second birthday, he will probably have completely adjusted his nap schedule. At two, he will likely take just one nap a day, either in the late morning or the early afternoon.

When One Nap Is Not Enough (But Two Naps Is Too Much)

The period between 18 and 24 months is one of the most difficult—for both parents and child—of all the preschool years. Not only will your child struggle toward independence while clinging to dependence, move from tentative walking to running and climbing, and increase her vocabulary from a couple of dozen words to hundreds, but she will achieve these milestones despite being overtired—and cranky—much of the time.

The transition from two naps a day down to one does not usually proceed smoothly. Throughout these months, your child will need one and a half naps a day—but of course, she can't take one and a half. She's stuck with one or two. So as the morning drags on—and again later in the evening—your toddler will become increasingly tired, whiny, miserable, and nearly unbearable.

Not only that, but because your child's body will no longer respond as well to her brain signals, she will become less and less physically coordinated—and more and more frustrated. In her overtired state, your toddler will have to work twice as hard (and thus tire herself out even more) to do anything physical: walking, climbing, or playing.

Not only will physical coordination become more difficult, but in her overtired state, your toddler will have little tolerance for such frustrations. Being overtired may make your toddler increasingly tense. So the more tired your child gets, the harder it may become for her to relax.

> **Q-Tip**
> Parents think that when their toddler gets overtired, she will slow down. Some toddlers do crash, but others continue humming along just as fast as usual, so if you're looking at the *level* of your child's activity, you may miss the signs of fatigue. Look at the *proficiency* of your child's activity. If tasks like running become difficult for your child or her tolerance for frustration falls, then she needs to rest.

You (who else?) will have to deal with your toddler's tiredness, crankiness, frustration, and irritability during these difficult months. Watch your child carefully for signs of tiredness—especially in the hour or two after the time when she used to take her naps. The signs are fairly clear—if you know what to look for.

For the child caught between one and two naps, rest does not necessarily mean sleep (though if it does, welcome it). You might have better luck trying to engage your child in restful "quiet-time" activities: reading, listening to music, drawing with crayons. Anything that gets your toddler to sit down and get some physical rest, some calm and quiet, will help restore your child's energy, strength, and skills. Even if your toddler resists naptime, she may nonetheless welcome rest time or quiet time. Indeed, she may even fall asleep in spite of herself.

How Long Should My Child Nap?

Another problem during this transitional period between one and two naps is how long to let your toddler nap. If you don't care when your child goes to sleep at night, then let him sleep as long as he wants. But if you want to preserve his bedtime as much as you can, on certain days you will probably need to wake your child from his nap prematurely. A four-hour nap may be a welcome break for you in the middle of the day. But rest assured—actually, rest not assured—you will pay for it when bedtime comes around that night.

Chances are, your toddler will not welcome the interruption of his slumber. So if you need to wake your child early, try to ease his passage gently and gradually back into the waking world. For example, very few toddlers will willingly go straight from waking to their midday meal. They just won't eat right away. Your toddler might consent to lying down on the changing table for a new diaper, but if changing his diaper right away after a nap tends to upset him, then don't even bother unless it's soiled or dripping. Just spend the first half-hour or hour in more quiet-time activities: cuddling, talking, and singing softly, or perhaps listening to some music or reading some picture books.

Sleep Disturbances

All toddlers wake up in the middle of the night. Those who aren't disturbed by something (cold, hunger or thirst, a soiled diaper, fears of being alone, of being in the dark, night-time noises, nothing to suck, and so on) simply drift back to sleep. But if something disturbs your infant, she will cry out.

> **Q-Tip**
> Many bedtime routines can be applied to naptime. But going to sleep when the sun is shining is different from going to sleep at night. You can give your child a naptime sleeping bag that she can plop down on the couch, on your bed, or even on the floor when it's naptime. If you try to make naptime a special time for your child, she may even lie down willingly.

So don't blame your child for waking you in the night. Your toddler is not doing it to get your attention (although she does want you to attend to whatever is wrong) or to drive you crazy. And she won't stop doing it just because you decide to ignore her midnight cries. (This strategy will actually make things worse.) Your toddler simply cannot help it. It's not a question of discipline; it's a question of disturbance. So if your child's cries wake you in the middle of the night, try not to take your anger and frustration out on her. Instead, figure out what's disturbing your toddler and try to correct it. In all likelihood, all she needs is a small dose of reassurance.

If something (perhaps hunger or a soiled diaper) bothers your child in the middle of the night only once in a blue moon, you can deal with the cause of the disturbance when it occurs. But if a particular disturbance becomes a pattern, waking your toddler several nights in a row or even several nights in the same week, then you'll do better to try taking some preemptive action. If your toddler regularly wakes due to:

> **Baby Talk**
> "In point of fact, we are all born rude. No infant has ever appeared yet with the grace to understand how inconsiderate it is to disturb others in the middle of the night."—Judith Martin (Miss Manners)

➤ **Cold**   Try putting a blanket over her after she falls asleep.

➤ **Hunger**   Feed her dinner earlier, rather than just before bedtime, when she may be too tired to eat well. Then offer her a snack or a bottle before bed.

➤ **Thirst** Encourage her to drink as much as he wants right before bed. If she wakes in the middle of the night anyway, offer her a bottle of water (because juice, milk, or formula will promote tooth decay). Or if your child can suck through a straw, rig up a makeshift "gerbil bottle" by taping a travel mug—the kind with a straw—to one of the crib railings.

➤ **A full diaper** Change your baby right before bedtime (*after* her bottle, not before).

➤ **Fear of being alone** Teach your child to go to sleep by herself (explained earlier in this chapter). Her fear may be reinforced by the habit of always going to sleep either in your arms or with you in the room.

➤ **Fear of the dark** Plug in a nightlight, give your child a flashlight, or install a lighted fish tank, which will provide not only soft light, but also soothing sights and sounds. If none of these nightlights do the trick, try letting her sleep with a lamp on. Or familiarize your child with the magical mystery of nighttime: After dark but before bed, take your toddler on a walk through the neighborhood—or sit or lie together in your yard and count stars and fireflies. This will help your child learn that nighttime and darkness don't have to be scary.

➤ **Noisiness** Put up heavy curtains to muffle outside noises or try a white-noise generator or a rotating fan to interfere with outside noises. Keep visitors (including you) out of your toddler's room when she is sleeping. Don't check on her every time you hear movement (unless you also hear distress), because you might be what's waking her up. Instead, leave your child's bedroom door open enough so that you can peek in at her without actually coming into the room.

➤ **Nothing to suck on** If she enjoys a pacifier, litter her crib with several in the hope that she'll find one.

If you check on your child and none of these problems seem to apply, you may find it most effective to use the same method you'd use to get her to sleep on her own. Soothe her as quickly as possible, then leave. If she immediately starts crying again, wait a few minutes before returning, then check her every five minutes or so, offering words of reassurance and perhaps a brief rub or pat on the back. Though the crying may seem to go on forever, try timing it. You may notice that the crying does not last as long on subsequent nights.

If your toddler's crying increases in volume, intensity, or duration, however, be flexible enough to alter your plans accordingly. Check again and see if something is really wrong.

When you do check on your child, try to avoid picking her up out of the crib (unless she is hysterical or needs a diaper change). Your toddler needs to learn how to comfort herself, if possible, and go back to sleep on her own.

Monsters Under the Bed: Dealing with Nightmares

To a toddler, who has at best a tenuous grasp of the difference between reality and imagination, nightmares can be horrific experiences. When a nightmare wakes your child up, you may find him sitting straight up in bed in screaming terror or curled up in a sobbing, miserable ball.

If you can get to your toddler quickly enough and offer soothing words and caresses that comfort him, he will probably drop off again in less than a minute—and not even remember it the next day. If you take more time, however, perhaps thinking that it would be best if he would fall back to sleep on his own, he will become even more terrified and most likely require 15 or 20 minutes or more of comforting.

As every good Freudian knows, nightmares most often spring from stress and anxiety. When your child wakes with a nightmare, try to guess what the source might be:

➤ Has he experienced any major change(s) recently?

➤ Did he recently start daycare—or switch to a new daycare setting?

➤ Did you or your partner just start going back to work?

➤ Did you or your partner have to spend a night or two away from home?

➤ Did you just have another baby? Or have you helped your toddler understand that a new baby is on the way?

➤ Have you and your child clashed at all over his struggle to reconcile dependence and independence in eating, walking, and so on?

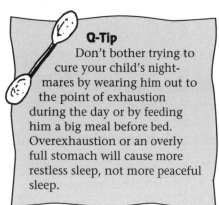

Q-Tip
Don't bother trying to cure your child's nightmares by wearing him out to the point of exhaustion during the day or by feeding him a big meal before bed. Overexhaustion or an overly full stomach will cause more restless sleep, not more peaceful sleep.

You probably cannot "fix" any of these lifestyle changes to your toddler's satisfaction: You can't make them go away. But you can make it easier on your child. Show him even more loving attention. If you are putting new demands on him, ease up for a while. (If he is unable to meet these demands, your child may fear your rejection and abandonment. These fears could be the source of his nightmares.) Tolerate more "bad behavior" during these difficult transitions. And above all, talk—even if your child is barely verbal—about what you've guessed is the source of his anxiety and about what dreams are. In acknowledging and understanding the cause of your toddler's stress and offering reassurance, you may help relieve it entirely.

The Midnight Rambler

Walking while half-asleep—or barely conscious running, which is the way most toddlers search for their parents in the night—can be very dangerous to your child. The best way to prevent midnight rambling is to stop it before it starts. If you never give your child any reason to get up in the middle of the night, she won't. How can you avoid it? By going to your toddler immediately whenever she cries out for you in the middle of the night. It's just common sense: If you go to your child, she won't need to come to you.

If possible, intercept your toddler even before she climbs out of bed. (You can hear your child stirring if you keep a baby monitor on at night.) If you don't hear your toddler getting out of bed but do hear her coming down the hall, try to catch her before she reaches your room and return her to bed at once.

Your child will have little motivation for midnight rambling if she never gets rewarded for it. So if your toddler does come to you in the middle of the night, don't entertain or indulge her. Scoop your child up right away, take her back to her own bed right away, and stay with her for a minute or so to calm her. If you decide to let your toddler crawl into your cozy bed with you instead, prepare yourself for more visits in the future.

Finally, if midnight rambling becomes a persistent problem, try rewarding your child for *not* coming into your bed at night. You might want to create a star chart: Give your child a star for every night that she stays in her own bed. When she has five or ten stars, reward her with a small prize or a favorite activity.

The Family Bed: An Alternative Sleeping Arrangement

If your child's sleep is disturbed often enough, or if he regularly comes into your room in the middle of the night, you may decide to "give in" and let your toddler crawl into bed with you. Keep in mind, however, that if you do this often enough, you will have a tough time getting him to sleep anywhere else. Especially if your toddler is already out of a crib and sleeping in a bed, he will pop up in your room almost every night.

Some parents find it a more practical solution simply to establish a "family bed," where everyone sleeps together. (By putting a guard rail on one side of the bed, you can ensure your toddler's safety without necessarily having him sleep between you and your partner.) In addition to offering your child a special degree of warmth and security, a family bed eliminates two nighttime problems:

➤ The safety risks posed by a toddler who wanders the halls in the middle of the night

➤ The annoyance—and sleep deprivation—of parents who need to get up to go to their child's room when he cries in the middle of the night

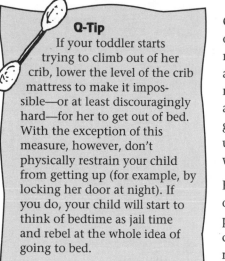

Q-Tip
If your toddler starts trying to climb out of her crib, lower the level of the crib mattress to make it impossible—or at least discouragingly hard—for her to get out of bed. With the exception of this measure, however, don't physically restrain your child from getting up (for example, by locking her door at night). If you do, your child will start to think of bedtime as jail time and rebel at the whole idea of going to bed.

Of course, your child may still wake you up in the middle of the night even if he's sleeping next to you. But he also may just snuggle up closer to you without waking you at all. Even if he does wake you, soothing your child by rubbing his back for a few seconds and then rolling over and going back to sleep is far easier than getting up and going to another room. You may not even need to wake up fully to reassure your child. So both you and your child will have far fewer sleep disturbances.

Family beds are not beds of roses though. The most obvious drawback is a lack of privacy. You and your partner will need to find your own separate place to cuddle. Also, sacrificing a private space of your own may make you feel somewhat claustrophobic: You can't get away from your toddler even when you're both sleeping.

The other major drawback of the family bed is its irreversibility. Although you can establish a family bed at almost any time in your child's preschool years, it's next to impossible to reverse course if you change your mind. After getting used to the cozy closeness of sleeping in your bed with you, your child is not likely to see any advantages to sleeping in "his own" bed and will probably resist the switch in any way he can.

Although some parents feel perfectly comfortable with a family bed, you should put a good deal of thought into it before trying it yourself. Don't back into this decision in a semiconscious state simply by "giving in" to your desperation for uninterrupted sleep. Talk to your partner and make a conscious decision about whether you want your toddler regularly sleeping in your bed. Remember: If you decide later that it's not working for you, it will be extremely hard to get your child to agree with you.

The Least You Need to Know

➤ The more consistent the bedtime routine (including timing), the easier your child will drop off.

➤ For several months after your child starts cutting down from two naps a day to one, she will be quicker to get angry, quicker to cry, and quicker to get frustrated as the day goes on. Quiet time activities can help.

➤ Sleep disturbances almost always happen for a reason. If you can find out why your child keeps waking up in the middle of the night, you can probably eliminate the cause.

➤ The quicker you respond to nighttime disturbances, the quicker both of you will get back to sleep.

Chapter 5

No, No, NO! Setting Limits

In This Chapter

➤ Setting limits on your toddler's behavior

➤ Is punishment appropriate?

➤ Mealtime manners: Do they matter at this age?

➤ How to positively guide and influence your child's behavior

Your toddler is an explorer and an adventurer and you don't want to curb your child's adventurous spirit or her thirst for discovery. But at the same time, you surely can't let your toddler do everything she wants to do. If you did, she'd be eating your money, painting your sofa, and jamming ice cream into your CD player.

During your child's second year, you'll need to establish some rules that impose limits on your toddler's behavior. Unfortunately, with the exception of "No!", your child will probably not understand any of your rules. The rules certainly won't make any sense to her, especially if they thwart her desires. And why would they? You cannot expect your toddler to understand your rules unless you take the time to explain them—and even then she may not acquiesce. "I won't hurt myself," your toddler will insist as she blithely teeters on the back of the couch.

Inside Your Toddler's Mind

A one-year-old cannot possibly comprehend your apparently arbitrary distinction between "good" and "bad" behavior. It's okay to pour water from a cup in the tub, but not okay to pour milk on the kitchen floor? Throwing a ball is good, but throwing mashed potatoes or a toy truck is bad? Pulling a wagon is fine, but pulling the cat's tail is mean? Who made up these rules anyway?

It's easy to forget that your child doesn't yet know the difference between right and wrong. After all, your toddler seems to understand much more than he actually does.

Your toddler not only lacks the understanding, but also the ability to take responsibility for his actions. Yes, he's no longer a baby, so you can expect more from your toddler now. But in truth, your child's still not much more than a baby. He's not even close to achieving the social maturity of a preschooler. So you cannot possibly hold your toddler up to the same standards of behavior that you might apply to a preschooler. He cannot be expected to know, for example, that pulling someone's hair hurts—or that walking near a swing set is dangerous when someone is swinging. Your child needs a great deal more experience—as well as your teaching—to develop a finer understanding of the effects and consequences of his actions and to learn how to behave himself accordingly.

Because your toddler still has a very short memory, he cannot carry the lessons of one experience into a similar situation later—or even the same situation. All toddlers lack foresight. You may have told your child a dozen times not to pull the cat's tail. The cat may have even scratched your toddler to defend itself. But toddlers live entirely in the moment. So the next time your child sees it, the lure of that twitching tail is just too much for him to resist. He just has to reach out and grab it.

> ### Kid Stuff
>
> The founder of Methodism, John Wesley, recalled his mother constantly reprimanding him when he was a small boy. His father once asked his mother how she had the patience to keep telling that blockheaded boy the same thing twenty different times. "Don't be silly, Samuel," Susanna Wesley replied, "had I told him just nineteen times, I would have been wasting my breath."

Ain't Misbehavin'

Because your child does not yet know the difference between "good" and "bad," it's not fair or reasonable to discipline her as if she did (that will come later). If you try punishing or threatening your toddler, her persistent refusal to "do as she's told" will stem not from defiance, but from a combination of a lack of understanding and a need to assert her independence.

When your child doesn't behave the way you would like her to behave, it's not that she doesn't agree with your rules. She's almost certainly not trying to be defiant. The truth of the matter is that your toddler neither agrees nor disagrees with your rules, she doesn't understand or remember them—especially in the heat of the moment, when she sees something that he wants to do.

A one-year-old will "behave herself"—that is, act the way you want her to act—only if she wants to do that. This does not mean that you should let your child willfully behave any way she pleases. You can still provide guidelines of acceptable behavior and cleverly steer your child to want to "be good." But you'll need to remain flexible enough to allow and even encourage your child's struggle for independence without damaging her confidence.

Where do you draw the line between acceptable and unacceptable behavior? The rules you develop to set limits for your child will probably aim to achieve one of the following:

➤ **Keep your child safe.** For example, hold a grown-up's hand in the street, no jumping on the bed, or no playing in the garbage.

➤ **Keep others safe from your child.** For example, no hitting, no kicking, no hair pulling, no biting, or no eye gouging.

➤ **Keep your property intact.** For example, no painting the rocking chair, no food in the living room, or no throwing of fragile objects.

If all your rules fall into one of these three categories, then they probably all set reasonable and necessary limits.

Your toddler is in a difficult spot: Her desire to please you, to love and be loved by you often conflicts with her dawning urge for independence. At this age, there's no question but that she wants to please you. Yet she has only a very vague idea of what you like her to do. At the same time, your child is no longer a compliant infant, but a toddler with a will and desires of her-own. Your toddler now recognizes herself as a separate being rather than as an extension of you. And naturally, she wants everything her own way. So take your corners and wait for the bell. The clash of wills that will periodically pop up and sometimes even dominate your relationship over the next seventeen (or more) years is about to begin.

"No!" Is Not Always Enough

How do you enforce limits? Most parents start by saying, "No!" The tone you use (even more than the word itself) will probably stop your toddler dead in his tracks, instantly conveying the message that his action was unacceptable and that you don't like it when he does that.

If possible, try to sound stern without yelling or getting angry. Of course, you may consider frightening your child an appropriate response after he's poked another toddler in the eye or frightened you by running across the street, but scaring your toddler is actually counterproductive. After you've scared him, the rest of your message will be totally lost on him.

Don't worry too much about occasional angry outbursts directed at your toddler. After all, you have every right to get angry at your child, especially when he does something unsafe or something that hurts others. So at times, you may lose your temper and blow off steam by yelling at your toddler.

Unless it becomes habitual, however, an isolated angry outburst may frighten your child for a few minutes, but will do no lasting harm. Indeed, it may do less harm than holding in your anger. Bottled-up resentments can linger for a long time, eating away at your good relationship with your toddler. But an outburst blows over, quickly allowing you and your toddler to enjoy each other's company again.

Though saying "no!" is a good first step, it's often not enough to stop your child from doing something that hurts others or puts himself or others in danger. A toddler's "bad" behavior sometimes demands swift action as well as sharp words. You may need to remove a dangerous object from his grasp or you may need to remove your child from the dangerous situation.

Q-Tip

Any corrective action you take with your toddler must be swift, consistent, and well-explained. If your toddler hits another child comfort the injured child, then scoop up your child and say, "Your hitting hurt Zak. See him crying? No hitting!" If you wait too long between your child's action and your response, your toddler will already have forgotten hitting his friend.

After restoring calm, explain directly to your child why you've separated him from the friend he was biting or the glass bottle he wanted to bang on the floor. Your child may not understand every word you say. In any case, your toddler probably won't remember your words the next time it occurs to him to bite someone or to play with something dangerous, but in the long run, these brief explanations will lay the groundwork for teaching your child the differences between safe and unsafe behavior—and between right and wrong.

"No!": Don't Overuse It

Like all toddlers, your child needs to be allowed to explore her environment. This exploration is part of her growing independence, confidence, and separation from you. (Don't worry, your child won't separate too much for many more years to come.) If you want your toddler to make the most of her early adventures, you'll need not only to provide her with the opportunity to make new discoveries, but actually to encourage exploration and experimentation.

Constantly having to tell your toddler "No!" will do exactly the opposite. It pointedly discourages your child from exploring her environment—at least parts of it.

In addition, the sternness and suddenness with which you say, "No!" will probably frighten your child. Many toddlers burst into tears, falling apart whenever their parents say, "No!" In general, your toddler doesn't like to do anything that displeases you. Oh, your child certainly has a will of her own. And when push comes to shove, your toddler would much rather get what she wants than sacrifice it for the sake of avoiding your displeasure. Nonetheless, conflict with you, a clash between your desires (for her safety, for example) and hers (for free reign) is very scary for your toddler. It feels dangerous to displease you. In your child's mind, the thought of your disapproval is equated with rejection, and therefore intensifies any abandonment fears.

> **Q-Tip**
> Be positive. Parents often forget that a toddler's social behavior is motivated not only by a desire to avoid displeasing others (especially parents), but also by a genuine desire to please. All too often, parents offer behavioral guidelines only in negative terms. If you take the time to praise good behavior often enough, your child will eventually make an effort to repeat it.

So try to avoid saying, "No!" all of the time. Whenever you do say it, follow up by comforting your child. Explain in concrete terms why you wanted your toddler to stop doing what she was doing (danger to herself, danger or harm to others, and so on). Above all, emphasize that even when you get angry at her, you still love your child. Toddlers, so richly anchored in the present, often have a hard time realizing this.

Does Punishment Work?

What punishments are appropriate for a one-year-old? Let's take a look at two strategies that don't work very well with young toddlers:

➤ Time-outs (separating your child from the site and circumstances of his misbehavior by putting him in a specially designated "time-out chair") work more effectively with older children than with early toddlers. Your child probably doesn't like to sit in one place for more than a second. This makes time-outs very hard for you to enforce. If you do try using time-outs and your child gets up from the time-out chair, gently but firmly return him to the chair—or ignore him as he tries to win your attention. Go about your business until the time-out is up (the standard rule of thumb is one minute for every year of your child's age). When the time-out is over, remind your child why you've put him in time-out.

➤ Spanking or hitting your child—to stop him from hurting others, for example— makes no sense at all. Put yourself in your one-year-old's place and try to figure out the logic behind eye-for-an-eye punishment: I can't hit because it hurts people, so you hit me and hurt me. Wait, that can't be right. It makes no sense.

If your aim is to steer your early toddler toward "good" behavior and away from "bad" behavior, neither time-outs nor spankings will do the trick. In fact, a one-year-old learns very little from any kind of punishment. Your toddler doesn't really understand the concept of punishment for unacceptable behavior. He can't yet make the connection between his own actions and your reactions.

Because your child at this age has just the barest grasp (if any) of the links between cause and effect or action and consequence, it makes no sense to threaten or spank him or withdraw pleasures or treats as punishment. Your toddler won't see these punishments as a consequence of his own actions. He will think only that you're being unfair, arbitrary, and cruel. Such punishments won't teach your child anything either, because by the next time a similar situation comes up, he will have long forgotten that he got punished for doing the same thing last time. So punishment will have no positive impact whatsoever on your one-year-old.

On the flip side of the coin, it makes no sense to bribe or bargain with your child to get him to behave. Your child cannot keep promises or uphold bargains. What's a promise to your one-year-old? It's his saying, "okay," to anything you say in get what he wants. But your toddler's verbal assent doesn't mean that he will then keep his end of the bargain— or even appreciate that he has made any sort of promise. Even if he does, when the time comes for your child to keep his promise, he won't remember having promised anything.

Breaking promises, however, is *not* a moral failing for a toddler. Your child does not yet have the ability to make or keep promises. In agreeing to a bargain, your toddler had no intention of being deceitful. Your child did not set out to trick you. He just wanted you to give him what he wanted or let him do what he wanted to do. And agreeing with you seemed to be the only way to get what he wanted.

Is Punishment Warranted at This Age?

Most actions that a toddler takes that might warrant punishment in an older child are things that she cannot help doing. By nature, toddlers are curious about things, explore them, and experiment with them. So before you punish your one-year-old, stop to consider: Does she really deserve punishment and was it truly your child's fault?

Did your toddler break something or play with something that was dangerous? Well, how did she get ahold of it in the first place? Who left it in her reach?

Did she pull someone's hair? If so, do you really think it was mean-spirited? Early toddlers most often hurt others not out of aggression, but as part of the process of exploring other people as if they were objects. When your toddler sees anything new, including a new person, she will want to explore it: She'll push it, pull it, poke it, scratch it, bang on it, kick it, and of course, bite it—just to see what happens. In all likelihood, your child did not intend to cause harm—and in fact, may still be incapable of intending much of anything, including hurting someone.

Baby Talk
"Thank God kids never mean well."
—Lily Tomlin

Until your child more fully understands the dynamics of cause and effect, of actions and their consequences, punishment and fear of punishment will do nothing to promote good behavior or deter bad behavior. And in the final analysis, is it fair to punish your toddler simply for being a toddler and behaving like one?

Manners and Mealtime Just Don't Mix

Mealtime for toddlers is never a good time to introduce the concepts of manners and discipline, yet many parents and toddlers have more conflict over eating habits than almost anything else. Maybe you want your child to eat everything on his plate or perhaps he refuses to eat what you're offering. Maybe you insist that he eat his vegetables before having any dessert or perhaps you've decided it's high time that he started using his spoon instead of his fingers to feed himself.

You want to make sure that your children eat well and don't disrupt family meals. But battling with your toddler over mealtime habits will probably not cause your child to eat any better—and is sure to create an enormous disruption. Whether they take the form of pleading, arguments, ultimatums, or all three, the more battles you have over your child's

Baby Talk
"Ask your child what he wants for dinner only if he's buying."
—Fran Lebowitz

Q-Tip

Most toddlers (and preschoolers) do not have very exotic tastes. So if you and your partner prefer foods that your child doesn't like, try to make something simpler for him.

eating habits, the more likely he will be to stage an encore performance. Look at the attention he's getting. Look how much you care what he eats. Look how helpless you are to force him to eat what he doesn't want to eat—or to eat in a way that you want him to eat. That must make your toddler feel powerful.

As in any situation that you think demands disciplinary action, first ask yourself whether your expectations of "appropriate behavior" are reasonable. Frankly, most parental expectations and concerns regarding their toddler's mealtime manners don't make sense when looked at from your child's point of view—or even from a detached, disinterested point of view.

Here are some typical concerns that cause chaos at the dinner table:

➤ You want your child to eat a balanced diet. So offer your toddler a balanced selection of foods, then let him eat what he wants. If you watch what your child eats in a single day, you may conclude that your concern is warranted, but if you watch what your child eats over the next week or two, you'll start to ease up on the nutritional demands you make of your child at each meal. Day by day, children do not always balance their diets. Over the long haul, however, as long as you continue to provided balanced foods, your toddler will most likely eat a balanced diet. This may mean nothing but bread today, nothing but cheese for the next two days, and nothing but fruit for a day after that. It will all even out. Research has shown that one-year-olds who are given the chance to choose their own meals (from a balanced offering of foods) do create a balanced diet for themselves in the long run.

➤ You're concerned that your child may not be eating enough. No toddler would ever choose to starve himself. As long as you provide enough food, he will eat what he wants and needs, but this doesn't mean he needs to eat everything you offer. Trust your toddler to know when he's had enough. If he lets you know by word or by gesture that he's already full, why would you want him to finish everything on his plate? As your parents may have told you, children are indeed starving in Africa, but what good will it do them for your toddler to clean his plate?

➤ You want your child to stay at the table because mealtime is "family time." Why not just stick bamboo shoots under your toddler's fingernails or hook him up to the rack instead? Sitting is torture for a toddler. Even while your child is eating, and apparently enjoying his food, you may notice him straining to get out of his highchair every few minutes. A toddler wants nothing more than to get up and get moving—even when he's engaged in an activity that demands sitting. So even though eating is usually fun for your child, sitting around after he's done definitely isn't. You'll have a more peaceful family time if you acknowledge this fact by letting your toddler roam about as soon as he's done eating.

➤ You want your toddler to observe proper mealtime manners. Forget about it—at least for now. Your child can hardly use a spoon by himself, still has trouble stabbing things with a fork, and has only the roughest idea of what to do with a knife. Let your toddler get his food to his mouth any way he likes. His confidence and sense of independence will increase the more you allow him to feed himself. But this means putting up with the way he chooses to do it—whether this means a spoon, fingers, or shoving his face down into the plate like a pig at a trough.

> **Baby Talk**
> "A man finds out what is meant by a spitting image when he tries to feed cereal to his infant."
> —Madeline Cox

Food Is Food (Not a Bribe, Reward, Threat, or Punishment)

Parents condition their children to think of certain foods—usually candy, dessert, and other sweets—as special treats. Certainly children have a predisposition to sweets as well. But parents often make their toddler's "sweet tooth" even more powerful by offering candy and dessert as rewards for good behavior. Sweets become a symbol of your love and approval. If you elevate the status of sweets in this way, your toddler, who craves your love and approval, will continually badger you to buy her some candy or give her some ice cream as a sign of your love. If you turn her down, your toddler may feel unloved and unappreciated.

So whether you're at the dinner table or away from the table, try to avoid using food to reward "good" behavior or to punish "bad" behavior. Don't bribe your children with food to do what you want her to do—whether it's eating her broccoli, picking up her toys, or keeping her pants on in the grocery store. And don't withhold certain foods to punish your child—or threaten to withhold them in an attempt to extort good behavior.

Look at it from your toddler's point of view. You shout, "Okay, that's it. No ice cream for you today because you ran out into the street." Or you suggest, "As soon as you put your dirty clothes in the hamper, you can have some strawberries." But even after hearing you say it, your child won't make any sense of it. She cannot see the connection between her behavior, good or bad, and the food you give her as a reward or deny her as a punishment. To your child, your denial (or reward) of food will seem totally arbitrary. And when you actually stop and think about it, your toddler is right.

Let's face it. Food and discipline are like oil and water; they just don't mix.

Molding Your Child's Behavior in a Positive Way

Bribes and rewards, punishments and threats don't work at this age. So if you want your toddler to behave in a certain way, you'll have to resort to trickery (though some might call it "guidance"). Remember, your willful one-year-old will "be good" only if he wants to do what you want to do. So all you have to do is figure out a trick that will make good behavior something your toddler wants to do.

Baby Talk
"To every job that must be done, there is an element of fun. Find the fun and, snap, the job's a game."—Mary Poppins (Bill Walsh and Don DaGradi, screenwriters)

Like Mary Poppins convincing Jane and Michael Banks to clean up their room, or like Tom Sawyer tricking other boys into whitewashing a fence for him, you can often get your toddler to do what you want without shouting, threats or bribery. It's simple really: If you make it seem like fun, your toddler will want to do it.

Do you want your toddler to pick up his toys? If you try ordering him to do it, your child will probably fight you every step of the way. You can yell, punish, grab your child's hand and lead him over to the toys, even wrap his fingers around one of the toys you want off the floor. But nothing you can do will make him pick up those toys unless he wants to.

Psst! Here's a little secret: You're more clever than your toddler is. So you can probably figure out a way to make him want to do what you want him to do. Try singing a clean-up song, like the one on *Barney*. Or make a game of picking up the toys. Open up the toy chest and see how many toys he can toss into it. Or challenge your toddler by saying, "Bet you can't clean up all these toys by the time the next song is over."

Another strategy that works well with toddlers is redirecting their energies. You can get your child to stop doing something unsafe or unacceptable by providing him with safe alternatives. If, for instance, your toddler picks up a breakable object and starts to throw it or drop it, offer him a trade. You might say, "Oh, do you want to throw something?" or "You want to play catch?" Then offer him a soft ball or something else safe to throw and take away the more fragile and dangerous object. Or if your child climbs up on the piano, pick him up and say, "Pianos are not for climbing, slides are for climbing." Then immediately bring him over to the plastic slide and get him interested in that.

A third strategy that works involves distraction. Your one-year-old still has a relatively short attention span. You can use this to your advantage by employing distraction to lure your child away from unsafe or unacceptable behavior. If you get your toddler interested in something else that's safe, he may soon forget what he had wanted to do before.

As a parent, it's your job to protect your child from himself and to safeguard others from your toddler's harmful impulses. If your child tries to do something that's unsafe for him or for others, it's your duty and responsibility to frustrate his intentions. But this doesn't mean you have to abandon your toddler to his state of frustration. If you simply tell your toddler that he can't do something that he wants to do, your child will probably create a scene. He may cry, he may kick, he may scream. But don't give in. Explain your reasoning and then quickly use trickery, redirection, and/or distraction to guide your child to more acceptable behavior that he also enjoys.

Childproofing

If your child becomes fixated on doing something dangerous, you'll have to make it impossible for him. Childproofing (see Chapter 3) is not a one-time deal, but an ongoing process. As your toddler explores his world, he will discover perils that you never even imagined. Remove these dangers so that you won't have to curtail your child's explorations again and again.

Calling a Cease-Fire

You will be wise to avoid most battles with your one-year-old over behavior. In the coming years, your child will learn the difference between being "good"or "bad." At that point, she can deliberately choose between doing or not doing what you want her to do. By making it fun to behave well now, you will pave the way for fewer discipline problems in the future. The more loud and angry clashes you have with your one-year-old over behavior, the less likely she will be to cooperate and do what you ask of her later: as a preschooler, as an elementary schooler, and as a teenager.

Faced with what seems like constant disapproval, your child may stop seeking your approval altogether. Remember, your toddler cannot yet understand that you can be angry with her and still love her. So she will mistakenly interpret repeated disapproval—and especially anger—as an obvious sign that you don't love her anymore. If, during this crucial year in her development, your toddler forms an impression of you as arbitrary, angry, and unloving, she will probably not put much effort into trying to please you later in her childhood. Why should she? If all she heard as a toddler was "No!", if she was constantly being punished for being a one-year-old and doing what one-year-olds do, it will seem as if there's no pleasing you anyway.

If you steer clear of battles over behavior and make your toddler feel secure, loved, and worthy of approval, she will continue to want to please you (though not all of the time). You'll still lose count of the number of times when your child behaves in ways you'd rather she didn't. But more often than not, she will try to behave well.

The Least You Need to Know

➤ A one-year-old has no understanding of good and bad or right and wrong—and therefore no morality.

➤ Punishing an amoral toddler makes no sense. You can't reasonably punish a toddler for being a toddler.

➤ You'll have enough trouble getting your toddler to sit down long enough to eat, so don't worry too much about mealtime manners yet.

➤ You're smarter than your child. You can therefore steer your child away from dangerous or hurtful behavior and trick her into behaving the way you want.

➤ Try to get everyone going in the same direction. Cooperate with your partner in setting appropriate limits and determining appropriate disciplinary measures. Enlist grandparents, babysitters, and any other caregivers in adopting the same program— at least with your child.

Chapter 6

Breaking Up Is Hard to Do: Easing Separation Anxiety

As you certainly know by now, your toddler is no longer a baby, but he is not a secure and independent child yet either. The toddler finds himself caught between infancy and childhood—not unlike the adolescent who is caught between childhood and adulthood. And like the later passage from childhood to adulthood, the transition of the toddler between infancy and childhood does not always go smoothly.

Like the teenager, your toddler wants to do more than he can. He wants to be independent. He does still depend on you for a lot, but this dependence frustrates and at times infuriates him. Because neither of these transitions are easy, it's not surprising that both toddlers and teenagers feel an enormous amount of anxiety. (Look on the bright side—at least your toddler doesn't have to worry about pimples!)

What's Your Toddler So Afraid Of?

Separation anxiety usually becomes strongest in children from about 9 to 18 months. In most cases, this anxiety first appears around the time your child begins crawling. This is no coincidence. As your baby becomes increasingly mobile, she may recognize how much her sense of security depends on staying close to you. This hazy recognition transforms your early toddler into a yo-yo: She will wander away, but never far, and then she comes rushing back.

Baby Talk
"Fond as we are of our loved ones, there comes at times during their absence an unexplained peace."—Anne Shaw

As your toddler becomes more and more independent in terms of her movement, speech, and desires, she realizes how much she still depends on you. Your toddler still needs you very much. You provide the sense of security and safety that allows your toddler to become more and more independent.

The Toddler's Dance

Your toddler wants to be independent, to become her own person, to free herself from your control. Yet at the same time, she wants to continue to depend on you absolutely to protect and care for her. She wants to be a big kid, but she also wants to be babied.

So the drive for greater independence proceeds in fits and starts: two steps forward and one step back. Your child's urge for independence will seesaw with her need for security. The result: a toddler's dance. Your child will separate, then quickly reunite; withdraw, then come back; push away, then cling; shout, "All by myself," then whine, "Help me!"

At times, your toddler will seem willful and contrary, but within minutes, the icicle will melt. Your child will suddenly latch on to your legs and refuse to let go, or she will climb up and cuddle in your lap, clinging to you and asking for comfort.

At any age, increased independence often leads to generalized feelings of insecurity. So despite your child's growing desire—and need—for independence (in fact because of it), she still needs you to provide her with that essential feeling of security that allows and encourages separation. Your toddler wants independence, but she doesn't feel safe to be apart from you. Whenever you drift out of your child's sight, she may panic. She may burst into tears and collapse to the ground or she may run around at random screaming for you. To avoid this panic, your toddler may try desperately to keep you in sight every minute of the day.

As your toddler's anxiety increases, any separation from you may bring on a momentary regression to infancy. She suddenly becomes inarticulate and cries bitterly. In time, her anxiety may become so severe that your toddler cries every time you start to leave the room.

The signs of separation anxiety are pretty easy to spot. Your toddler will constantly want to be a part of you rather than apart from you. For this reason, she will:

➤ become clingier in general;

➤ often follow you from room to room;

➤ insist on holding your hand when walking with you;

➤ repeatedly elbow her way onto your lap;

➤ try to be on her best behavior (in other words, if she knows or can remember what pleases you, she'll try to do it);

➤ seem more wary or shy of others;

➤ try to withdraw into you in crowds or unfamiliar places;

➤ whine more often; and

➤ seem more like a baby.

Reasonable Doubt (and Fear)

Why shouldn't your toddler feel anxious and upset when you leave him or he loses sight of you? You are the source of your child's security, so when he can't see you, he feels unsafe. Your toddler's fear of separation is basic and primal: He's afraid you'll never come back.

Remember, your toddler still has an extremely limited memory and virtually no ability to anticipate the future. Your child lives entirely in the moment. What's happening now is all that matters to him—and indeed almost all he knows. And at that moment when anxiety floods through him, all your toddler knows is that you've left him (or are leaving him) and that he is (or soon will be) all alone. (Oh, sure, there's a babysitter or other caretaker—but no one really counts except you.)

Your toddler probably feels not only fear, but anger as well. He doesn't like you to go anywhere without him. In fact, he probably doesn't even like the fact that you can go somewhere without him. With his increasing mobility, your toddler is now beginning to understand that you and he are not the same person. Sometimes, this discovery excites him. He has fun experimenting with his newfound ability to go away and come back. But at other times, especially when you're going somewhere without him, your toddler deeply resents your ability to do the same.

Making the Separation Easier—for Everyone

Let's start with a basic assumption: You can't make it all better. No healthy toddler can avoid going through the difficult process of separation and individuation. You cannot stay with your child every minute of every day and even if you could, that wouldn't take care of everything. Separation anxiety stems from the conflict between your child's urge for independence and her need for security. You can't make that conflict go away no matter what you do. But you can help your child in her struggle with that conflict.

First of all, try not to get annoyed by your toddler's whining and clinging. Instead, take it as a compliment. If you had failed to form a warm and loving relationship with your child, she probably wouldn't care if you left. So bear with the tears and tantrums. The fact that your toddler makes such a fuss when you leave shows that she loves you.

Probably the most important thing you can do to ease your child's anxiety about separation is to offer her a balance between freedom and security. Independence springs from the combination of these two conditions: having the opportunity to venture off on one's own and feeling safe enough to do it.

If you increase your toddler's freedom but deny her a sense of security, your child, filled with anxiety, will flounder. (So don't just leave your toddler alone in her room for extended periods of time thinking it will make her more independent. It won't.)

On the other hand, if you provide your child with plenty of security but little freedom, your child will likely become either extremely timid or very rebellious. Either way, you will transform your child's struggle for eventual and inevitable independence into a hard-fought battle.

The Balancing Act

Because neither freedom nor security alone will facilitate your child's independence, you need to strive for a balance between the two:

➤ Try to be there for your child whenever he needs you. You're still the "home base." Whenever your toddler asks for it, he needs to know that you will give him the security he needs. This knowledge will in turn bolster your child's courage to venture out independently.

➤ At the same time, provide your toddler with safe environments that allow him almost free reign.

➤ When separation anxiety seems particularly painful for your child, pamper him to help him feel more secure. Your toddler may need a little babying, which is fine as long as it doesn't go on forever. Treat him just as you would if he were sick: Shower him with extra attention and care.

➤ Your toddler's anxiety may lead to nightmares or sleep disturbances—especially the obvious one of not being able to get to sleep without you in the room, preferably holding him. He may kick and scream and cry for hours if you leave him alone in his crib. If so, give yourself permission to sit beside him until he falls asleep; do this for a week or so. Then, as his anxiety begins to wane a bit, gradually return to the sleep routines that allow you more freedom of movement. (See Chapter 4 for more on sleep disturbances.)

Childproofing
Try to avoid making major lifestyle changes during your child's second year. Putting him into a different situation will dramatically increase his insecurity and separation. For example, if you can manage it, put off taking a job that requires you to change your child's day-care provider (or put him in day care for the first time) until after your child's second birthday.

Don't Minimize the Fear

Your toddler feels fear intensely. It does not matter that her fears are groundless, that she remains safe in your absence, and that you will return soon. Your toddler's feelings are real and reasonable—at least until she develops a greater ability to remember (your dependability in the past) and anticipate (your promised return in the future). So don't ignore your child's tears or the fear that you suspect underlies them.

The more you try to minimize and deny your toddler's fears, the more anxious she will become. This heightened anxiety will only make her cling more tightly to you, begging for your continued understanding, protection, and support.

Keep in mind that though she may seem worlds apart from it by now, your toddler was a baby just a few months ago. She is still not capable of taking care of herself physically or emotionally. She can neither control nor cope with her own emotions. In fact, she's probably not even comfortable yet with her emotions or their intensity. So if you deny the validity of those emotions that overwhelm her, if you refuse to recognize and acknowledge them, your toddler will become even more desperate for your love, presence, and attention.

Don't bother trying to defeat your toddler's fear with adult logic. Fear is a constellation of emotions, and powerful feelings seldom respond very well to appeals of reason. Before you try to talk your toddler out of her fear, consider your own fears. Are you afraid of anything? Snakes? Heights? If so, are your fears based in logic and reason? Does reason (knowing that a particular snake is harmless or that a guard rail will prevent you from falling) make them go away? Of course not. So accept your child's fear as real, too—regardless of whether you think it's warranted.

Don't tell your toddler not to be afraid. Because she has no control over her emotions, she can't possibly put her fears away like that. Instead, acknowledge your child's fear and respond to it.

For example:

➤ Tell your toddler that there's really nothing to be afraid of. ("Nothing bad will happen to you while I'm away.")

➤ At the same time, appreciate the reality of your child's fear. ("But I can see that you're scared.")

➤ And respond to it. ("So I'll stay a few minutes longer to help you feel more comfortable.")

Ultimately, you'll still have to leave. But your toddler may draw some comfort from the fact that you—her chief protector—understand her feelings and are trying to accommodate them. Just having someone else—especially you—put her inarticulate fears into words may help dissipate them a little.

Don't Overprotect

When separation anxiety strikes, you'll need to baby your child a little. But overprotectiveness—too much babying—may cause either excessive dependence or an explosion of anger, frustration, and rebelliousness from your toddler. Remember, your child does want to be independent. Responding to that need—and the anxiety it creates—demands a delicate and constantly shifting balance.

Overprotectiveness sometimes causes parents to appear hesitant to turn the care of their child over to another person. Yet your toddler is watching you carefully, trying to gauge your feelings as a template for his own. Your child will sense how you feel about the separation, too. If you telegraph your own anxiety or ambivalence, or if you say good-bye three or four different times, your child will feel even more anxious about the dangers that will beset him after you leave. So put on a happy face and reassure your toddler that everything will be okay. It will actually help your child if he sees you cheerful and confident about the separation.

Childproofing

If your child's separation anxiety does become severe enough to pull him out of day care, you might find it worthwhile to consult your pediatrician or a child psychologist to try to find out what's behind it.

It may help to make a moderate appeal to the bravery and independence that your toddler strives for. However, because bravery by definition involves doing something frightening, you will first need to acknowledge and respect your child's fears. Show your toddler that you recognize and understand his feelings and encourage him to express them. Praise your child for the bravery and effort it takes to try to control his fears. Encourage and compliment him whenever he shows signs that he is ready to give up just a little more dependence.

Try to avoid extreme measures. Don't pull your child out of day care, for example, unless he's truly terrified and panic-stricken—not just at parting, but for most of the time when you're away. Talk to your babysitter or day-care provider to find out how your toddler seems while you're gone.

Helpful Reassurance: Preparing Your Child in Advance

More than anything else, your own attitude can help your child to overcome her fear. Your confidence will increase your toddler's confidence. Your cheerfulness will help reduce her tears. Your fearlessness will help her let go of her own fears. Your encouragement will heighten her sense of competence.

Besides projecting an air of confidence, you can take a number of other steps that might be effective in easing your toddler's separation anxiety even before you step out the door:

➤ Play peek-a-boo or hide and seek often with your toddler. Games of disappearance and reappearance will help strengthen your child's grasp of "object constancy." They provide concrete evidence that you can "go away," but you will always come back.

➤ Let your toddler know how much you love her and will miss her while you're away. When you return, praise your child's courage. Tell her how proud you are of her, how brave she was, and again how much you love her.

➤ Acknowledge and, as much as you can, try to ease your toddler's fears and sadness. (Though your child will still be afraid, your efforts may reduce the intensity and duration of her fear.)

➤ Plan special activities for your babysitter and your toddler and then let your child know how much fun she'll have while you're gone.

➤ Ask your babysitter to take your child out to your child's favorite park or playground before you leave. It may be easier for your child to leave you than to have you leave her. (Be sure to let your child know that you won't be there when she comes back from the park. This could be an unwelcome surprise.)

➤ Make good use of the electronic babysitter. Videotape yourself reading one of your toddler's favorite books or singing some favorite songs. Your (human) babysitter can play them while you're away.

➤ If it's not bedtime—or beyond—when you return, plan a special activity that you will do with your child as soon as you get home. Let your toddler know your plan in advance.

➤ Make sure that your first few outings apart from your child are short ones (no more than an hour). This will give your toddler a chance to get used to the idea that you can go away and come back relatively quickly. As your toddler gets more used to the idea—if not more comfortable with it—you can gradually increase the time you stay away.

Short and Sometimes Sweet: Less Painful Partings

One of the keys to less painful partings is your toddler's familiarity with, and affection for, your babysitter or day-care provider. Things will go much easier for you, for your baby, and for your sitter if your toddler knows and likes the person who will be caring for him while you're away. An unfamiliar sitter will further frighten your toddler and create even more anxiety.

So if you're using a new sitter, ask her (or him) to come and meet your child once or twice before you leave the two of them alone. The opportunity to play with the sitter for an hour or two while you are still there will give your child a chance to grow more comfortable with her (or him).

Similarly, visit your day-care center (or the home of your day-care provider) several times together before you begin dropping your toddler off by himself. Try to spend the first two or three days at the day-care center with your child. Stay close by, but encourage him to play while you remain "offstage" as much as possible. These days together will offer your child the extra security he may need to form some attachments to the place, to the day-care provider, and perhaps to some other children.

After you and your toddler have become more comfortable with the sitter or day-care provider, it's time for the big date. Try to avoid having to hand off your child and rush out the door. Ask your babysitter to come a half an hour early (paid, of course). Especially with a new sitter, this time will give your toddler a chance to remember and become comfortable with the sitter before you "abandon" him. Even with a known and loved sitter, this extra half an hour will allow your toddler and the sitter to become engaged in something fun or fascinating by the time you leave.

The same thinking applies to day-care situations. Try to arrive five or ten minutes early at your day-care center. That way you won't have to rush off. Instead, you can help your child get involved in play—or enlist the day-care provider's help—before you leave.

Q-Tip
If your toddler falls apart every time you leave the day-care center, consider the possibility of copping out. Ask your partner or someone else to take your child to day care. (Again, your child may find it easier to leave you than to see you leave.)

Comfort items and rituals can help make parting less painful, too:

➤ Let your toddler hold on tight to a comfort object (a security blanket, a favorite stuffed animal, and so on) when it's time for you to go.

➤ Develop a special parting ritual—some combination of hugs, kisses, good-byes, thrown kisses, waving, and so on. Though the new ritual may not help the first few times, as it becomes more established it will help your child recall memories of past partings (and hopefully of later reunions as well).

➤ Don't draw out the ritual endlessly. Remember, your toddler may want to repeat it exactly every time you go anywhere without him and this could go on for several years to come.

➤ When the time comes for you to leave, say good-bye with affection, confidence, and happiness. Your child will want to see clearly what your mood is like. If you look unsure or anguished, your toddler will feel insecure, too.

Sneaking Away

How much should you distract your child, diverting attention away from your leaving? To sneak or not to sneak, that is the question.

Sneaking out while your toddler is engaged with the babysitter or day-care provider may initially seem easier than the otherwise tearful good-byes. But your child is no dummy. Eventually she will notice that you've gone. What message does that send? That you're unreliable, that your toddler can't trust you, even to stick around. If you wait for the chance to sneak off unnoticed, she'll start watching you like a hawk from now on and will follow you from room to room even more closely than before.

You—and your child and your sitter—will be much better off if you take a more straightforward approach. Tell your child where you're going and remind her that you'll be back in a little while. Try to be loving but firm. You need to inform your child that you're going out; you don't need to ask her for permission. Though your honesty may prompt tears, at least it lets your toddler know that you're leaving, rather than letting her discover it later and freak out with the babysitter.

Childproofing
The fear that motivates long, tearful good-byes is genuine. However, by their second birthday, some toddlers learn to use their fear to manipulate their parents. If your toddler sees that you will do almost anything to calm her down, she will gain a tremendous sense of her own power over you. Your child will demand more concessions from you before she will cooperate—not just with leave-taking, but with anything you want her to do. Eventually, you'll have to draw the line and say, "No more."

After You've Gone

After you've left your child for the evening (or the morning), you may need to begin dealing with your own separation anxiety. Don't be reluctant to call your day-care provider or babysitter, even after only half an hour or so. If your child knows and likes the sitter, your child will probably calm down within a few minutes after you leave. You may want to be reassured that your toddler has indeed calmed down. If you call and find out that your child is still upset, you may decide to alter your plans (by coming home a little earlier or even coming home right away and trying again another time). You may have to build up more gradually to a full night or morning out.

Finally, try your best to come back when you said you would, even though your child can't tell time yet. Remind your child beforehand that you always do come back whenever you go away. Then, develop a ritual announcing your triumphant return: "See? I told you I'd come back. And here I am!"

The Least You Need to Know

➤ Your toddler teeters between the urge for independence and the need for security.

➤ Your child's fear is real. Whether the danger he fears is real is irrelevant.

➤ Overprotectiveness will telegraph your own ambivalence and anxieties to your child and make his separation anxiety even worse.

➤ Talk to your toddler about his fears. Show him that you love him and understand his fears.

➤ Give your child time to get to know his babysitter or day-care provider *before* you leave them on their own.

➤ Establish predictable routines for both parting and reuniting.

Playtime!

Play is fun for both you and your toddler, but for your toddler, play is much more than fun. Through play, your child explores her world, discovers new things, sees how different objects feel or move, learns new abilities, and practices and masters new skills.

Play is neither a waste of time, idle indulgence, or mere busy work for your child. Play is how your toddler best learns and develops. For your toddler, everything involves learning. No matter what she's doing at any moment, your child is learning something. Play just means that she also enjoys what she's doing. And what could be better for your child than enjoying learning?

You and your partner are your toddler's first and best teachers. And toys and play are your best teaching tools. Through games, toys, and play, you can stimulate all of your child's senses as well as her physical and mental development. You can help your toddler learn about the natural and human worlds, find out how things work, and build skills she'll need throughout her life. By choosing age-appropriate games, toys, and play, you can make learning fun, interesting, and enjoyable for both you and your child. And the love for learning you create in your child now can establish a pattern that will last for the rest of her life.

Rules of the Game: Playing with Your Child

During your child's second year, you will remain his favorite plaything. He will enjoy jumping on you, climbing all over you, and having you toss him up in the air (please catch him, too). He will love dancing with you, chasing you, and having you chase him. He will listen intently as you talk and sing and he will delight in trying to make you smile and laugh.

Baby Talk

"Lambs skip and bound, kittens and puppies seem wild with the joy of life; and little children naturally run, leap, dance and shout in the exuberance of that capacity for happiness which the young human heart feels as instinctively as the flower buds open to the sun. To repress their natural joyousness, not to direct and train it for the good, seems to be the object of most parents."—Sarah Josepha Hale

Set aside special times to play with your child, but even aside from these playtimes, try to make everything you do with your child fun. While you change your child's diaper, sing a silly song or give him a toy to play with. When you dress your child, play a quick game of peek-a-boo as you pull a shirt over his head. When you cook dinner, let your toddler serenade you with selections from his pots-and-pans percussion band. When you do the laundry, play a little basketball, letting him throw and slam-dunk clothes into the washing machine.

Try not to worry too much about how much your child is learning through his play. All your attempts to teach your child at this age should have an element of fun in them. But not all fun needs to have an element of teaching. Your toddler will learn something—that water is wet, that blocks don't roll, that balls drop down, that balloons float up, and that bubbles waft up and then sink down—whether or not you make a conscious effort to teach him something. That's what toddlers do.

Trust your toddler to learn through play. Give him the time and freedom he needs to explore toys and playthings on his own. Sit on your hands if you have to. But try not to disrupt your child's experimentation with a new plaything by showing him how to do it. You're an adult. Of course you know the "right" way to play with that toy or game. Yes, you could probably fit that puzzle piece into the hole faster than your toddler. But your child has distinctly non-adult ways to play with it, too. So unless your child asks for your help, back off and let him steer the direction of his own play.

This does not mean you should leave your child entirely to his own devices. You can play a number of valuable roles that will help your toddler get the most out of his play:

➤ **Cheerleader**   Applaud your child every time he achieves his goal or masters a new skill.

➤ **Playmate**   Your toddler can't play certain games without a partner. You can roll the ball back to him or play "chase me," for example.

➤ **Research Assistant** Bring your young scientist the things he needs for his experiments.

➤ **Expert** Answer your child's questions about what he's playing with or show him how to do something if he asks.

➤ **Psychologist** Help your child deal with the frustration of wanting to do more than he's physically capable of doing. Talk to him, encourage him, comfort him, and offer your help if he wants it.

Baby Talk
"The illusions of childhood are necessary experiences: A child should not be denied a balloon because an adult knows that sooner or later it will burst."
—Marcelene Cox

Pay attention to how your toddler is playing and what he is doing with a toy. For the most part, let your child's own instincts guide him in how and what to play. If you do see another way he could play or if you think of something that might also be fun, offer your guidance only as a suggestion. Then let your child decide whether he's interested in taking you up on it. After all, your notions about how to play are neither more important nor more valid than your toddler's ideas.

Choosing Appropriate Toys and Games

Your one-year-old is an explorer. And because almost everything is still new to her, she will not get bored easily. She'll have fun with almost anything you give her.

Simple toys (blocks, stacking cups, balls) are by far the most versatile and long-lasting. Your one-year-old can discover several different uses for stacking cups: building towers, nesting one inside another, hiding smaller toys underneath, pouring water, scooping sand, and so on. And she'll find still more uses for them when she's two, three, and four years old.

In selecting playthings, choose a variety of toys that stimulate all five of your toddler's senses: sight, hearing, smell, taste, and touch. Try to select toys that offer your child different colors, different textures, a variety of shapes, and different sounds.

Baby Talk
"All…, sweet child of nature, is pleasing to thee, because all is new: O youth, what a season of delight is thine."
—Sydney Owenson Morgan

Whatever you do give your toddler, make sure that it's safe. Avoid any plaything that:

➤ has sharp edges;

➤ has loose parts (for example, the eyes of stuffed animals);

Q-Tip

Not all of your child's playthings need to be store-bought toys. In fact, you may find that your toddler sometimes prefers the box to the toy that came in it. You can find dozens of suitable—and often versatile—playthings throughout your house. Look in the kitchen. Fruits and vegetables can be fun to play with. Your toddler will love wooden and plastic spoons; measuring spoons; spatulas; pots, pans, and lids; plastic colanders; funnels; plastic bottles and jars; and cups and plates. Cardboard tubes from paper towel and toilet paper rolls, cardboard boxes, and plastic containers can entertain your toddler for hours. Look in a desk drawer. You'll find plastic rulers, protractors, pieces of paper (crumpled or flat), and transparent tape that you can wad up into a big, sticky ball.

Q-Tip

Your toddler is still almost as easily distracted as she was when she was a baby. So if she is playing with something you need—a spatula or other cooking utensil, for example—give her another plaything instead. By offering your baby a trade, you will retrieve the object you need with little or no fuss. She quickly will shift her focus to the new toy and drop the old one.

➤ has small parts;

➤ is less than two inches in diameter (a choking hazard);

➤ has a pull-string longer than one foot;

➤ has holes that her finger(s) might get caught in;

➤ is made of glass;

➤ is already broken;

➤ is toxic; or

➤ will hurt her toes when she drops it (as she eventually always will).

Try rotating your toddler's toys every week or so. Put some of them away and pull out forgotten ones from the bottom of the toy chest or the shelves she usually neglects to search. If you give your child the same toy again and again and again, you'll deny her the opportunity to explore the world in all its diversity.

If your toddler does get bored with a particular toy or game, try something else instead. Encourage your child, but don't pressure her. Don't get so set on teaching your toddler how to build a tower of blocks, for example, that you ignore her boredom or frustration. Try to remain flexible. Let your toddler make up the rules that govern her own play. (You can play with your child's toys any way you like after she's gone to bed.)

Skill Building Through Play

Before his second birthday, your one-year-old will learn, practice, and perhaps even master a remarkable number of skills. He will move from crawling to walking to running. He will go from babbling to chattering. On his first birthday, he could just barely pick things up and grasp them. By his second, he can pick objects up with ease, rotate them, throw them, catch them (well, some of the time), and stack them. Toys play a critical role in these developments. The best toys for your toddler give him an opportunity to practice all these new skills in a variety of different ways.

Balance, Walking, and Climbing

Even before your child can walk, he can use toys and games to strengthen his leg muscles and improve his balance:

➤ Ride-on toys with wheels (cars, trucks, scooters, various animals) can help your child do both. Your one-year-old also will enjoy the mobility these toys provide: By pushing down with his feet, he can scoot along without having to stay on the ground. This gives your toddler an entirely new perspective on the world inside your home.

➤ After he's started walking, a pushcart or push-along corn popper can help him practice. Pushcarts are sometimes designed as shopping carts, trucks, baby carriages, vacuum cleaners, or lawn mowers—which make them not only useful to the early walker, but also fun for later toddler games of make-believe.

Make sure any pushcart you choose has a low center of gravity. It needs to be stable enough for your early toddler to use the handle to pull himself to a standing position. If your child is not yet steady on his feet and the pushcart is lightweight or top heavy, it will flip over on top of him.

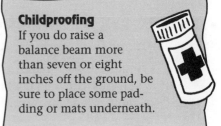

Q-Tip
When you choose pushcarts or other toys for your toddler, be careful about sexual stereotyping. There's no reason why your son won't enjoy a shopping cart or your daughter, a truck.

Childproofing
If you do raise a balance beam more than seven or eight inches off the ground, be sure to place some padding or mats underneath.

➤ A makeshift balance beam can help your toddler improve his balance and the coordination of his feet. At first, just set a six-foot length of board directly on the floor. As your child's balance improves enough to let him negotiate the length of the board successfully, then you can start to raise it a little by putting several books under each end of the board. By your child's second birthday, you may be able to raise it all the way to chair level.

➤ As your toddler's standing balance and walking both improve, he will acquire the ability to turn his head while walking. At this point, a pull toy will entertain him, especially if it makes clicking or other noises. Noisy pull toys allow your child another opportunity to observe cause (movement) and effect (noise). Another good pull toy is a train that links up cars using hooks and rings. This encourages experimentation (will a ring connect with a ring?) while improving your toddler's manual dexterity.

➤ Near the end of your child's second year, he will enjoy "kicking" a large, soft ball. Actually, he won't really kick the ball, because he cannot yet sustain one-legged balance. But he'll use his legs and lower body to bump it along in front of him and he'll have a lot of fun doing it.

➤ Games and activities can help improve walking skills, too. "Ring-around-a-rosy" will let your toddler practice sitting, standing, squatting, jumping up, walking sideways in a circle, and maintaining his balance throughout. Dancing to any kind of music also will improve balance and walking skills.

➤ A toddler slide or toddler steps that are safe for your child to climb are also good ideas. Having a safe alternative will help curtail your toddler's urge to climb on more dangerous chairs, benches, sofas, tables, and shelves.

➤ After your toddler has mastered a variety of walking and climbing skills, set up an obstacle course using cloth tunnels, sofa cushions, cardboard boxes, toddler slides, and so on. Your child will love to crawl, climb, stand, and walk through, around, over, and under all the obstacles you create.

Hand-Eye Coordination

Toys that challenge your toddler's ability to manipulate objects will provide her with practice using her hands and seeing how they work. Your child will be amazed to discover that hands can build (and take apart), stack (and knock down), and put one thing inside of another (and take it out).

Q-Tip
Toddlers especially like large blocks, which allow them a feeling of power as they build towers as large as themselves. Large cardboard bricks do the trick. You can construct lightweight blocks by filling old diaper boxes with newspaper and taping them shut.

➤ By about 15 months, your toddler will probably be able to build a three-block tower—or line up five or six blocks in a row. Blocks of various kinds are very versatile learning tools (as well as fun toys).

➤ Toys that fit together also let your toddler practice new manipulative skills. Stacking and nesting cups (which also can be used to build a tower) are classics. Six or eight plastic bowls of the same size work especially well for the early "nester," because they can fit together in any order.

➤ Your toddler will enjoy filling and dumping containers, too: sand buckets, plastic bottles, shape molds, and those same stacking cups and plastic bowls.

Your child will love experimenting with the different properties of water, sand, and snow that she discovers through filling and pouring. She can practice these skills in the bathtub or kiddie pool, a sandbox, or even a large pan filled with uncooked rice.

➤ Wooden (or plastic) jigsaw puzzles will give your toddler lots of practice at complex hand-eye coordination. At first, choose puzzles that have a knob on each piece, which will make it easier for your child to grasp and rotate. Besides helping improve your toddler's manual dexterity, puzzles can increase your child's understanding and appreciation of different shapes.

But don't wander off when your child's doing a puzzle. She may initially need your help figuring out how to turn and fit the pieces. Or you may want to help by sorting pieces and limiting your child's choices—which may cut down on her frustration level while still allowing her to do the puzzle herself. Even when she insists on doing it herself, your toddler will probably show more patience and persistence if you stay with her and cheer her on.

➤ As your toddler nears her second birthday, a shape box (a box with cut-outs on the sides for inserting different shaped blocks) is also terrific for improving manual dexterity. Like jigsaw puzzles, however, shape boxes demand mastery of a complex set of skills: Your child not only has to match the shape of a hole and the shape of a piece; he also needs to rotate her wrist to fit the piece through the hole.

➤ Your child will start sorting objects (though not always according to a classification you will understand) in the second half of her second year. What's alike? What's different? Your toddler may organize all her balls or stuffed animals. Or she may separate all the cows from the pigs in a toy farm set.

➤ Though your child probably can't catch yet, that doesn't mean you should ignore the play possibilities of balls. Given a large enough ball (about half the size of a beach ball—or a beach ball itself), your toddler can kick it, roll it, and stop it with her hands when you roll it back.

A large balloon also makes a great lightweight ball that cannot hurt your child. Your toddler can spend lots of time trying to catch it—or at least keep it up in the air by chasing it down and swatting it. If you add a cardboard tube from a roll of paper towels, you'll have a perfectly safe bat and ball set for indoor or outdoor play.

Childproofing
Always supervise your child when she's playing with a balloon. If it pops, it will not only startle your child, but also become a choking hazard.

85

Arts and Crafts

Even one-year-olds take satisfaction in creating works of art and love to admire and show off the products of their work. You can encourage your young artist by giving him plenty of supplies:

➤ Throughout the second year, your child will find scribbling with crayons and chalk fun and easy. At the beginning of the year, you might do well to start with thick crayons and sidewalk chalk, but by the end of the year, he should be able to handle smaller crayons as well as chalkboard chalk.

➤ At one, your child will probably enjoy finger painting (unless he's exceedingly fastidious about clean hands), which allows a direct and sensual experience of creating art. A little later in the year, you can let him try his hand with a thick brush. You might want to give your toddler some valuable practice by giving him a large paint brush and a bucket of water so he can "paint" the sidewalk.

➤ Sculpting also offers your child a sensual experience of art. Media like molding clay and playdough—whether homemade or store-bought—will give your toddler a hands-on opportunity to create shapes, mix colors, and discover the delightful sensation of squishiness.

Childproofing
Make sure that all art supplies used by your toddler are non-toxic—and hopefully washable, too.

➤ If you don't want your toddler decorating the walls, floors, tables, and chairs, you'll need to provide him with plenty of surfaces on which he can create his work. Blank paper, the back of junk mail, and cardboard can all yield works for your permanent collection. For temporary exhibitions, try a chalkboard, washable placemats, your walkway, your driveway, or the sidewalk.

Language and Music

For a year now, you've been singing songs to your child: lullabies at bedtime, silly songs at playtime, active songs like "If You're Happy and You Know It" and "Wheels on the Bus" in parent-baby play groups. Now it's time for the two of you to start singing together.

Certainly you should continue to sing lullabies and play songs to your child, but encourage your toddler to join in the clapping, stomping, and rolling wheels of active songs. Start to invite your child to sing along with you. (Many young children seem to know many more words in songs than they do in everyday conversation.)

Your child also can begin to make music with various musical instruments. Pot-and-pan "drums" allow your child to make delightful sounds—at least to your toddler. Other favorites include such simple musical instruments as a small xylophone, a toy piano, or an electric toy piano.

By the end of your toddler's second year, she may not just be banging at random any-more. Instead, she will start experimenting with carefully selected notes to see what "melody" they produce. (It may not necessarily be anything you would recognize, but it will be music to you child's ears.)

Continuing to read or recite nursery rhymes, like singing play songs and lullabies, will help improve your toddler's language comprehension and verbalization skills. Other games that can help are:

➤ **Where's...?** Ask your child to point out certain objects or animals in the room or in a book. This game encourages your toddler to know the names of all the things in her immediate world.

➤ **Touch 'Em** Ask your toddler to "touch your ears, touch your nose, touch your mouth, touch your toes," and so on. This lets your toddler demonstrate her ability to understand (and eventually to say) the names of her body parts.

Story Time and Make Believe

Your child will probably love reading and hearing short stories during his second year. Books are probably the second best language builders (talking with you naturally comes in first). Reading opens up so many possibilities. It offers opportunities to teach your toddler about the world and about colors, shapes, and textures.

Despite the notoriously short attention span of the typical one-year-old, your toddler will probably settle down for more than two minutes if you sit with him to read. (He probably won't sit still for very long if you just give him a book to "read" by himself.) Quiet quality time spent reading with you also offers your toddler a break from always being on the go.

If you really want to encourage your child to enjoy reading, schedule special times to read every day (naptime or bedtime are good times). Even though your toddler won't understand them word for word, simple storybooks are fine for one-year-olds. But try

Q-Tip
Your one-year-old will probably love the simple stories and bright, colorful, and clear illustra-tions in the books of the following authors: Sandra Boynton, Margaret Wise Brown, Eric Hill, Helen Oxenbury, Jan Pienkowski, Richard Scarry, Rosemary Wells, and Vera B. Williams.

to remain flexible. Don't be a fanatic about reading every word on every page of the book. When your baby seems to be getting bored with one page, turn to the next even if you haven't finished reading. (He may even reach over and start to do it for you. If he does, take the hint.)

Toddlers love repetition. So don't be surprised if your child wants to read the same book or hear the same story over and over again. In fact, you may not have even finished the last page of a favorite book before your toddler asks you to read it again. Try to maintain your enthusiasm—and your sense of humor—no matter how many times your child asks you to reread a book.

Give your child plastic books, bath books, sturdy board books, and texture books—especially ones with bright colors and large, simple pictures (one object per page, clearly illustrated or photographed). These books allow your baby to explore them on his own without destroying them. By about 18 months, your child will probably have the manual dexterity needed to flip through books on his own. (Okay, so he'll usually turn more than one page at a time, but he'll make progress nonetheless.)

Q-Tip

Consider making story-time part of your child's bedtime or naptime routine. Tape yourself reading some of your child's favorite books. After reading one special book, say goodnight and turn on the tape. Homemade story tapes also come in handy on long car trips or when you have to put your toddler down for 10 or 15 minutes to get dinner going.

Also, place the books where your toddler can reach them. Many parents (and most daycare providers) fear that toddlers will destroy their own books (and often with good reason). So they put all books high up on a shelf where toddlers can't get them. But this prevents toddlers from choosing to play with books if that's what they want to do.

If your toddler is consistently ripping books apart, then okay, move them out of harm's way. But keeping books away from your toddler as a regular policy will literally and figuratively distance your child from reading.

Imaginary Play

Don't ignore the value of dolls, stuffed animals, and puppets. Besides keeping watch over your children at night, dolls and stuffed animals can perform several valuable functions for your toddler. They encourage imaginative play for both boys and girls.

Late in his second year, your toddler will probably show an interest in playing "Let's pretend." She'll want to make believe she's the mommy or the daddy. Role-playing games like these give your toddler valuable practice in expressing emotions, sharing, and caring for others (through feeding, dressing, putting a doll to bed, and even "disciplining" a naughty doll). In addition, dolls allow your child to vent aggressive feelings that you won't let her inflict on other people: hitting, biting, kicking, pinching.

Toddlers love to play at being adult. Imitating adult behavior will help promote your child's confidence and sense of independence. Children's cooking sets, tea sets, garden sets, telephones, all give your toddler a chance to try to "be like you." Miniatures (cars, doll houses, farm sets, and so on) also allow your toddler to re-create adult worlds with scenes and activities that he's observed.

Splish, Splash, Taking a Bath

Bathtime (or pooltime) is fun time for your toddler. Playing with water is both fun and fascinating. Your child can see it, and he can touch it, but he can't hold it for more than a second before it washes out through his fingers. And pouring water, which can flow so smoothly, is not at all like dumping sand or any other solid. Old favorites such as rubber duckies or other floating animals will of course delight your toddler in the bath or wading pool. But almost anything else that floats (so long as it's safe) will also be a big hit. Try these for water play:

➤ Plastic stacking cups or other unbreakable containers (like plastic measuring cups or bottles) which are great for filling and emptying with water.

Childproofing
Never leave your toddler alone in the bath or wading pool—not even for a second.

➤ Watering cans or cups with one or more holes in the bottom which allow him to create his own stream or, if you hold it above his hands, play "catch the water."

➤ Floating balls, boats, bath books, and foam toys are fun to set sailing and then to try and catch.

➤ Bathtub activity centers that spin or rise or make noise when your toddler pours water through them.

➤ Bathtub crayons, which are great for the budding artist.

➤ Bubble baths, which are just plain fun.

Try not to rush your toddler in and out of the bath. Let your child continue to have some time to play naked. Of course, you'll have to make sure that the room—or the day, if you're playing in the outdoor wading pool—is warm enough for your toddler. If so, naked play will give your toddler the chance to experience an array of sensations that he can't get any other way: The contrast between a splash of cool water and the warmth and softness of the towel you wrap around him; the warmth of the sun on his back; the touch of a breeze on his belly. Would anyone want to deny these pleasures to a child?

The Great Outdoors

Besides splashing about in wading pools, your toddler will enjoy lots of time outdoors. Just running around, climbing, jumping, and swinging will help your toddler establish greater control over her body. And because even the largest of homes get a little cramped for all the activity of a toddler, the best place to get all this exercise is the great outdoors.

Childproofing
Make sure that any playground you visit with your child is in good condition. Equipment should be free of chipping or peeling paint and should rest on top of sand, wood chips, or a cushioned surface.

If you have safe playground equipment in your yard, make the most of it. If you don't, find the nearest playground—especially if it's designed for younger children, so that your child won't be intimidated by older kids. Toddlers love swings, slides, seesaws, swinging gates, sandboxes, and safe equipment to climb.

Public playgrounds also give both of you the rare opportunity for social interaction. Your child at this stage will probably not take full advantage of this opportunity, but you can meet with other parents of toddlers, share ideas, and perhaps even arrange some play dates.

Don't ignore nature's playground either. Parks, fields, and meadows provide plenty of safe space for your child to run, jump, tumble, roll, and have fun. And because they offer wildflowers, grass, mud, leaves, and sticks for your child to collect and analyze, wide open spaces also can stimulate your child's continued thirst for exploration, discovery, and learning.

The Least You Need to Know

➤ For your toddler, play is not idleness. It allows her to develop new abilities and explore the world.

➤ Your toddler doesn't need a lot of store-bought toys. Safe household objects are just as much fun and give her just as much opportunity to grow and explore.

➤ Simple toys that allow a variety of applications will get more use than more complicated toys that have only one function.

➤ Don't rule over your child's play with an iron fist. The way your toddler wants to play is just as important as the way you want her to play.

Part 2
The Terrific, Terrible Twos: 25–36 Months

Like an alien from another planet—a stranger in a strange land—your two-year-old descends on your household. She comes in peace, seeking only to further her understanding of the odd sorts who inhabit this world. She finds it frustrating not to speak their language—and to be able to do all that she wants to do.

Two-year-olds are the only children who come with warning labels. After all, everyone has heard about the terrible twos. But despite their reputation, two-year-olds are fun and fascinating creatures. If you can somehow manage to maintain your patience and your sense of humor, you and your child will have a terrific time this year.

Chapter 8

I Wanna Do It Myself! Development at Two

> **In This Chapter**
>
> ➤ The birth of a gymnast: your two-year-old's physical development
>
> ➤ The frightening force of your child's feelings and fears
>
> ➤ The blossoming of your toddler's thinking and language skills
>
> ➤ Your two-year-old's drive toward independence

Two-year-olds get a bad rap. What's so "terrible" about becoming your own person? Between his second and third birthdays, your toddler will transform himself from your darling to an independent, self-willed, headstrong preschooler.

By his second birthday, your toddler had certainly begun his long struggle for independence. But he still looked ready to totter at any moment; his emotions were simple and raw; his ability to express himself was extremely limited. In short, your toddler needed you more than he could say (literally).

Don't worry, your child will still need you—a lot—after his third birthday. But he will be able to do so much more on his own that he won't need half as much everyday assistance. During this third year, your toddler's strength and physical coordination will increase rapidly. His language skills and mental abilities will expand exponentially. And the combination of his physical and mental development will enable him to develop a solid sense of self.

Of course, this isn't easy for you or your toddler. Certainly, his incessant curiosity will make you wonder why you ever taught him the word "why." "No" will become one of his favorite words. His blossoming sense of self and the willfulness that comes with it will often clash with your own. His emotions will become increasingly powerful, often exploding in tantrums. But without this turbulence and turmoil, your child would never emerge from your shadow.

See What I Can Do? Physical Development

During this year, your toddler's physical abilities will grow in leaps and bounds. Remember that little one who not so long ago tottered across the floor toward you and fell down with a plop? By two, your toddler walks with much more confidence. As the year goes by, her gait, once as stiff as the Frankenstein monster's, will become smoother and more fluid. Midway through the third year, your toddler will bend her knees and ankles more when walking and will swing her arms at her sides rather than holding them out for balance. In addition, she can now walk on tiptoe and can probably walk backward almost as well as she walks forward.

Fairy Tales
During this second year of toddlerhood, your child will love walking backward, but take care! Walking backward was considered unlucky for children in mid-19th century England. The dire consequences were not just bumped heads, but also everything from failing to complete their errands to the imminent death of their mothers. So consider this before letting your child walk backward: You may be putting your own life at stake!

Walking or running, your child is no doubt very steady on her feet by now. She can probably even look over her shoulder while walking without losing her balance and ending up on the floor. While running, your toddler has much more control now than at age one. Your two-year-old runner can probably stop on a dime or make a pretty sharp turn without having her forward momentum pitch her into a wall or knock her onto the floor (well, most of the time, anyway). Also during this year, your toddler will jump for the first time!

Your two-year-old's improved balance also will enable her to stand on one foot for short periods of time. This means that your child can actually kick a ball now, rather than just shuffling into it to nudge it forward.

Your toddler's hand-eye coordination and manipulative skills also will show marked advancement. She will, for instance, become better at catching large balls, spooning food into her mouth, and turning the pages of a book.

But the most remarkable advance will be your toddler's newfound ability to turn her wrist. This means that your child can now screw the lids of jars on and off and pull on a pair of shoes if they're not too tight. Throughout this year, your toddler will perform all of these skills with greater skill, dexterity, and confidence.

Childproofing
Your child's ability to rotate her wrist also means that she can now turn doorknobs—and therefore open doors. So you may want to begin bolting your door(s) from the inside to keep your toddler from wandering out—or falling down the basement stairs. Always stay alert and know where your child is at all times.

Toy Time

You can accelerate your toddler's continued development of hand-eye coordination by challenging his new abilities with practice tools (mostly toys). After all, he needs to practice his skills so that they continue to improve. (You will find information on toys that will help build hand-eye coordination in Chapter 13.) Don't give him practice tools that are too easy, because working past low-level frustration to master a challenge is a fundamental principle of growth and development. It will give your child a sense of accomplishment to do something that's hard for him. He will learn through this process.

At the same time, however, make sure you don't give your toddler toys that are too big or too hard for him to manage. Watch your child closely to evaluate his abilities and provide toys of the right size and complexity. If you give your two-year-old a toy that's too big or too hard for him, it will eat away at his self-confidence and may even damage his self-esteem in the long run.

Even with toys you think your child can manage, try to monitor his play closely to see how he's doing. If his frustration level gets too high, your toddler will lose control completely and end up in a tantrum (see Chapter 11). But if you watch your child carefully, you can sometimes avoid a tantrum by stepping in before the frustration level boils over. Offer your child some guidance and possibly even some assistance, but try to avoid taking over completely and doing whatever he's trying to do for him. Your toddler won't learn nearly as much that way.

The Danger Zone: Emotional Development

Why are they called the "terrible twos"? Probably because of the way two-year-olds express their emotions. Feelings are raw and powerful at age two. Most toddlers put their emotions right out there where you can see them clearly. So when your toddler is feeling happy and loving, she will throw her arms around you, she will beam and giggle and chortle, and she may even say in a singsong voice, "I love you." When your child feels sad or lonely, her face contorts with pain, and tears stream from her eyes as she desperately searches for your comfort and company. And when your child feels angry or frustrated, she screams and kicks and bites like a rabid animal. You've probably never seen such a naked expression of emotion as the display put on by your two-year-old.

Baby Talk
"Why are they sad and glad and bad? I do not know go ask your dad."—Theodore Geisel (Dr. Seuss)

And you're not the only one seeing the raw power of your child's emotions. Throughout the third year, your child will become increasingly aware of herself—and her emotions. What must it be like to notice emotions for the first time? Your child doesn't yet have the words to describe it, but she probably feels confused, overwhelmed, and frightened by the sheer power of her own feelings. For she knows that they are uncontrollable: that she cannot manage them by herself. They seem to come from out of the blue and possess her.

Your child probably doesn't even have the words to describe the increasing range of her emotions. Oh, sure, your toddler knows the basics: sad and glad and mad. But does she know the words for the more complex shadings that she now feels: scared, ashamed, guilty, jealous, kind, considerate, empathetic, embarrassed, resentful, disappointed, relieved, and proud?

Emotional Rescue

Your toddler needs your help to manage his emotions. He needs your help to find the words that express his needs and emotions. Your child also needs your help to cope with this new array of feelings. Perhaps you might dissipate your child's anger, helping to change the mood with a joke, a smile, or a treat. Or maybe you'll relieve some of his sadness or fear with a warm hug, kind words, and a soft voice.

Observe your child with care during this third year. Your two-year-old will send clear signals that telegraph his emotions. But he still needs you to receive them and translate them for him. Until your child has a greater facility with words, he needs you to help define his emotions. So do your best to pay attention and help your child acknowledge his feelings.

Try not to deny your toddler's feelings in your well-intended attempts to bolster his courage or relieve his pain. Eliminate from your vocabulary phrases like:

➤ "You're not scared of that pigeon, are you?"

➤ "Don't be sad."

➤ "There's nothing to be jealous about."

➤ "You don't have any reason to be angry."

➤ "Buck up, you're not hurt."

Your two-year-old is probably having a hard time just trying to comprehend his emotions in the first place. You make it that much harder if you deny that these feelings even exist—or if you deny their legitimacy. Children feel sad, mad, jealous, and hurt. Whether we have a right to feel the way we do, or whether our feelings are reasonable, we feel what we feel when we feel it. Your child has become a person, too. So don't deny what he finds so real, so powerful, and sometimes, so frightening.

The Only Thing We Have to Fear Is Fear Itself

Your toddler's emotions are not the only things that will frighten her. Throughout the year, her imagination will expand dramatically. But this increased potential for fantasy brings with it a range of possibilities to fear. Among the most common objects of fear for two-year-olds are:

➤ the dark (perhaps the most common);

➤ separation from you (still a major focus of fear);

➤ loud noises, especially thunder;

➤ animals, especially big dogs and insects; and

➤ monsters (often ones that come in the dark).

What Are You Afraid Of?

If you want to help your child confront her fears (and it will help a lot if you do), always remember this fundamental rule: The fear is real. Regardless of whether the fear is reasonable, rational, or well-founded, it is very real to your child—and perfectly all right for her to feel. So reasoning with your child will not help. Neither will belittling your child for her fears: Your toddler is not being a coward or a crybaby.

The most important thing you can do to help is no easy task with a toddler: Get your child to talk about her fears. Help her to find the words she needs by asking questions. Be careful not to lead the witness though. Don't guess, ask. Your two-year-old is likely to agree with almost any suggestion you make, so you might put fears into her head that she had not even considered before. Instead, use general questions to nail down the specifics:

Q-Tip
If your child can produce somewhat recognizable drawings and words fail her (that is, she just doesn't have the words she needs to describe her fear), have her draw a picture of what she fears. Use this picture as a focus to help you both talk about it.

➤ "Are you frightened?"

➤ "What scares you?"

➤ "Are you afraid something will happen?"

In talking to your child about her fears, draw on your own experience. Share memories of your fears from childhood—and how you got over them. Or if you don't remember that far back, ask your parents and your partner's parents to tell their grandchildren about what you feared as a child. This will help to make the point that everybody—even you—feels fear now and then.

Q-Tip
Encourage your child to use a security blanket or other objects that offer "magical" protection against fears.

If fear doesn't totally overwhelm your child, help her to confront her fears in a safe, secure atmosphere. Is your child scared of water? Let her watch mama splash around. After she sees it's fun, offer to hold her tight and promise not to let go so that she can have fun in the water, too. Afraid of the dark? Have her sit on daddy's lap in a dark room. Listen to the sounds together. Let your eyes adjust to the darkness until you can both make out some of the things you see.

Boom Booms and the Big Bad Wolf

Specific fears may demand specific solutions. After all, your child can't avoid occasional thunder or separations from you forever—and can't avoid the dark for more than a day. We've already talked about what you can do to relieve your child's fear of the dark (in Chapter 4) and his fear of separation (in Chapter 6). If, however, your child suffers from:

➤ **Fear of thunder** Two possibilities may help: distract him from the thunder or focus attention on it.

You might want to distract your toddler with your own singing or a loud cassette tape.

Or you might want to acknowledge the thunder by playing games with it. You could do a call and response, answering back the thunder with your own, even louder, booms. Or use the thunder to mark the rounds in a game in which you both take turns trying to do something (for example, finish a puzzle or sing a song) before the next clap of thunder.

➤ **Fear of monsters**   Again, two distinct strategies suggest themselves to help with this situation.

Some parents refuse to acknowledge the existence of monsters. To offer any sort of "protection," they object, suggests that you too believe that monsters are out there somewhere. So they banish the monsters to the realm of make-believe, stories, and movies. ("Monsters don't exist except in....")

If you do feel comfortable with it, however, magic can work wonders. Give your child an amulet of some sort, cast a "magic spell," or offer your own protection to ward away any and all monsters.

In helping your child overcome his fears, make sure to let him know that you're making these concessions not because there's anything to be afraid of, but because he is afraid and you know that's no fun. Don't even suggest that you too are afraid of the thing that frightens your toddler.

Phobias

If your child (with your help, of course) cannot deal with her fears, they can become phobias—more generalized and all-pervasive fears. Phobias can terrorize a child even when the object of the fear is not immediately present. The fear itself generates more and more fear of the object, real or imagined.

In time, a toddler with a phobia focuses general feelings of anxiety on that specific object. Phobias cannot be overcome rationally. The phobia becomes so strong that it cannot be tackled head on. Bringing a child who has a phobia of snakes into contact with a harmless snake, for instance, will only terrorize the child.

If your child becomes phobic, you will need to deal first with the general anxieties that fuel the phobia. Watch for signs of general anxiety, which are most often communicated through renewed demonstrations of strong dependence on you. These include clinginess, pronounced shyness about new situations, and kowtowing (fear of offending you through misbehavior).

Childproofing
If your child's phobias become so pronounced as to disrupt her life and prevent her from enjoying activities or places that she once loved, consult your pediatrician or a child psychologist.

Then try to discover the source of your child's general anxiety and stress and deal with that. You may need to baby your child for a while—at least in some situations—to relieve some of that anxiety.

The Dawn of Reason

At age two, your child will finally begin learning from his experience. Memory, more than anything else, makes the difference. Your child's ability to remember the past will grow stronger as the year goes on. In addition, his ability to observe and analyze the concept of cause and effect also will increase.

The combination of these two skills—memory and analysis—will allow your child at two to anticipate things that may happen and plan his own actions. Oh, he may make the same mistakes more than once, but with each repetition, he will grow more and more wary of doing it again. He will begin to apply the knowledge gained from past experience to similar situations in the present—and sometimes even to anticipated circumstances in the future.

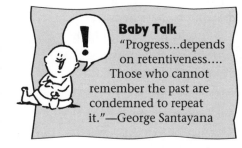

Baby Talk
"Progress...depends on retentiveness.... Those who cannot remember the past are condemned to repeat it."—George Santayana

Besides applying his analytical skills to the notion of cause and effect, your two-year-old also will begin to examine objects for similarities and differences. In the months before his second birthday, your child may have sorted objects according to similarity of type (animals with animals, blocks with blocks, food with food, shoes with shoes, and so on). Now, in the third year, your toddler will separate objects because of differences.

This marks a significant leap in your child's level of understanding. At the beginning of the year, your child can probably sort some objects by name or by basic function—for example, he knows that a ball is not a piece of cake. But by the end of the year, he will be able to discriminate among objects according to qualities such as color, size, shape, or more specific functions. So by his third birthday, your child will know how to identify a red ball, a big ball, a green ball, a little ball, a basketball, or a ping-pong ball.

Curiouser and Curiouser

Insatiable curiosity and the application of knowledge are the hallmarks of the two-year-old mind. Your child will thirst for knowledge, and demonstrate curiosity about almost everything. She will pour forth an endless stream of questions. Many of them have obvious answers ("What's that?" or "Where's dada?"), but some require more esoteric knowledge or a quick and vivid imagination to answer ("Why do birds fly?" or "Why does the rainbow have so many colors?"). Now that your child knows what so many things are, she will want to know how and why things work.

Your toddler's curiosity, analysis, and application of knowledge are all entirely self-centered. Her curiosity focuses on how other things relate to her and how she can use them. When she analyzes objects and information, their similarity or difference to *her* is what matters most. Similarly, your toddler applies her knowledge and experience almost exclusively to her current circumstances.

Of course, the level of your toddler's understanding—though growing more sophisticated each day—is still limited. She is, after all, just two years old. Your child may, for example, recognize or even memorize the sequence of numbers or the letters of the alphabet. But for most of the year, she will not demonstrate any understanding of what numbers or the alphabet mean or what she can do with them.

Similarly, though your child's awareness of past, present, and future are becoming clearer, she will probably be three-and-a-half or older before she can talk about time with any precision. Your two-year-old can distinguish between day and night—and perhaps among winter, spring, summer, and fall, too. But when your two-year-old says, "Remember yesterday I goed to the store and falled down," she could be talking about any time in the past. That's what "yesterday" means to a toddler. Likewise, "tomorrow" really means anytime later than now. And though you may be able to get your toddler to memorize the names of the days or the months, chances are these words mean almost nothing to your child.

Just My Imagination

Another exciting mental development in the third year is the dawning of make-believe. Your two-year-old's imagination and creativity run wild. From an initial fascination with dolls and miniature worlds around his second birthday, your child progresses to pretend play involving dress-up costumes, creatures, and toddler-sized versions of adult tools (cooking sets, workbenches, and so on). Before his third birthday, your toddler may even play with imaginary friends. Entertaining invisible guests represents a huge imaginative leap from the dolls and toys he used as stand-ins just a year earlier.

Your toddler's growing imagination will prompt him to invent creative ways to play with old toys: A toilet paper roll becomes a horn or a telescope. A bowl becomes a hat. Stacking rings become bracelets. This kind of inventing and pretending—especially if he comes up with them on his own—shows a remarkable degree of creativity and imagination.

The Explosion of Language

One thing about most two-year-olds: You can't get them to shut up. Your toddler is constantly talking, talking, talking. Your child wants you to understand her experience, just as she herself is beginning to make sense of it. So she is constantly trying to communicate with you.

Your toddler's language skills expand dramatically in this third year. On your child's second birthday, she probably spoke around 200 to 300 words. By her third birthday, your toddler's vocabulary will jump to well over a thousand different words! What's more, vocabulary becomes a focus for your toddler's curiosity. Your two-year-old wants to be able to say more and understand more—and to do that, she needs to learn more words.

Childproofing

Early or precocious use of language is not necessarily a sign of your child's superior intellect. Likewise, comparatively slow mastery of language skills does not necessarily indicate inferior intellect. Remember that Albert Einstein didn't speak until very late in his toddlerhood.

Early in the third year, your child will employ language as one of her play materials. She'll use it just the same way she pounds and pounds on play dough: to come up with different shapes and see what she can make. Your child loves chanting, singing, and speaking the same words (or even just sounds) over and over again in a sing-song way.

Around her second birthday, your child may begin to put together two or three words to communicate a simple idea. At first, she'll sound like an old Western Union operator sending a telegram: "Dada, ball (STOP). Sara play (STOP)." But soon, your child will put together three-, four-, and even five-word sentences.

These sentences become increasingly complex throughout the year and may even begin to contain more than one idea. By her third birthday, your toddler may be telling you "stories"—perhaps narrating her life story to you, just as you did to her when she was younger. (In fact, if you listen closely, you might hear echoes of yourself and your partner as your child adopts some of your most-used phrases.) And, of course, your two-year-old will also ask you questions—incessantly.

How You Can Help Your Chatterbox

The best way to help your child's language skills is, of course, to continue to talk to your child—and listen to him. He can communicate ideas and experiences to you now, so you can have real conversations with him. Again, just as you did when he was a one-year-old, respond to your child using proper "adult" words (except perhaps for a handful of favorites that your child invented) and grammar. But don't bother correcting your child's word choices or sentence structure.

What you talk about with your child matters more now than it did when he was one. Then, your purpose was to introduce your child to the sound of language and the notion of communication. But now that your child is two, understanding becomes much more important to both of you. As the year goes on and your toddler's language skills continue to mature, you can move from simple words and phrases to the more complex.

Try not to talk too far over your child's head. Certainly, you'll want to stimulate and encourage his desire to learn more. But this won't happen if you overwhelm him with a deluge of unfamiliar words. So talk about the way a ball bounces without getting into the intersection of the force of gravity with the Newtonian principle of energy conservation.

> **Q-Tip**
> If you want to make sure your child understands what you are saying, look directly at him when speaking to him. If your toddler's eyes begin to wander, you've probably lost him.

Word Power

To build your child's vocabulary and encourage more abstract thinking, make a point of talking about the specific qualities of particular objects. Rather than just naming the objects as you did when she was one, use more adjectives: a "red sweater," a "tall tower," a "slow turtle." Talk about the shapes of things. An orange is round, but so is a circle, a ball, a teething ring, the mouth of a play tunnel, and so on. Talking about these qualities helps your child make these connections.

Also talk about the relationships between objects. This helps your child to understand:

> **Q-Tip**
> Board books with brightly colored pictures provide terrific learning tools for vocabulary building.

➤ Spatial relationships (over, under, in front, behind, in, out)

➤ Size relationships (bigger, smaller, taller, shorter, skinnier, fatter)

➤ Temporal relationships (before, after, first, second, third, last)

By appealing to your two-year-old's natural inclination to expand her vocabulary and increase her understanding, you can stimulate her to analyze what she senses, and to make comparisons and connections.

Above all, don't make language building a chore. Have fun with language and help your child have fun with it, too. Be ridiculous. Whether you're reading a story, singing a song, or pointing out the sights on a walk, make silly mistakes to see how your child reacts. Point to a picture of a cow and say, "Look, a duck!" Your toddler will think you're delightfully silly and have lots of fun correcting you.

When you're reading a favorite book, singing a familiar song, or reciting a nursery rhyme, leave some of the words out, and then pause for your child to finish the sentence. If your child has heard it enough before, she can probably fill in the blanks perfectly.

If you're doing this while reading a book and she tries to fill in a blank, comes close, but doesn't repeat the words exactly, that's even better. That shows that she is trying to make sense of the words she's hearing and the pictures she's seeing. So don't bother correcting this kind of daring "mistake"—even if your child's word seems totally off base to you. Instead, applaud your child's courage.

The Continuing Struggle for Independence

Your two-year-old persists in the struggle that began when he started walking: The struggle toward some degree of separation, autonomy, independence, and the ultimate issue—identity. This means that you will have to try to meet your child's growing need for independence, while at the same time offering him all the support, comfort, and even babying that he needs.

Your child's growing independence will show itself in a variety of contexts: eating, dressing, perhaps using the potty seat, playing with toys, drawing, and so on. On some days your toddler will want to do many of these things all by himself; on others, he will need your help for all of them. For this reason, any of these everyday adventures can become a furious battleground.

Baby Talk
"There is this to be said about little children: They keep you feeling old."
—Jean Kerr

Despite your child's improving ability to dress or eat or play independently, he may resist if you pressure him or insist that he do them himself. This resistance also demonstrates your toddler's independence. To assert his own will, your child all too often opposes your own. And that's why they call it the "terrible twos." Two-year-olds often seem willful, contrary, and negative. And to top it all off, when they don't get their way, they throw a tantrum.

Tantrums (see Chapter 11) also spring from your child's growing desire for independence. Despite your toddler's rapidly developing abilities, he no doubt still wants to do much more than he can handle physically and mentally. This frustrating incompetence will drive your two-year-old over the edge. When his frustration reaches a certain level, it explodes as a tantrum.

Though it hardly seems like it much of the time, your toddler is actually trying to control himself. And despite all the turbulence, your child will become increasingly self-aware throughout this year. By his third birthday, this self-awareness will probably awaken a previously unseen ability in your toddler: awareness of and identification with the feelings of others. So in the end, your child's sometimes painful journey toward self-awareness will give birth to a degree of empathy.

Dressing Independently

By about two-and-a-half your child will begin to express interest in dressing and undressing herself some of the time. By all means, encourage her to do so if she wants to. The practice helps to improve both her coordination and her confidence. Until your child is three, she will probably need help with her socks, shoes, and mittens. Tying shoes is almost impossible for a two-year-old, but your toddler may be able to master shoes with Velcro straps. By her third birthday, your child may be able to dress herself completely in a few easy-to-put-on outfits. Just be patient and give your child all the time she needs. Let your child pick out her own clothes if she wants, too—and ignore your own sense of fashion. It won't really hurt anyone if she chooses striped pants with a plaid shirt. And it also won't do any harm if your toddler chooses the same clothes day after day.

Try to avoid buttons and zippers as much as possible. Despite their name, snaps are no snap either. So buy pants with an elastic waistband (not too tight) rather than a zipper and a snap. If you cannot avoid buttons, snaps, and zippers, large ones will be easier for small fingers to practice on. It also might help to get your child a dress-up doll with buttons, zippers, snaps, and Velcro.

> **Q-Tip**
> Here's a good trick for toddlers. Lay your child's coat on the floor. Have her stand at the neck or hood of the coat (so that it's upside down from her perspective). If your child then sticks her arms in the sleeves and flips the coat over her head, it will be on. Most toddlers find this trick enchanting proof that they are big kids now.

Helping by Not Helping (Much)

The best way you can help your two-year-old achieve a healthy degree of independence is to stay out of his way—but at the same time, stay close enough to help when he really needs it. Here's what you can do:

➤ Be patient! This is probably the most important guideline for parents of two-year-olds. Your child cannot possibly complete a "simple" task as easily as you can. But if you give your toddler the time and opportunity to learn through trial and error—with a few pointers from you—he will soon become competent and confident in a variety of skills.

➤ Leave extra time for everything. If you want your child to practice independent skills, it's not fair to hurry him through them. So get ready to leave ten or fifteen minutes—okay, half an hour—before you actually have to go anywhere.

➤ If time becomes short, trade off tasks. "You put your socks on and I'll get your shoes on." Or perhaps, "You do that shoe, I'll do this one." Or, "You put your coat on, I'll zip it up."

➤ Empower your child. Try to come up with ways to increase your toddler's sense of competence, strength, ability, and power. You may, for instance, let your child decide where to hang his latest artwork (building his sense of pride and confidence). Or you may encourage him to move the chairs around to set up a play tent (building his sense of strength).

➤ Rather than forcing, directing, or commanding your child to do what you want, gently steer him toward doing it. For instance, give your toddler some choices about what to do next. (Hint: If all the options you offer are things your child likes to do and things you want him to do, he—and you—can't lose no matter what he chooses to do first.)

➤ If your child can do it, let him do it. Your toddler's various skills only will improve if he gets a chance to use them. And the more practice you give your child, the faster he will master a task. So after your child can put on his jacket, let him do it most of the time. Not only will he become more and more skilled, but you will have less and less to do yourself.

➤ Intervene only if your child becomes frustrated or asks for help. Avoid the temptation to take over just because you think your toddler has been trying long enough. If he's still trying and is not tearing his hair out, then he is still confident that he can complete the task. If you lose patience and do it for him, you will undermine your two-year-old's confidence and transform everything he's done up to now into wasted effort.

➤ Remember your child is only two. Although your child is much more independent than a one-year-old, he is by no means fully independent. Expect your child to go through spells of clinging and anxiety, though they may occur less often and be less pronounced than they were in the first year of toddlerhood. So give your child the attention and help that he does want. Your independent-minded toddler wouldn't ask for it if he didn't really need it.

Baby Talk
"I figure if the kids are alive at the end of the day, I've done my job."—Roseanne

➤ Praise the effort. It's not easy for your two-year-old to do things himself. So even if he doesn't quite succeed, reward your child with praise and encouragement. If your child comes close to succeeding at the task—maybe he buttoned his coat, but missed a button—don't redo it. There's really no reason he needs to do everything perfectly when he's just learning.

➤ Don't pressure your child. If you nag or harass him, he will resist doing it at all. That's another way your child can assert his independence.

The Least You Need to Know

➤ Your two-year-old is trying, yes; but "terrible," no.

➤ Your toddler's feelings and fears are intense and sometimes frightening (for both of you). Don't deny or minimize them.

➤ Your two-year-old wants to know and to understand much more than she can say.

➤ No degree of independence comes easily. With each step toward greater independence, your toddler will struggle with herself—and you.

Chapter 9

Disposing of Diapers: Toilet Training

In This Chapter

➤ When and how to start toilet training

➤ The dos and don'ts of toilet training

➤ Avoiding "accidents" and dealing with them when they happen anyway

➤ How to know when your child is ready to stay dry through the night (most nights)

Think about toilet training from your child's point of view. What exactly is in it for him? When your toddler learned to feed himself, he got an immediate and tangible benefit: relief from hunger. When he learned to walk, he became more mobile and open to adventure. When he learned to talk, he became better able to communicate his needs. But why on earth should your toddler *want* to learn to use the toilet? After all, your child will continue to urinate and defecate whether or not he ever learns to use the potty.

In fact, it's much easier for your child to stay in diapers. As long as your toddler's in a diaper, he can relieve himself whenever he wants without worrying about where the nearest bathroom is. Your child doesn't have to clean up the mess himself or even wash his hands. You do.

You certainly have plenty of motivation to toilet train your child, but your two-year-old child does not have much of an incentive, except:

➤ He gets to feel more grown up—probably the strongest stimulus for an independently minded toddler.

➤ Doing so will please you—a motivation that will grow more important to your child as the year goes on.

➤ He doesn't have to endure a soggy or soiled diaper—though some kids seem to revel in this.

If you want to motivate your two-year-old to use the toilet, appeal to the independence your child will gain. The discomfort of a full diaper is at worst only a temporary annoyance. And until midway through his third year, your child probably can't make any sustained connection between his own actions and your pleased response. However, demonstrating that he is a "big boy" or she is a "big girl" is becoming increasingly important to your child. Certainly you should encourage this urge for independence. But try as you might, you can't force it on your child. If you transform toilet training into a battle of wills, you'll lose. Defying you in this area will not only allow your child to demonstrate his independence, but also to see tangible evidence of his victory. So if your child isn't ready or interested, don't push. You'll only be paving the way for fights, tears, disappointment, and shattered self-esteem all around.

Childproofing

Before your child is ready to begin potty training, she must progress from spontaneous and uncontrollable urination and defecation to voluntary control over her bowel—and then her bladder. In general, if your child can coordinate the muscles and balance needed to run, then she can control her bowels or bladder. Of course, just because your toddler has the muscle control does not mean she will use it.

When to Begin Toilet Training

Believe it or not, your child will let you know when she's ready to begin toilet training. Until that happens, don't try to force the issue or rush your child into it. If you urge your child to take up potty training too soon, she will fail—and feel anxious for having disappointed you—and the whole process will take longer. Besides, it makes sense to let your child decide when she's ready. The whole objective of the process is to have your child gain control over her bladder and bowel movements. So from the very beginning, it will help if your toddler feels in control of the process.

For most toddlers, the process begins some time between the second and third birthday. But a rare few start even earlier and many more don't start until they are three.

Kid Stuff

Kids often find their own motivation to get out of diapers, but they follow their own timetable. Megan switched to underwear at a precocious 21 months, when her brother was born. She convinced herself that only babies wear diapers. Ian, her younger brother, did not stop wearing daytime diapers until he was three years and three months. He himself set the date (his sister's fifth birthday) and then had little trouble keeping the bargain he had made with himself.

In general, girls tend to gain control over bladder and bowel movements sooner than boys. But regardless of when they start using the potty, few children master this skill until close to their third birthday. Even early starters tend to have at least occasional accidents until age three. And late starters tend to have fewer accidents, perhaps because they're more mature physically by the time they begin. So why be in a hurry to get your child on the potty?

The key to determining when your child is ready for toilet training is your toddler's self-awareness. Your child has to know when she is going to relieve her bladder or bowels before it happens. Toilet training will fail if your child becomes aware of the need to go to the toilet only after the pee or poop is running down her leg.

Watch for these signs that your toddler might be ready:

➤ Your child's diaper is often still dry a couple of hours after it was changed.

➤ Your child shows that she understands simple requests or instructions.

➤ Your child demonstrates the ability to mimic adult behavior.

➤ Your child has the verbal ability to let you know when she needs to go to the bathroom.

➤ Your child shows a marked dislike for wet or soiled diapers.

➤ Your child offers a tip-off when she's about to have a bowel movement. It may be a facial expression; she might stand straight up, as still as a statue; or she might head for a particular location.

Q-Tip
Don't start toilet training when a younger sibling is about to be born, when day care is just beginning, when a family member is very ill, or when some other monumental life change is occurring. Your child should not have to deal with more than one change at a time.

> ### Kid Stuff
>
> A month or so before she started toilet training, Molly would stop what she was doing and stand perfectly still whenever she needed to fill her diaper. She would silence her parents by barking, "Mama, Dada, don't talk to me!" (Translation: "I'm about to poop, so let me focus on this.")

Toilet Training 101

Toilet training begins with the introduction to the potty seat or the toilet itself. As a beginner, your child can use either a potty seat (essentially a small chamber pot with a lid) or a specially designed ring that fits over the toilet seat and narrows its opening, making it the perfect size for toddler tushies. (There's also a transition seat that combines the two—first fitting over the potty and then sitting on top of the toilet.) Each has its advantages.

The potty seat is:

➤ less intimidating in size and easier for your child to use than the toilet;

➤ less frightening because it doesn't flush away the waste (some kids fear they'll be the next to go); and

➤ much more portable around the house than the toilet ring, which must of course stay on the toilet.

The toilet ring, however, is:

➤ much easier for you to clean up, because your child's waste is already in the toilet, where you can easily flush it away;

➤ often much more portable on the road than a potty seat, because many models fold into quarters and can thus fit in a large purse or diaper bag; and

➤ an immediate transition to the toilet, which your child will eventually need to use anyway.

If you choose the toilet ring, you'll also need to put a sturdy step stool next to the toilet to make it more accessible to your toddler. If you choose the potty seat, buy one that is relatively comfortable and solid enough to avoid tipping over no matter how much your child squirms around while waiting for some results.

Getting to Know the Potty

If your child will be using a potty seat, you'll find it worthwhile to familiarize your toddler with it long before you think he's actually ready to begin using it. Don't assume that your child will know what the potty seat is or what it's for. After all, a potty seat doesn't really look like the toilet he's seen mommy or daddy use. So tell your child what it is and what it's for, but don't put any pressure on him to begin using it.

Take a low-key approach instead. Tell your toddler that all children eventually stop wearing diapers and that when he's ready, the potty will be there for him. Then let him become comfortable with the potty—and the idea of using it. If your child wants to play with the potty seat, sit one of his dolls or animals on it, or try sitting on it himself—with or without diapers and other clothes on—that's fine. Let your child know that if he wants to practice using it sometimes, that's fine, too. But be forewarned: Just because your toddler urinates or defecates in the potty once does not necessarily mean he's ready to do it all the time (though for a rare few, it just might).

Q-Tip
Even before your child starts wearing underwear, let him pick out several pair. Your child can choose from a variety of colors, prints, and favorite cartoon characters. Having the new underwear may inspire him to practice potty training.

Observation and imitation provide the most direct lessons about what to do on the potty or toilet. In fact, your two-year-old probably already knows how to use the potty, because he's no doubt seen you or your partner on the toilet. However, if you think your child needs more in the way of introducing the concept, your library should have a number of good books and videos that will engage and instruct your child. Remember though that if your child isn't ready, it does not matter how many videos or books you buy, rent, or borrow—or how often he barges in on you while you're in the bathroom. If your toddler has not shown any interest, you cannot possibly begin successful toilet training.

Even after your child has demonstrated interest, let him take the lead. Encourage his interest certainly, but let your child dictate the pace with which he feels most comfortable. Suggest, but don't insist; encourage, but don't press.

Have a Seat

You—and your child—will probably have more success if you start toilet training only with bowel movements. Your toddler may seem more aware of emptying her bladder, but she has more control over her bowels. As you well know by now, bowel movements usually come pretty much on schedule. Your child probably poops just once or twice a day, at fairly predictable times. This makes it much easier to anticipate and plan for bowel

113

movements when you're starting to toilet train. You won't need to spend all day watching your child like a hawk in a futile attempt to prevent accidents. You'll just need to devote an hour or two a day, training only when you expect your child to poop.

Childproofing

Don't use laxatives to try to control the timing of your toddler's bowel movements. There is no excuse for disrupting your child's natural regularity.

Childproofing

When food goes into the stomach, the gastrocolic reflex makes the colon contract. Because this produces an urge to have a bowel movement, you may find it effective to suggest some potty time right after mealtime.

Another reason to begin with the bowels is that your child probably signals the coming of a bowel movement in some way or other. So even if your child is wearing a diaper, you—and she—can usually tell when she is about to poop. And because the tip off often comes a minute or more before the actual defecation, you'll have enough time to ask, or even suggest, that she might want to poop in the potty rather than in her diaper. So if your child is ready, you can offer a lot of help. But if your toddler says, "No, I don't want that," respect that decision. Your child is clearly telling you that she's not ready.

Urination does not offer the same kind of lag time as a bowel movement. "I'm going to pee" comes just moments before—or even simultaneous with—the outpouring of urine. Also, because urination does not come on as strict a schedule as bowel movements, it is harder to anticipate. And because toddlers pee so often, accidents will be frequent.

Nonetheless, after you and your child have achieved some success—not perfection, just overall success—at bowel control, then it's time to move on to bladder control.

Surprisingly, naptime is a good time to start bladder training. If your toddler regularly wakes up dry after a nap, start foregoing the naptime diaper. Ask your child to use the potty just before lying down for a nap, then ask her to use it again right after she wakes up. If you aren't spending most afternoons changing sheets, you might then encourage your child to go without diapers from naptime to bedtime—and then all day. (Regardless of her daytime success at toilet training, however, you would be wise to keep your child in diapers at night for some time yet.)

Ease of Access

When you're ready to start toilet training your toddler, do everything you can to ensure your child's success. Make sure that you keep the potty relatively close to the room in which you'll be spending most of your time. If, for instance, the only bathroom is on the second floor and you'll be playing on the first floor, move the potty downstairs. Or give your toddler more control over the whole process by letting him decide where the most convenient place for the potty would be.

You'll want to make it as easy as possible for your child to get to the potty, get undressed, and get on the pot. So for the next few months anyway, make sure that you dress your toddler in clothes—or at least pants—that he can get off quickly and easily. Better yet, have your child wear no pants at all, if the season and the weather allow it. (The spring and the summer are certainly the most convenient times to begin toilet training—but only if that's when your toddler wants to do it.)

The best way for any toddler to learn how to use the toilet is probably to go bare bottom (whenever possible) for the first several weeks. If circumstances make this impossible, you can use training pants—specially designed paper underwear that your child can pull on and pull off by himself. Or get special toddler's underwear that has extra layers of padding to prevent accidents from becoming floods.

> **Q-Tip**
> Start toilet training at home, but let your day-care provider, if any, know that you've started. All of your child's caregivers need to be on the same page. If you send your child to day care in training pants or underwear, your day-care provider needs to know—and probably also needs several extra sets of dry clothes.

If you can allow your child to go without training pants or underwear, it will increase his awareness of his own bladder and bowel movements. If you do go this way, however, watch your child very carefully for a while and look for any advance warning. If you aren't monitoring him constantly, you'd better have a mop or washrag ready.

Coaching Your Child's Training Program

If your child starts telling you when she needs to use the potty—or goes by herself—consider yourself blessed. More likely, you will need to help your toddler out at least some of the time.

In her first weeks out of a diaper, watch your child like a mother hen. You will easily recognize your child's body signals:

➤ holding her legs together;

➤ pressing her hand against her groin;

➤ a certain look that passes over her face; or

➤ hopping up and down on one foot.

Whenever your toddler seems like she's ready to go, take her directly to the potty or toilet—or better still, just ask your child if she needs to use the potty. In doing so, you can help alert your child to her own body signs, too: "Clio, you're holding your legs together pretty tightly there. Do you need to go to the bathroom?"

Patience and persistence are the key to successful toilet training. Once every hour or two, suggest sitting on the potty seat to your child. Your "suggestions" should begin from the moment your child wakes up. Even though your child still wears a nighttime diaper, she should get into the habit of going to the bathroom first thing in the morning. After all, your child's bladder will not be completely empty and you don't know exactly when she last urinated. The other mandatory times for your child to try are right before and after her nap—especially if she naps without a diaper.

Q-Tip

Use a calendar as both an incentive and reward for your toilet-training toddler. Post a calendar next to the potty seat. Whenever your child makes it through a day of doing it "all by myself," put a special sticker on the calendar for that day. The sticker itself may be reward enough, or you may decide to up the ante a little by providing a special treat after your toddler earns a certain number of stickers—but not necessarily in a row. You don't want to make it too hard.

You may need to entice your child to sit on the potty. Sit down next to your toddler and sing some songs or read some books to help your child relax. You might even want to turn on the water in the bathroom sink to see if the sound of running water prompts your child to run some water, too. If your child doesn't want to sit or sits for only a moment and then hops off, saying, "All done," don't force her to sit longer. Just keep the potty handy.

Whenever your child sits on the potty or toilet for more than a minute, applaud her effort—whether she actually pees or poops. Certainly, you should encourage your toddler to feel proud of her accomplishment—or even her "unsuccessful" tries. But at the same time don't go overboard with your praise. If you overpraise your child for successfully using the potty, she will feel much worse about the inevitable accidents that will follow. Even if you don't make a big deal about accidents when they happen, your child will miss the praise and know she's disappointed you.

Let's not kid ourselves. Cleaning up your child's potty after she's used it is no joy. But no matter how "yucky," "gross," or "disgusting" you think your child's poop is, keep your comments to yourself. First of all, it's a natural human function. But even more importantly, your toddler probably won't feel it's yucky at all. She'll most likely think it's wonderful and fascinating. Your child will feel very proud of the product of her "labor." After all, she made it all by herself. If you then let your toddler know that you think her creations are gross, she may feel as if you are rejecting her efforts.

After the first few weeks, when your child has begun to get the hang of it, ease up a bit. There's a thin line between reminding your child and nagging. Nagging provokes resistance on the part of a headstrong toddler. Besides, after your child knows what she's doing, reminding her six or sixteen times a day to sit on the potty is not toilet training. Your child needs to be given control.

Accidents Will Happen

While your child is learning bladder and bowel control, you can safely anticipate that accidents will happen. Like so much of your toddler's learning (eating, walking, running) toilet training is mastered through trial and error. Some kids pick it up very quickly; others find it much harder, but *all* toddlers have accidents.

Toilet training is never a matter of instant mastery. Your toddler was aware of his bladder and bowel movements long before he demonstrated any control over them. Even after he demonstrates some degree of control, your child will be far from infallible. Finally, after several months, your child will achieve mastery. Even then, however, he will probably still have occasional accidents during his first year or two out of diapers, so just expect to clean up urine and bowel movements.

> **Q-Tip**
> Never ask your toddler to wait before urinating or having a bowel movement. Because your toddler is not in complete control of his bladder and bowel movements, asking him to wait is dooming him to failure. Even if you don't make a big deal of the accident, your child may feel like he let you down by not being able to wait.

No matter how inconvenient they become, accidents should *never* be an occasion for shaming or blaming, shouting or scolding. Toilet training is not a moral issue. Your toddler is not being "bad" or "naughty" when he makes a puddle on the floor, so don't chastise your child after an accident. After all, your child would no doubt prefer to please you. Don't think that he's having these accidents maliciously or on purpose. Trust that your toddler is doing the best he can.

When accidents do happen, try to take them in stride. Accept accidents in a low-key manner, offering sympathy rather than censure. "Oh, that's too bad. Well, it's easy enough to clean up." Then just calmly suggest to your child that he try using the potty next time.

Listen to your child. When your toddler tells you that he needs to use the bathroom, take him right away. And please take your child seriously if he tells you, "I can't wait!" Your child is doing everything he can to communicate the urgency of the moment. It will do little good to exhort your toddler to control himself for more than about a minute more. He simply cannot do it.

Along similar lines, it may do little good to urge your toddler to try to go to the bathroom before going out to do errands or going on a car trip. Most children cannot urinate on command until some time during the fourth or even fifth year. Asking your child if he needs to use the bathroom makes sense. But if he answers that he can't or doesn't need to go, take his word for it.

Q-Tip

Keep an extra potty in the trunk of your car for travel-time "emergencies." On long car trips, you may want to put your child back in a diaper to avoid frequent stops. If your child objects, promise him that it's only for the ride. Or, if your child's car seat cleans easily, give him a chance—but bring along an extra set of clothes!

Avoid urging your child to "Hurry up and go to the bathroom!" when you want him to empty his bladder. Parents usually say this just before they step out the door to go out somewhere. But urging your child to hurry will likely cause him to try to push and strain to empty his bladder. This tension will make it harder for your child to relax the sphincter muscle to empty his bladder completely. For this reason, this kind of exhortation may make it even more likely that accidents will happen along the way. (It also may lead your child to misunderstand the mechanics of emptying his bladder. If your toddler thinks he needs to push rather than relax, he may develop further urinary problems down the road.)

Puddles and Piles: Problems with Toilet Training

By the time your child has started toilet training, you are probably more than ready to say goodbye to diapers forever. But certain times will still demand the use of diapers.

Diapers Again

You should probably return your child to diapers whenever:

➤ You'll be in the car for more than an hour or so and would prefer to stop as little as possible;

➤ You're attending a special occasion (a wedding, a funeral, a concert), where you would really resent having to leave to attend to an accident;

➤ Your two-year-old or three-year-old goes to bed for the night—or for a nap if she still urinates during naptime; or

➤ Your child has quite a number of accidents in quick succession.

This last item gets a little tricky. Toilet training does not always work the first time. If your child doesn't seem to be getting it, if misses far outnumber hits, if accidents happen, but they happen all over the place, then you may need to put a halt to the experiment for a while. There's no law that says you need to toilet train your child by a certain date or to succeed the first time. So put it off for a few weeks—or even a few months.

But at the same time, try not to use the "dreaded diapers" as a threat. Remember that accidents should not be used to shame or blame your child. It only makes your child feel small to hear you saying something like, "If you don't stop wetting yourself, you'll have to go back to wearing baby diapers." Try to keep in mind that it's really not your child's fault if she has frequent accidents. That's an indicator that your toddler doesn't yet have control, not that she's not trying. Maybe you tried toilet training too soon, before your child was really ready.

If you do decide to curtail your child's potty training for a while, try to ignore "helpful" relatives and friends who insist your child should be on the potty by now. Your child will eventually master this skill. If she's not ready, does it really have to be right now?

Ready... Aim... Wait!

Recognize that until you began toilet training, your child never needed to aim anything. All he had to do was let the pee or poop come out. So don't expect your child's aim to be perfect from the start.

Two- and three-year-old girls sometimes have a problem with aim because they don't always remember to sit forward. If your girl leans back on the potty or toilet, her urine will spray out in an arc that lands on the floor or all over her pants and underwear.

Boys obviously have a bigger problem with aim, because they can point their penis in almost any direction. You can help your son learn to aim by providing him with a target (a piece of toilet paper, a tissue, a Cheerio, anything that floats and will later flush down the toilet). Then teach your boy not to start urinating until he has started aiming. You also should let your son know that both girls and boys can sit while peeing. Let your child decide what's most comfortable for him.

Toilet Hygiene

You cannot depend on your child to wipe herself properly—at least until she is four or five years old. So you will have to do the bulk of the wiping yourself— at least at the beginning. Even after your child has begun wiping herself, ask her to have you check her wiping every time she has a bowel movement. Otherwise, your child might end up with a very nasty diaper rash—even though she's out of diapers.

Always wipe from front to back, especially if your child is a girl (to avoid a bladder infection). After wiping, flush the contents down the toilet and clean out the potty (if any) with disinfectant. Be sure to wash your child's hands as well as your own.

> **Q-Tip**
> Keep flushable diaper wipes next to the potty for your child to use on her own. Toddlers find wipes easier to use—and you won't have to worry about her using an entire roll of toilet paper to wipe up a small trace of urine.

You might find it easier to clean the potty afterward if you keep an inch of water in the pot (or line the bottom with a few sheets of toilet paper). However, you should never keep bleach in the potty! Besides being toxic to ingest and dangerous even to touch, the mixture of bleach and the ammonia in your child's urine will cause a dangerous chemical reaction.

Make it easy for your toddler to wash her hands after using the toilet or potty. Put a small stool in the bathroom if your child needs help reaching the sink. And make sure your child knows which tap is hot and which is cold before she begins turning them on by herself.

> ### Kid Stuff
>
> Nick refused to even try wiping his bottom for months after starting to use the toilet. As it turned out, what Nick wanted to avoid was not dirtying his hands so much as having to clean them. He just hated taking the trouble to wash his hands. When his parents figured out the connection, they began insisting that Nick wash his hands every time he went to the toilet—whether he wiped himself or not. Within a couple weeks, Nick decided that as long as he had to wash anyway, he might as well wipe himself.

Playing with Poop

Disgusting though it may seem, some children like to play with the products of their labor. Try not to overreact if your child is one of them. For a toddler, pee and poop are fascinating stuff—and besides, he made it all by himself. So of course he wants to play with it.

If your child begins handling his feces or urine, calmly stop him from continuing. You can tell your child that his waste carries germs. But avoid labeling your child's behavior (or your child) as dirty or disgusting. Just wash his hands thoroughly with antibacterial soap and water, and dispose of the feces or urine.

Fear of Flushing

Even if your toddler uses the potty almost all the time, you would be wise to let your child practice using the big toilet at least some of the time. If you don't, someday you'll be out somewhere and find that your child literally doesn't have a pot to pee in.

Using the big toilet can be scary. To your child, her own fears seem very reasonable. You may know that she won't fall in and get flushed away—but your child doesn't know this. She also might fall off the toilet and land on the hard tile floor.

A child's toilet seat that reduces the circumference of the rim can help ease some of your toddler's fear of the toilet. You also might want to try turning your child around. Some two- and three-year-olds, both boys and girls, feel more comfortable facing the toilet tank and straddling the seat rather than facing forward. You also might find it helpful to suggest that your child hold onto the sides for balance. Offer a sturdy stool so that your toddler can step up to the toilet.

The noise of the toilet can be frightening, too. So always ask your toddler if she wants to flush the toilet herself, or if she would rather that you wait to flush until she has left the room.

All Through the Night

Staying dry throughout the night will not happen anywhere near as soon as daytime control. Give your child a break. After all, he's just starting to learn how to control his bowel and bladder during the day, when he's fully awake and conscious of his body's signals. It will take your toddler more time before he maintains control when he's unconscious, too. (Nighttime urination tends to occur during the deepest stages of sleep.)

Bedwetting is a nuisance and although you can't avoid it altogether, you can significantly reduce the frequency.

Start by keeping your child in diapers (or even double diapers) at night long after he has started—and even mastered—daytime toilet training. But every night, just before he goes to bed, encourage your child to empty his bladder. Only when your toddler wakes up with a dry diaper for several nights in a row should you consider taking off the nighttime diaper. This probably won't happen until your child is three—and perhaps not until he's four. (See Chapter 18 for a detailed discussion of preschoolers and bedwetting.)

Because accidents will still occasionally happen after you've eliminated nighttime diapers, put a plastic or rubber sheet as well as a mattress pad between the sheets and mattress of your child's bed.

Q-Tip
If accidents happen frequently, try doing a double dip: Make your child's bed with two layers of rubber sheets and fitted bottom sheets. Cleaning up will be twice as easy because you'll only have to strip off the top set; you won't have to remake the entire bed with new sheets.

If several accidents happen in the same week, ask your child what he thinks about returning to a nighttime diaper. If you handle this situation with sensitivity and avoid blaming your child, or making the return to diapers seem like a threat, or implying that he's being a baby, only good will come from this opening. Your child has two possible responses: He may realize that he's not yet ready to go without nighttime diapers and opt to try again later. Or it may strengthen your child's resolve not to need diapers anymore. Whatever your toddler decides, go along with it.

The Least You Need to Know

➤ Don't force your toddler to begin toilet training. Demanding that your child use the toilet before she's ready will inevitably lead to failure. So let your child control the timetable and the process as a whole.

➤ Be alert to your child's cues. When you start noticing signals that indicate she's about to dirty her diaper, that's when you can help her notice the signals, too. And that's when to start toilet training.

➤ Expect accidents and setbacks, and never blame your toddler for them. Preparing yourself for accidents will make them less inconvenient.

➤ Be patient. Controlling her bowels and bladder is a developmental skill. Your child eventually will master it.

Best Behavior

During the first two years of his life, your child lacked any substantive memory and lived from moment to moment, drawing no lessons from the past and giving no thought to the future. The principles of cause and effect were totally foreign to him. These factors made it impossible to get your child to do what you wanted through threats or bribery—and grossly unfair to punish or reward your child for his behavior. So prior to age two, discipline consisted almost entirely of:

➤ setting limits on your child's immediate behavior;

➤ saying "no" at the moment of some misbehavior; and

➤ using wiles, trickery, playfulness, and a sense of fun to get your child to do what you wanted at any particular moment (see Chapter 5, "No, No, NO! Setting Limits").

All of these methods of curtailing "bad" behavior and encouraging "good" behavior still apply—and for the most part, work very effectively—at age two. However, your toddler is now beginning to recognize cause and effect. Your child can now remember events from his past, some of them very vividly, and can learn through experience (though he generally needs more than one lesson before experience can have an impact on behavior). His memory of past experience allows your two-year-old to anticipate the future, though somewhat sketchily.

Your toddler's new mental abilities and his more sophisticated thinking processes—including his dawning capacity for reason—make the third year a good time to begin introducing the notion of good behavior and proper manners.

Especially in the second half of this year, the focus of discipline should shift from particular incidents to general rules of behavior. Your child can now generalize from particular events and also can follow simple rules of behavior. Your child knows, for example, that because knives are sharp and stoves are hot, they can hurt him. So he stays away from them— (at least for the most part). He knows that to get a shirt on, he has to push his arms through the sleeves and his head through the neck. So you no longer need to tell your toddler to lift his arms each time you want to change his shirt.

Social Graces

If your child can learn about these objects and activities and generalize rules of behavior from them, then she can certainly learn that if she says, "please" and "thank you," you are more likely to give her what she wants. She can learn that when you're on the phone or doing something with someone else, you will listen to her more readily if she says, "Excuse me." And believe it or not, she can learn to share, too.

Of course, you also can expect many lapses in your two-year-old's behavior. You need to remind her on occasion to raise her arms to get her shirt on. She does pick up a sharp knife now and then. And your child will also behave territorially on occasion and sometimes forget to say the "magic" words.

While encouraging your toddler's development of good behavior habits, try to treat these lapses lightly. Like everything else she does, she learns good behavior through repeated practice, and through trial and error. If you applaud the successes and tolerate the errors with good grace and humor, your child will develop habits that please you.

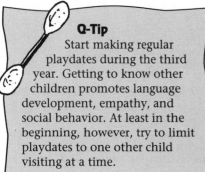

Q-Tip
Start making regular playdates during the third year. Getting to know other children promotes language development, empathy, and social behavior. At least in the beginning, however, try to limit playdates to one other child visiting at a time.

Q-Tip
If you have the luxury of deciding when—or if—you will begin sending your child to preschool or day care, two and a half is the ideal age. Spending part of the day in preschool will expose your child to other children and help get her used to playing and sharing with others.

During the first two years, you set certain limits on your baby's behavior primarily because it endangered the safety of your child or of others. Safety concerns remain important throughout your child's preschool years. But as you attempt to guide your child's behavior in this third year, another element becomes important: promoting social behavior.

Play Patterns

With a little guidance (okay, sometimes a lot of guidance), your child's ability to get along with others may take great strides forward this year. Throughout this year, your toddler will become increasingly social. It may not seem that way at first. Around his second birthday, your child will most likely engage in some sort of parallel play if thrown together with other two-year-olds. This means that your toddler will play near another child, without actually playing together with the other child.

At first glance, it may seem as if not much interaction is going on. Though closely juxtaposed, each child seems to be entirely immersed in his own little world. Each toddler is totally self-centered, hardly ever looking at the other. Yet parallel play opens up your child's social world. Over the course of the third year, such get-togethers will let your toddler (and his new friends) practice getting along with others and help him learn such social skills as sharing.

Though your child will remain essentially self-centered through most of the year, playdates or day care will help him discover the importance of getting along with others.

Around the middle of the third year, your child may begin to show more and more interest in what other kids do. He will start to enjoy playing near other children and will often imitate and adapt behaviors that he observes in other children. The other child starts smashing clay into a pancake; then your child does the same. Or your child starts making car noises; the other child makes similar sounds.

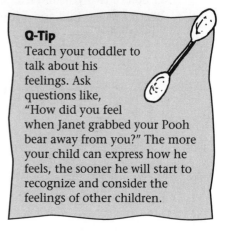

Q-Tip
Teach your toddler to talk about his feelings. Ask questions like, "How did you feel when Janet grabbed your Pooh bear away from you?" The more your child can express how he feels, the sooner he will start to recognize and consider the feelings of other children.

Just as he watches and copies your adult behavior in fantasy role-playing as the mommy or the daddy or the doctor or the fire fighter, your child also will watch and copy behavior that shows him how to play the role of a child: the behavior of other children.

By his third birthday, your child may actually play with others, at least for brief periods of time. He may even begin to form fledgling friendships. Around this time, he also will become capable of feeling at least some degree of empathy toward others. With your help, your child can begin to recognize and respect the feelings of others. This nurturing of empathy is the key to courtesy and good manners. Without empathy, your toddler would never even consider how his behavior might effect the feelings of others.

Negotiating the "Mine!" Field

Your toddler's language development advances the formation of empathy and first friendships. During the second half of the third year, language becomes more and more of a social tool. Playdates give your child the opportunity to communicate with other children her own age—instead of constantly talking to adults.

Social language with other children begins with a marking out of territory. Your toddler is becoming her own person. And to forge her own identity, she needs to lay claim to what's (at least in her own mind) rightfully hers: her toys, her bed, her home, and her mommy and daddy.

When another toddler trespasses on this territory, your child will yell, "Mine!" The other child will scream, "Go away!" You might as well get used to mediating these territorial battles ("Mine!" "No, mine!" "Mine!"). They will be played out for several months—and will recur from time to time for many years. Though it certainly doesn't seem like it, these skirmishes are just the first stage in a process that will teach your child how to share and how to be fair.

As the year goes on, your toddler's friendships will probably get stronger, but even the closest of two-year-old friends still need consistent adult supervision. Left to their own devices, your child and a friend will almost certainly be fighting soon about some perceived unfairness or refusal to share.

Q-Tip

Your child may be more willing to share with a playmate if you allow him to put away several toys that he just can't bear to share. Knowing that his most cherished possessions are safely stowed away may give your child a greater push toward generosity with the rest of his toys.

Share and Share Alike

Toddlers do not share without prompting. It is by no means the natural behavior of a selfish, self-centered two-year-old—and that's the only kind of two-year-old there is. So if you want your child to begin sharing, you need to teach him how to do it—and repeatedly encourage him to share. Try to be patient with your child as he learns (and repeatedly forgets) and relearns the value of sharing.

If your child—and you—are hosting a playdate, try to prepare him in advance. Tell your toddler that you expect him to share his toys. But stress this point: Just because the visiting friend plays with the toys doesn't mean the other toddler gets to keep them. Your child may feel more secure throughout the playdate if you keep reminding him that his toys will still be his when the playdate is over. It may help if you offer (in advance) to replace any toys that your guest might break—and then of course keep your promise if anything does.

Oddly enough, helping your child and a guest share fairly and peacefully begins with getting the toddlers to understand the difference between possession and ownership. On playdates, no matter who actually owns a particular toy, possession is nine-tenths of the law. This doesn't mean your guest can take your child's toys home with her. But it does mean that your child cannot be allowed to grab the toy away from the other toddler—and vice versa, of course.

Baby Talk
"The law of grab is the primal law of infancy."
—Antoinette Brown Blackwell

If your toddler does grab a toy (or food or anything else) from another child, you'll need to step in immediately. Quickly and firmly, but without anger (if possible), return the toy to the child who had it first and tell your child, "No grabbing!" Then remind your child that if he wants something that someone else is already playing with, he must:

➤ wait his turn;

➤ ask for your help in setting up turns;

➤ ask the other child nicely and get permission to use the toy; or

➤ offer the other child a trade so that both children end up with something they want to play with.

If the other child will not under any conditions part with the toy that he has, or if your child cannot wait a second longer for his turn to begin, you'll need to turn down the heat even more. Though two-year-olds are not nearly as distractable as one-year-olds, you may still succeed in distracting your child. Try shifting his attention to another toy or game—and if necessary, to another place.

Q-Tip
Don't make playdates for toddlers last too long. Even if the parent of the other child stays, one to two hours is probably close to the limit for any two toddlers, at least at first.

If a particular toy becomes the sole object of full-scale warfare: take the toy away; bring out a duplicate (if you have a close enough match); or call an end to the playdate.

Good Manners

Besides helping your toddler get along with other kids, you can now teach her proper manners, which will help her get along with adults, too. If you make the effort to help

your child learn common courtesies now, politeness will most likely remain an integral part of her personality as she grows older.

Teaching your child politeness is a matter of instilling good social habits. You already brush your child's teeth at least twice a day. If you're toilet training, you've encouraged your toddler to get into the habit of washing her hands every time she goes to the bathroom. Common courtesy is a habit just like these.

The Magic Words

In teaching your two-year-old how to behave politely, concentrate on the "magic words." This teaching will feed into your child's already strong urge to learn and master new words.

You can heighten your child's motivation to use these words by telling her that each phrase has a secret power. Toddlers want to feel powerful. So let your child know that with just one or two words, she can exercise a very special and magic effect on other people—and that these magic words give her the power even to influence grown-ups. All of them, when spoken by a toddler or preschooler, tend to make adults smile. But each has specific powers as well:

➤ "Please" makes grown-ups much more willing to help your toddler or to give her something she wants.

➤ "Thank you" pleases grown-ups by letting them know that your toddler likes what they have given her or done for her —and makes them even more willing to do more favors in the future.

➤ "Excuse me" or "Pardon me" allows your child to get the attention of an adult who is having a conversation or is otherwise absorbed in something other than the child herself; also has the power to move adults who are blocking your toddler's way or to win forgiveness from someone she bumps into.

➤ "I'm sorry" perhaps the most magical of all, because it actually helps to fix hurts, whether your child has injured someone by accident or on purpose.

After your child learns that these words have magical powers, she will want to use them even more.

After you've taught your child the basics about how to use these words, you'll need to follow through if you want to encourage her to use them. Don't respond directly to what your child is saying if she leaves these "grease" words out. Of course, you'll probably need to remind your two-year-old (and your three-year-old and your four-year-old, etc.) many, many times to use these words.

If your child screams, "I want juice!", explain that you'll be happy to get her what she wants—but only if she asks for it politely. Then stick to your guns. Don't cave until your child stops yelling. If she changes her tone but still forgets to say, "please," help her out by prompting her a little. Then and only then should she get what she wants.

Or if your child starts talking to you while you're on the telephone, do not respond to her except to remind her to say, "Excuse me." When she does, excuse yourself from the phone for a few seconds either to tell your toddler that you'll listen to her in just a minute or to address her concern quickly.

Magic, Not Miracles

If you want to help politeness become a habit for your child, you'll have to offer him some reward for using the right words and intonation. Of course, this doesn't mean you need to give him everything he wants as long as he says "please" and "thank you." Your child has to learn that the magic words, while powerful, are not all-powerful. But though the magic words do not provide a free pass, they do earn your toddler a reasonable consideration of his request.

Though you can't give your toddler everything he wants, you can reward his politeness with your attention and praise. Listen alertly for these words. If you hear your child speak any of them, respond to them quickly and politely. Congratulate him for speaking so politely and honor your toddler's polite requests as often as you think appropriate. If you must refuse your child, do so firmly but politely.

> **Q-Tip**
> A lot of times, you can avoid saying "no" by mastering the art of "yes, later." For instance, "Yes, you can watch some more TV after dinner." Or "Yes, I'll be happy to read you that book as soon as I'm done talking on the phone." Your toddler may find it much easier to accept a qualified yes than a "No, not now."

Model Manners

Of course, the best way to instill proper manners in your child is to set a good example yourself. Are you polite and respectful to the people—adults and children alike—whom you meet during the course of the day? If not, your toddler—and later your preschooler—will catch you up in your hypocrisies and throw them back in your face.

> **Baby Talk**
> "It is not a bad thing that children should occasionally, and politely, put parents in their place."—Colette

If you want your child to behave with common courtesy, you will need to model that behavior. Your child needs to see you treat other adults—and children, too—with respect. Do you serve as the drill sergeant in your house, constantly barking orders at your child?

"Get your coat on! Pick up those blocks! Put away those books! Get out of the bath!" If you do, you're not likely to get much politeness in return.

Baby Talk
"Don't demand respect as a parent. Demand civility and insist on honesty. But respect is something you must earn—with kids as well as with adults."
—William Attwood

So if you want your toddler to do something for you, at least start by asking and using the magic word, "Please." Then if she does what you wanted, acknowledge your gratitude with a "Thank you." (Of course, if you ask a couple of times and your child doesn't move, then it may be time to start issuing commands.) None of us is perfect. But if you behave with common courtesy most of the time, your child will see it as expected everyday behavior—and model her own behavior after it.

Table Manners: Why Even Bother?

Eating with your two-year-old can spoil your appetite. Your toddler no doubt eats with his hands (and would do so with his feet if he could), plays with his food, and devises repulsive combinations of foods—and then eats them. He also smears food on his face and wipes his hands and face on his clothes. If he doesn't want something you've served him, he's likely to push it away with such force that it spills—or even worse, deliberately throw it at the wall or on the floor.

Baby Talk
"A child should always say what's true

And speak when he is spoken to,

And behave mannerly at table;

At least as far as he is able."
—Robert Louis Stevenson

Yet with the exception of throwing food and possibly banging spoons you should probably ignore most of this misbehavior if you can. Table manners are still not critical—or even very appropriate—at age two. Just be grateful your child is now feeding himself so that you have your hands free at dinnertime. Don't fret that your toddler is feeding himself like a pig at the trough or a monkey in a tree.

Your two-year-old cannot yet feed himself and behave himself at the table. Certainly, you should discourage your toddler from throwing food (or banging a spoon on his plate or the table). But at least for now, continue to let your child eat in any way that he enjoys.

If your child repeatedly disrupts the dinner hour with his antics, then consider feeding him at a different time, apart from the rest of the family. But as soon as he seems capable of eating with you without wreaking havoc, bring your toddler back into the fold. At two, most children should be sitting down and eating with their parents, rather than eating before.

Eating with you lets your toddler observe the way adults behave at the dinner table. And your child will learn more about table manners from watching you than from any other way you might try to teach him.

Q-Tip
For easier clean-ups, put a tarp or a large plastic sheet under your toddler's highchair. Put a bib or napkin on your child. Put food on the tray, step back a little, and enjoy watching your child feed himself.

If you consistently model good table manners, your child will begin wanting to emulate your behavior at meals. It may take another year or two, but eventually it will happen.

The Least You Need to Know

➤ Mastering good behavior is a trial-and-error process. Expect frequent lapses and don't make a big deal out of them.

➤ Sharing is *not* natural behavior for your toddler. To share even a little, your child will need repeated prompting, encouragement, and praise.

➤ Good manners and common courtesy are just social habits. Repeated practice will make them habitual.

➤ Even at age two, an emphasis on table manners may discourage your child from eating. Discourage your child from dangerous table habits, but otherwise let her eat in any way she pleases.

Girls (and Boys) Behaving Badly

In This Chapter

➤ The roots of your toddler's misbehavior

➤ The importance of appropriate and consistent discipline

➤ The use of time-outs

➤ How to control your own anger before disciplining your child

"All children are essentially criminal."—Denis Diderot

To a child of two, "bad" behavior has a certain undeniable appeal. Contrary to what Diderot suggested (if you're preparing for your appearance on *Jeopardy*, he was an 18th-century French philosopher), toddlers are not sociopaths. They don't misbehave simply because it's bad. In general, toddlers misbehave for one of two reasons:

➤ the inability to control or comprehend emotions and impulses; or

➤ the drive toward independence.

Your two-year-old has just started to be aware of her emotions. Yet awareness of feelings is only the first step toward exercising some degree of control over them. Given some time and your guidance, your child will learn to express her emotions—especially her anger and frustration—without violence or other misbehavior. But she isn't there yet.

As part of your child's drive toward independence, she needs to separate herself from you, at least to some degree. Much of your toddler's misbehavior can be seen in this context. She wants to establish that she is no longer under your complete control. By behaving contrary to your wishes, your two-year-old stakes out her own territory. Though she doesn't come right out and say, "You can't make me," that's what your child is trying to prove. The drive to become her own self also makes your child very protective of what she regards as her possessions or birthrights.

Bad Behavior

The combination of these two factors—poor impulse control and the struggle to become an individual—leads to the most common behavior problems among two-year-olds. These problems include:

Baby Talk
"There was a time when we expected nothing of children but obedience, as opposed to the present, when we expect everything of them but obedience."
—Anatole Broyard

"The thing that impresses me most about America is the way parents obey their children."
—King Edward VIII of England (Duke of Windsor)

➤ Hitting, biting, poking, and other violent acts

➤ Tantrums

➤ Stubbornness

➤ Defiance and a refusal to cooperate

➤ Screaming

➤ Grabbing

As you start to discipline your child for misbehavior, remember that your child is not bad, no matter how bad his behavior gets. Actually being contrary, willful, and even defiant is an essential part of your toddler's growth and development. It helps your child separate himself from you.

You can almost see the wheels clicking inside your child's head as he looks you right in the eye and defies you. He clearly heard you say, "No more puzzles now because it's time for bed," but he slowly, deliberately moves toward the shelf of puzzles. The whole time, he keeps staring at your face to see how you're reacting. He might flash a mischievous smile to see if you think it's cute. If you don't stop your child, he will go all the way to the puzzles and take one out despite your prohibition.

Why does your child so blatantly defy you? Because with this single act, your toddler accomplishes two important ends:

➤ He shows himself that he can do something even though you don't want him to do it. Your child discovers he has some control over what happens. He clearly demonstrates that he is not you.

➤ He also tests you to see how you will respond. Your child wants to know exactly what behavior he can get away with. He wants to establish a clear idea of the limits you will impose on him (and apparently the words "no TV until later" did not tell him clearly enough).

Try not to impose harsh discipline on every contrary act, because that will crush your child's spirit. Yes, urge your child to cooperate and find ways to motivate his cooperation. But unless your toddler becomes hurtful in words or deeds, try not to punish him every time he demonstrates his natural resistance to authority in general—and yours in particular. He needs to do this to establish a strong and healthy sense of self.

Playing by the Rules

As you did when your child was one, you will need to continue to set limits on your toddler's behavior. When your child was one, however, you focused primarily on stopping immediate problems rather than establishing hard and fast rules. Now that she's two, your toddler can appreciate the difference between good and bad behavior. But she still doesn't always know whether (as Dr. Seuss would say) "This one is that one or that one is this one or which one is what one or what one is who."

That's why your teaching of right and wrong becomes so important at this age. Your child needs you to define and prohibit unacceptable behavior—and to enforce the limits you set consistently and fairly. So always take the time to explain actions that you have taken either to prevent (before the fact) or to punish (immediately after the fact) behavior that was dangerous or hurtful. And be prepared to repeat the same moral lessons again and again. Your child will probably not pick up on your teachings instantly.

No, You Can't Do That

As your child's foremost disciplinarian, the most important guideline you can follow is the rule of consistency. If you set any absolute rules they must always be absolutes. "No" means no! If you don't mean it, then don't say it.

This rule applies both to unacceptable behavior and to requests your child makes that you feel compelled to deny. If you mean "No, not under these conditions," then add a qualifier. Say, "No, not now." Or to cast a more positive spin on it, try, "Yes, but not right now." But "no"—just plain "no," with no qualifiers attached—is an absolute term. So use it on its own only for things that are always forbidden—for instance, "no hitting," "no pushing," or "no grabbing."

If you do say "no" and then soon change your mind—or ignore it when your child goes ahead and does what you've forbidden—you will unwittingly teach your child that "no" doesn't always mean no. Obviously, your toddler will conclude, under certain conditions, "no" actually means yes. Is this really what you want to teach your child?

Of course, you should be somewhat flexible regarding your child's behavior or requests. That's another reason to limit your use of absolute terms like "no" and "never." If you realize later that you've been arbitrary or unfair, then feel free to change your mind—on rare occasions. But whenever you do, let your child know why you've changed your mind. If you leave it up to your toddler to make sense of your mixed and confusing messages, he'll guess that magic changed your mind: the magic of his wishing as well as his screaming or hitting or other misbehavior. Whatever your child was doing between the time you initially said "no" and the time you turned around and said "yes," you can expect to see a lot of in the near future because your child will think that's what changed your mind.

Cardinal Rules

Although some behavior is somewhat negotiable (how much TV she can watch, how many books before bed, whether she can use that magic marker of yours), other actions should be absolutely prohibited. Take a hard line on:

Baby Talk
"The nakedness of their bad character! We adults have learned how to disguise our terrible character, but children, well, they are like grotesque drawings of *us*. They should be neither seen nor heard, and no one must make another one."
—Gore Vidal

➤ protecting the safety of your child;

➤ protecting the safety of others;

➤ prohibiting violence (hitting, kicking, biting, pinching, hurtful squeezing, pulling hair, scratching, pushing someone off a chair or couch, poking with a stick, and so on);

➤ respecting the feelings, thoughts, rights, and property of others; and

➤ honesty as the expected and only acceptable policy.

The more you emphasize these cardinal rules—and model them with your own actions—the more your child will begin to assume responsibility for stopping herself from violating them. It may take more than a couple of months. Heck, it may take more than a couple of years. After all, your toddler's only two years old, so you can anticipate many lapses. But in time, your child will absorb these rules and adopt them as her own.

Punishment That Fits the Crime

Consistent enforcement of discipline becomes especially important now that your toddler can learn from the past and anticipate, at least to some degree, the future. If you are consistent, your child will come to know that his behavior has predictable consequences.

If he hits or bites, he gets put in time-out. Always, without fail. However, if you are inconsistent—if you yelled at him for hitting yesterday morning, spanked him for hitting yesterday afternoon, and put him in time-out for hitting this morning, he won't know what to expect if he hits someone tomorrow.

Granted, knowing the preordained consequences of his actions may not necessarily deter your child from hitting for quite some time. And even if the desire to avoid a certain punishment stops him from misbehaving on some occasions, it certainly won't deter him from every misdeed. But if you hope for your punishment to have any deterrent effect at all, it needs to be consistent and predictable.

> **Q-Tip**
> Because consistency is so important to a child learning right from wrong, ask your sitters or day-care providers to discipline the same behaviors in the same ways that you do.

Crimes and Misdemeanors

If your child's misbehavior is not causing injury to herself or others or serious damage to property, consider it a misdemeanor.

To put a stop to it, start by getting your child's attention. After you have her attention, you can either try to distract her with something else or simply tell her to stop doing what she's doing. Be sure to let her know exactly what the consequences will be if she continues.

If your toddler chooses to ignore your one or two "words to the wise," then quickly remove her from the situation—and do what you said you would do. Always have consequences (some call it punishment) well-defined and ready to impose. Even at two, children recognize—and quickly take advantage of—empty threats. So never give more than one warning. On the other hand, if your child finally does stop the inappropriate behavior, congratulate her on regaining control and showing the good sense to stop.

> **Q-Tip**
> To get your child's attention when she's misbehaving, try using a stage whisper instead of yelling. Whispering can sometimes cut through a lot of noise and get your child to focus on you and listen.

Besides explicitly telling your child the consequences of continued misbehavior, be as specific as you can about the behavior you disapprove of.

You don't teach your child anything by simply saying, "Bad girl, look what you've done!" First of all, she probably was looking at what she was doing. She may even have felt proud of it. And secondly, as pointed out earlier, bad behavior does not make her a bad child. Your child will learn much more from hearing you say, "No painting on the wall!"

137

than she will from hearing "No!" or "Bad girl!" In this case, even "No painting!" will confuse your child, because she knows that she's allowed and encouraged to paint at other times (on paper).

If you provide your toddler with more details, you'll give her information that she can use in guiding future behav-ior. (Whether she actually will use it is of course another question.)

Go Directly to Jail: Time-Outs

For more serious offenses, you'll need to sentence your toddler to some jail time. If your child behaves violently or destructively, toss him in the clink, send him up the river, give him a ticket to the big house. In short, separate him from the people he has victimized or the property he has destroyed. In the parenting trade, we call this a "time-out."

Pick one chair on each floor of your home (preferably one that isn't used much, at least by your child) and designate it as a time-out chair. When your toddler or preschooler behaves violently or refuses to stop misbehaving, put the child in time-out.

Generally, most parents accept the guideline of roughly one minute in the time-out chair for every year of a child's age. So your two-year-old needs to stay in the time-out chair for two minutes, a three-year-old for three minutes, and so on. If your child gets out of the time-out chair before his time is up, gently but firmly pick him up and put him back in the chair and begin timing again.

With a two-year-old, you will probably need to stay in the room to make sure your child stays in his seat. Even without the element of punishment, two-year-olds find it a tor-ment to sit in one place for very long. But your child's already powerful separation anxiety might escalate to a panic if you put him in a time-out chair and then leave the room. Because you are punishing him, your child already fears that you hate him. Don't make these feelings even worse by abandoning him, too. But while staying in the same room with your child, avoid interacting with him—except to remind him that he is in time-out, urge him to calm down, and put him back in the chair if he gets up—until the time-out is over.

Time-outs work remarkably well for most toddlers. They accomplish two things:

➤ They remove your child from the situation that prompted or exacerbated the misbehavior.

> ➤ They force your child to stop misbehaving, to achieve some degree of internal control by having an external control imposed upon him.

Time-outs are especially effective in cases of violent behavior. Because the time-out begins by removing the child from the situation or circumstances that sparked the violent outburst, it also takes him away from the high pitch of emotions (anger, frustration, and so on) that led to the hitting, biting, or other violence. A time-out lets your child cool his jets a bit. At the same time, it physically reinforces the notion that your child will not be allowed to play with others if he hurts them.

On Parole

When your child has completed her time-out, calm her down if she hasn't calmed herself down yet. Then, while she is still sitting, ask your child if she knows *why* you put her in the time-out chair—that is, what she did that was wrong. Although it doesn't always work that way in practice, a time-out should ideally be not just a punishment, but a learning process, too.

For the first few dozen time-outs, your child will probably answer back, "Why?" You can then provide a leading answer to your own question—or even just give her the answer. But certainly by her third birthday, your child should have an attention span long enough to remember the specific misbehavior that landed her in the hot seat.

After the time-out has ended, you should often take the time to remind your child that you still love her—especially if she still seems particularly upset. Your child's own anger is often so powerful that it blocks out all other thoughts and emotions. So when you punish her or express anger toward her, your child does not know that you can still love her. And despite all of her defiance and contrary behavior, your love is still your child's most valued possession. She needs to know that she still has it.

After serving her sentence for violent behavior, you might want to encourage your child to apologize to the victim (including you, if you're the victim).

Q-Tip
If certain situations recurrently provoke problem behaviors, try to avoid those situations for a while.

Q-Tip
When dealing with two- and three-year-olds, don't jump to punish behavior that one child alleges unless you actually saw it. For instance, when your two-year-old falls off a couch during a playdate, she doesn't believe that she could have fallen off through her own clumsiness. So she'll cry and scream, "Matthew pushed me!" In making this accusation, your child probably believes that it is the truth. But if you didn't see it, how do you know whether he did or didn't push? And if Matthew denies it, who are you going to believe?

Then quickly try to involve your toddler in an activity that's very different from the one that led to the misbehavior. If you put your two- or three-year-old back into the same situation, you'll almost certainly see a repeat of the same behavior—no matter how sorry she seems at first. Your child may know what she did wrong—but that doesn't mean that she knows how to control her temper—or her behavior—just yet.

Kid Stuff

At two, Danny had—with some justification—earned a reputation as a troublemaker. His four-year-old brother, J.J., soon learned how to exploit this reputation. One afternoon, his grandmother spied J.J. biting on his own arm. Less than a minute later, J.J. rushed into the room yelling that Danny had bit him.

To Spank or Not to Spank?

What exactly do you teach your child when you spank him or hit him for an act of misbehavior? Does it teach your child not to hit under any circumstances? Or does it teach not to hit anyone unless he's much bigger than them and can therefore get away with it? How contradictory is it for you to say that your child cannot hit or hurt anyone else—but that you can hurt him whenever you think it's appropriate? Will your toddler pick up a moral lesson here?

Baby Talk

"Never raise your hand to your children—it leaves your mid-section unprotected."
—Robert Orben

Before you spank or slap or hit your toddler or preschooler, remember that you are your toddler's first and best model of appropriate behavior. A parent's spanking, slapping, or hitting will therefore probably lead the child not to less aggressive behavior, but rather more. If you instead demonstrate kindness to any victim of your child's misbehavior and forceful disapproval toward your child, then that's what your child will eventually emulate (though certainly not right away).

The American Academy of Pediatrics opposes all forms of corporal punishment. All too often, corporal punishment is applied indiscriminately and arbitrarily. Spanking—and even more so slapping—most often occurs spontaneously, rather than after a minute or two of reasoned consideration. And because both are often administered in anger, spanking and slapping too easily slip over the line to punitive physical abuse. For these reasons, we cannot recommend corporal punishment as a disciplinary measure.

Arresting Violence

Your toddler's violence always demands an immediate response. Don't ever ignore acts of aggression by your toddler (or by other toddlers who might be visiting for a playdate). Violence cannot be condoned. If you ignore it, your child will think it's okay. So respond quickly and clearly to hitting, kicking, scratching, hair pulling, poking, pushing, biting, and throwing things.

Whenever your toddler hurts another child, go to the other child and offer comfort first, even before you discipline your own child. Correcting violence is not simply a matter of disciplining your child and teaching her right from wrong. It also is an opportunity to model empathetic, caring, and compassionate behavior toward others. So make sure that your toddler sees you offering comfort to the victim. In time, she will begin to emulate your behavior.

While offering comfort to the injured child, clearly state to your own toddler that hurting another person is not allowed. Show your child the teeth marks or scratches or bruises on the child she victimized. Point out the injured child's tears and tell your toddler what they mean: that your child hurt the other. Finally, proscribe the specific violent behavior of your child: "No biting—ever!" or "Hitting is never allowed!"

While focusing your initial attention on the victimized child, don't let too much time lapse before disciplining your child. A time-out should be automatic in instances of violent behavior. But if you delay too long before beginning the time-out, your toddler will have a hard time making a connection between the unacceptable behavior and the punishment.

During the second half of the third year, or earlier if your child appears ready for it, you may be able to enlist your toddler's assistance in caring for her victim. Before or after her time-out, your child needs to tell the other toddler, "I'm sorry." Encourage your child to offer some comfort, too: perhaps by kissing the injured spot or by getting a Band-Aid.

Even though your child may not understand every word you say, she will know from your tone and your facial expression that she shouldn't have done what she did. Speak sharply and sternly, but try to avoid yelling, which will only frighten your child (and also may scare the injured child you're trying to comfort). After you start yelling at your child, her emotional response to your anger will most likely block out any further message you want to communicate.

Baby Talk
"If you have never been hated by your child, you have never been a parent."
—Bette Davis

If a child bites, hits, or kicks you while you are disciplining her, put her in the time-out chair immediately, gently, and firmly. (No matter how tempted you become, don't throw her down into the chair.) Say, "No kicking!" and start the time-out at once. If you need to get your own anger under control before you can deal fairly with your child's misbehavior, then walk away for a minute or two.

Controlling Yourself

Controlling your anger and maintaining a consistent tone is important whenever you discipline your child—even for nonviolent behavior. If you punish your toddler in anger, you may end up behaving punitively or vindictively yourself. So unless your child's behavior is causing (or will cause) immediate harm or damage, count to five or ten yourself before taking any disciplinary action. If your child's behavior does hurt someone else, the act of comforting the victim will give you five or ten seconds to collect yourself and control your anger.

Childproofing
If you cannot quickly control your anger, ask your partner to discipline your child. Give yourself the time you need to cool down.

One of the things you want to teach your child through disciplinary action is to develop some control over his anger and other strong emotions. These feelings—which can be so powerful that they probably frighten even your child—can prompt impulsive and sometimes violent actions. Because you want to teach your child how to control his anger, you will need to model this behavior as best you can (without, of course, allowing further damage through your delayed response). So take a minute to calm down yourself if that's what it will take to insure a fair and somewhat detached response to your child's misbehavior.

The Least You Need to Know

➤ No matter how badly your toddler acts, she is not bad.

➤ Some misbehavior demands a hard line: dangerous behavior, disrespect, dishonesty, and violence.

➤ Timeouts offer an effective way to remove your toddler—or preschooler—from a dangerous or violent situation and allow her to regain some degree of control.

➤ If your child attacks someone else, model empathy for his victim as well as disapproval of your child's behavior.

➤ Try not to punish in anger. Calm yourself first to ensure fair and reasonable disciplinary measures.

Chapter 12

Taming Temper Tantrums

In This Chapter

➤ How to head off a tantrum before it starts

➤ Dealing with tantrums without having one yourself

➤ How to handle the height of embarrassment: a public tantrum

➤ Helping your child express anger without hurting himself or others

Tantrums are extremely common among two-year-olds. Almost every toddler has at least an occasional tantrum; the majority have one or more a day. Possibly, the more active and more intelligent your toddler, the more prone he will be to tantrums. Children with an active intelligence often have set ideas about what they want to do and how they want to do it. When this kind of toddler can't do what he wants—due to his own inability or to external constraints imposed upon him—he loses it.

Childproofing
Though uncomfortable and even frightening to witness, your child will not suffer any permanent damage from holding his breath until he faints. His fainting will actually force him to resume normal breathing.

So chances are, before your child's second birthday—and certainly before his third—you will see one or two (hundred) tantrums. Everybody has an idea of what a tantrum looks like. But actually not all tantrums look alike. Your toddler may throw himself on the floor, kicking and screaming and writhing as if possessed. Or he may run through the room screaming and out of control, crashing into furniture and anything else in his way (including you). Your child may scream so much that he makes himself throw up, turns blue, or perhaps even faints. After witnessing a few tantrums, you probably wouldn't be surprised to see your child's head start spinning around as he levitates above his bed.

Quick! Call an Exorcist: Taming Tantrums

Toddlers have tantrums primarily due to frustration and anger. Your toddler is probably very demanding and ambitious. Yet at the same time, she probably has a very low threshold for frustration. This volatile combination often leads to tantrums. When your child cannot do what she wants, or when you deny her something in what she considers a battle of wills, she naturally gets frustrated. But a two-year-old has few words to express her frustration. She may not even have the exact words to express what she wants in the first place. Denied verbal expression, frustration often comes out physically—through violence or tantrums.

Parents of toddlers need to keep one thing in mind when their child begins to have a tantrum: *Your child cannot help it.* Older children often use tantrums to show they mean business, to demonstrate how much they want something. But two- and three-year-olds do not yet have the capacity to manipulate in this way. When her frustration builds to a certain level, your toddler literally loses control. Think of your child as a pressure cooker: the steam of frustration builds and builds and builds inside her until it finally forces an explosion.

If it's frightening for you to see your toddler possessed by the demon of a tantrum, think how she must feel. It's not a pleasant experience to be overwhelmed by the force of one's own emotions. Tantrums—and the uncontrollable internal rage that fuels them—are very scary for your child.

An Ounce of Prevention

The best way to deal with tantrums is, of course, to stop them before they start. You will need to monitor your child's frustration and try to keep it at a manageable level. In doing this, you will function as the relief valve on your child's pressure cooker.

This does *not* mean you should do everything for your child so that he never experiences any frustration. For one thing, a certain degree of frustration is good for your two-year-old. Moving beyond frustration to succeed at a task is one of the most satisfying ways that your child can learn how to do things. If he can do it, working through frustration will teach your toddler a great deal about himself and about how to accomplish certain tasks. For another thing, your child may regard your interference as an added source of frustration. He wants to be able to master new tasks. If you won't let him try, he's just as likely to explode as if he had tried and failed.

You shouldn't protect your child from every experience of frustration, but you should try to keep it at a manageable level. To do this, you will need to pay attention to what your child is doing. Watch for signs of frustration and then try to head them off. If you do notice your child's level of frustration building, try one of the following:

➤ Offer help before your toddler reaches the tantrum stage. If he refuses your help, however, back off. Remember that you can add to your child's frustration by trying to take over.

➤ Encourage your toddler to take a rest and come back to it later with a refreshed attitude.

➤ Distract your toddler with a different toy, a snack, a book, or a video. This may be a good time to encourage some quiet time activities.

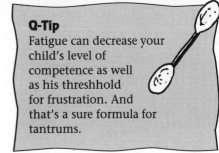

Q-Tip
Fatigue can decrease your child's level of competence as well as his threshhold for frustration. And that's a sure formula for tantrums.

➤ Constantly try to teach your toddler words that will help him express his anger and/or frustration. The inability to express these emotions in words heightens the likelihood of tantrums.

Besides monitoring your child's frustration level from a safe distance, recognize that the limits you establish can be another external source of frustration for your child. Certainly, you shouldn't have to roll over backward to avoid offending your little angel. But set limits on your child's behavior primarily to insure safety and promote socialization. Try to avoid laying down the law arbitrarily or—with noted exceptions (see Chapter 11)—absolutely.

Exorcising the Demons

When your child starts screaming, kicking, or turning blue, try to stay calm. Your toddler has already lost control of herself; she needs you to stay in control. Here are some things you can do:

➤ Don't yell. You may feel tempted to return your toddler's screaming with some yelling of your own. But seeing your anger when she's already got enough of her own will no doubt drive your child even farther over the edge. Your own yelling will tend to prolong your child's tantrum, because it will set her off again and again.

➤ Don't bother trying to reason with your child while she's having a tantrum. No toddler can listen to reason while caught inside the whirlwind of a tantrum.

➤ Unless your child is likely to hurt herself or others or break things, you should probably just ignore the tantrum until it goes away. If your presence seems to be aggravating your toddler's tantrum or you're getting angry and can't stand it any more, leave the room.

➤ Try to avoid long, drawnout scenes in which you beg, bribe, urge, or command your child to regain control of herself. If you allow the tantrum to become a big scene, you will be rewarding your child with "too much" attention. (Sometimes attracting even negative attention is better than no attention at all.) Creating a scene will not only prolong the tantrum, but it may provoke repeat performances in the near future. If, however, you deny your tantrum-torn toddler an audience, she will call off the performance as soon as she can.

➤ Later, when your child's comprehension improves, explain that her tantrum is making you angry (if you really are getting angry). Say that though you'd like to stay, you don't want to be in the same room when she's out of control and you're angry at her. Again, make it clear that you still love your child even when you're angry at her.

> **Childproofing**
> Never lock your toddler in a room either to discipline her or to calm a tantrum. Not only will this forced separation likely produce hysteria, but it also makes it impossible for your child to atone for her misbehavior: to come back to you and apologize.

> **Q-Tip**
> If you need to cut a tantrum short, try saying something silly to your child or making a ridiculous face at her. A particularly headstrong toddler will try to maintain her anger, but it won't be easy. Although your toddler may not want to let go of her anger yet, she can't laugh and have a tantrum at the same time.

What WON'T Stop a Tantrum

Never reward a tantrum! Don't ever bribe your child or give in on the limit you've set just to quiet a tantrum. (Even if you realize that a limit you've set is unreasonable, hold your ground. You can always apologize later for your unreasonableness, but continue to be unreasonable for some time after the tantrum has ended.)

If you reward a tantrum, you will condition your child just like one of Pavlov's dogs. Every time your toddler wants something, he'll throw a little fit. So don't buy your child the candy he wanted just because he makes a little scene—or even a huge brouhaha. Instead, try to demonstrate that the tantrum has no effect on you whatsoever. It will not change your mind one little bit.

Never punish a tantrum! A tantrum should have no consequences, positive or negative. It happens and then it's over. Life goes on.

The reasoning behind this rule is simple: tantrums should be treated like speed bumps. You may slow down and ease over them for a second, but then you get right back up to speed. They have absolutely no lasting power over you.

Besides, if your child is out of control, then he's out of control. Is this really a punishable offense? Probably not. The tantrum itself is probably frightening and punishing enough to your child without having you add further punishment to it.

Caution! Handle with Care

When tantrums turn violent or dangerous, you'll need to do everything you can to prevent your child from getting hurt, hurting anyone else, or destroying anything. You are your child's protector. If you let her do damage, your toddler will lose some of the sense of security you provide her. Already overwhelmed with her own uncontrollable emotion, she will now have proof that you can't control it, either. According to the magical thinking of a two-year-old, this means that she must be a demon, a horrible monster possessed of awesome and unstoppable power.

If your child becomes violent in a tantrum, or if she starts knocking things over as she careens about the room, try to hold her down as gently but firmly as you can in your arms. (If holding seems to make your child's tantrum worse, let her go—but quickly remove anything that might hurt her or that she might break, and run interference to try to prevent her from harming herself or anyone else.) Wrap your child up, envelop her in the strength and safety of your arms. Although it may take some time, your "horrible monster" will suddenly transform before your eyes, turning into a sobbing infant.

Airing Your Dirty Laundry

Parents of two- and three-year-olds find themselves most uncomfortable and embarrassed when their children have tantrums in public: in the grocery store, in the park, or—and this is the worst—in the (until then) silent sanctuary of the public library. Yet there's really no reason why it should be so embarrassing that your toddler is behaving like a two-year-old. Virtually every toddler has tantrums. So even if every head turns your way, and you think everybody is recognizing what a terrible parent you really are, just shrug your shoulders and say, "Two-year-olds."

Baby Talk
"The secret of dealing successfully with a child is not to be its parent."
—Mell Lazarus

Baby Talk
"I love children, especially when they cry, for then someone takes them away."—Nancy Mitford

The most difficult advice in the world for parents to follow is when they are told to ignore a public tantrum until it goes away. But tantrums shouldn't be treated any differently just because they occur in public. Don't reward, bribe, threaten, or punish your toddler. Don't get mad or start shouting back at your child. Just prevent any damage, encourage your child to quiet down, and wait until the tantrum plays itself out.

If you cannot possibly ignore it, scoop your toddler up firmly but gently and, with as little fuss as possible, take him outside, to the car, or to a bathroom. Make it clear to your child that he won't get what he wants by having a tantrum. Then either talk him down or just tell him that you'll both wait exactly where you are until he calms down. Don't be overly solicitous though. If you pay too much attention to your child in this situation, you are backhandedly rewarding him for his tantrum. Soon your toddler may start having a tantrum whenever he feels the need for attention.

Finally, try not to treat your child any differently in public in an attempt to avoid a tantrum. Don't go out of your way to avoid certain stores out of fear that your toddler will fly off the handle. And if you wouldn't give in to the same demand at home, don't give in to it in a store either. If you do, you can be sure that your child will notice the effect that your fear of tantrums is producing. In time, this discovery will lead to more deliberate and manipulative use of tantrums.

Take heart. This really is "just a stage" that almost all children go through. If you manage to handle tantrums well, your child will eventually grow out of them (at least as a regular event).

I'm SO Mad! Helping Your Child Express Anger Appropriately

Part of the reason two-year-olds have tantrums is because they don't have the words or other tools they need to express their anger or frustration fully or appropriately. For this, your toddler needs your help.

Thus the most important rule in handling tantrums is this:

Ignore the behavior, but don't ignore your child.

What is your toddler trying to communicate to you through her tantrum? Anger? Frustration? Ask your child what's wrong and at the same time, encourage her to calm down enough so that you can help her. Let your child know that if she's frustrated with something, you can't possibly help her unless you know what's wrong—but that you can't understand her when she tries to talk to you in the midst of a hysterical tantrum.

Don't ignore your child's expressions of anger. In fact, if they are appropriate, encourage them. Suppressed anger can become even more explosive. So don't encourage your toddler to rein in her anger or frustration. Instead, teach your child to express it in non-destructive or non-hurtful ways. Allow and encourage your child to express anger and frustration:

> **Q-Tip**
> Challenging your child by saying, "No laughing," may be a good way to transform anger into a burst of the giggles. Yet although this is a very useful trick at times, this approach also slights your toddler's anger. So if you decide to diffuse your child's anger in this way, be sure to take the time to encourage her to talk about her anger with you afterward, when she has calmed down.

➤ in words;

➤ by punching a pillow or mattress;

➤ by slamming clay around on a cutting board;

➤ by banging a drum;

➤ by running around outside;

➤ by doing something brief, loud, and angry: letting out a "primal scream," yelling, dancing, or singing about her anger; or

➤ by creating an angry work of art.

The lessons you teach your child about expressing anger and frustration may seem to have little impact during her third year—and perhaps even her fourth. Your toddler (and later, your preschooler) will no doubt still have angry outbursts, violent episodes, and uncontrollable tantrums at least occasionally. In time, however, your child will absorb these lessons. And learning how to handle anger without becoming destructive or hurtful is an invaluable lesson for anyone, child or adult.

The Least You Need to Know

➤ You can often head off a tantrum by trying to keep your child's level of frustration at a manageable level.

➤ Do whatever you need to do to remain calm during your child's tantrum. One of you needs to stay in control of yourself.

➤ Your child cannot help having tantrums—at least not at this age. So never punish a tantrum. But never reward one either.

➤ Try to treat a tantrum in public exactly the same way you would at home. You have nothing to be embarrassed about: All toddlers have tantrums.

➤ Help your child find ways other than tantrums to express anger and frustration.

Chapter 13

Raising Bias-Free Children

In This Chapter

➤ The difference between discrimination and prejudice

➤ Answering your child's questions about race, gender, ethnicity, and disability

➤ Confronting stereotypes aimed at children

➤ Creating an atmosphere that helps your child resist and reject prejudice

Listen to your child or other toddlers at the playground. You may surprised to hear comments like:

➤ "Girls can't be doctors. You have to be the nurse."

➤ "I don't want to play with her. I want to play with other children who have pink skin like me."

➤ "I'll be the brave cowboy. You be the wild Indian."

Almost all of us would like to believe that two- and three-year-olds don't say such things. Yet we hear our own toddlers saying these words. Sadly, children absorb stereotypes about girls and boys, men and women, African Americans, Asian Americans, Native Americans, disabled people, and older people at a very early age.

The Price of Prejudice

Some stereotypes are negative (for instance, women are weak, Asian Americans are "inscrutable") and some positive (for example, women are nurturing, Asian Americans are good at math). But even the "positive" ones limit adults and children alike. The "compliment" that women are nurturing, for example, suggests that:

➤ men are not capable of nurturing; and

➤ women should focus on nurturing—like being good mothers or teachers or nurses—to the exclusion of other talents.

Whether they portray a group in a positive light or a negative light, stereotypes can be damaging. All stereotypes disregard both:

➤ the similarities among all people that cross lines of gender, ethnicity, age, and

➤ the differences among individuals in a particular group.

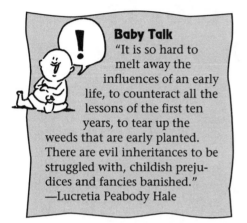

Baby Talk
"It is so hard to melt away the influences of an early life, to counteract all the lessons of the first ten years, to tear up the weeds that are early planted. There are evil inheritances to be struggled with, childish prejudices and fancies banished."
—Lucretia Peabody Hale

None of us want to close off our children from particular activities or areas of experience because of their sex, skin color, or cultural background. Yet when we allow our toddlers' stereotypes to persist, that's just what we end up doing.

What's the Difference? The Seeds of Discrimination

You may think that it's too early to begin teaching about discrimination and prejudice at two years of age, but if you wait too much longer, any bias that does creep into your child's mind will be that much harder to shake. You need to start teaching tolerance and correcting biases at age two because this is precisely the age when children begin noticing differences in sex, skin color, and other physical characteristics.

Discrimination, in the most neutral sense of the word, begins around your toddler's second birthday. That's when your child starts to discover differences and similarities and to sort things accordingly. Indeed, toddlers and preschoolers learn a great deal by "stereotyping": They draw general conclusions about people and things based on specific experiences with them or on knowledge they have acquired about them. By her third birthday, for instance, your child will know that:

➤ balls are round;

➤ a cracker is food, but a cracker box is not;

➤ girls and women have vaginas, while boys and men have penises.

All of this knowledge consists of stereotypes—and all of it is useful information. Stereotyping helps your toddler simplify and categorize—and therefore make sense of—the very complex world in which she finds herself. None of these stereotypes necessarily distort reality. But when stereotypes impose distortions, you will need to correct them.

Discrimination is natural. But while discrimination is an innate process, prejudice—the assigning of values to stereotypes—is learned.

During their third year, toddlers not only begin to recognize differences, but they also absorb values regarding those differences. As a toddler (and later as a preschooler), your child will become increasingly aware of both positive attitudes and negative biases toward race, gender, disabilities, ethnicity, and other traits. Your child may acquire these biases from many sources—from you and your partner, of course, but also from day-care providers, from friends, and from books and television.

Does this really have an impact? You bet it does. Research has shown that by age two, children notice differences in gender and skin color. (By age three or four, preschoolers also notice differences in ethnicity and become aware of disabilities.) By age three, prejudiced attitudes—distortions and misconceptions, fear and unease—begin to develop. And by age four or five, children begin rejecting differences, citing race or sex as reasons for not playing with other children.

This rejection is not necessarily vicious. Toddlers and preschoolers are extremely self-centered: Everything is defined in terms of how it relates to them. So your child may reject another person not so much because the other person's skin is pink, but rather because her own skin is brown, and the other person's is not like hers.

Needless to say, if parents and teachers do not intervene, biased attitudes can take root and develop into even more damaging forms of prejudice.

> ### Kid Stuff
>
> Megan was just under three when her parents started to interview new sitters. Mio—a bright, gentle 16-year-old—seemed perfect to Megan's parents. But when they introduced Mio and told Megan that she would be taking care of her for a couple of hours every afternoon, Megan said, "I don't want her to stay with me." When asked why, she replied, without malice but matter-of-factly, "Her skin is brown. I want someone with light skin like me."
>
> To her credit, Mio took this rejection in stride. But Megan's parents were aghast. Despite their embarrassment, however, they challenged their daughter's statement right away. They pointed out that her best friend, Sachan (a Japanese-American), did not have the same color skin that Megan did, but that didn't stop them from being friends. They also reminded her that she seemed to be having fun with Mio during this visit. Megan agreed to give it a try and the two soon became the best of buddies.
>
> By tackling their daughter's expression of bias immediately and directly, not with condemnation but with understanding, Megan's parents helped her to overcome it. By kindergarten, Megan's friends included: boys and girls, whites, African Americans, Chinese Americans, Japanese Americans, Korean Americans, and Indian Americans.

Simple Answers to Tough Questions

As much as we would like to be a color-blind, gender-blind, age-blind society, we aren't. So don't ignore the issues of racism and sexism (and ageism and other prejudices) just because they make you uncomfortable. Your toddler needs your help to resist biases and prejudice.

The best way to defeat the influence of bias is to talk about it with your toddler or preschooler. Listen to your child's questions and comments about others—and about himself—and answer them as directly and as well as you can.

If you show your child that you welcome open discussions about race and gender and age and physical abilities, you can expect him to start asking some tough questions:

➤ Why is Nana in a wheelchair all the time?

➤ Why is my skin so dark?

➤ If she takes a bath, will her skin get pink like mine?

➤ Why am I called white? My skin is pink.

➤ Why am I called black? My skin is brown.

➤ Why does Adriana sound so funny when she talks?

➤ Why don't I have a penis?

When your child brings up such questions, be straightforward and direct. Here are some pointers on how to answer tough questions:

➤ Listen carefully to the question, not only so that you will hear exactly what your child wants to know, but also so that you can gauge his feelings about the question—and about your answer.

➤ Answer briefly, directly, and matter-of-factly.

> **Q-Tip**
> In teaching your child respect and tolerance for different people, start with concepts they'll understand. African American? Latino? No. Your toddler doesn't understand these adult labels. Instead, start by talking about gender and skin color—the real color: not black and white, but brown, tan, beige, and pink. Then you can talk about the shape of eyes, the color and texture of hair, and other obvious differences.

➤ If you can't answer (either because you don't know or you're feeling thrown by the question), tell him that you need a little time either to think or to find out the answer. If you do put it off, however, make it a point to follow through.

➤ Don't ignore, evade, sidestep, or change the subject when your child asks about differences or biases.

➤ Do not chastise your child for asking the question, even if it seems inappropriate or embarrassing (to you). It's never bad for your child to ask about what he's observed. Besides, if you give your child the idea that it isn't polite to discuss these differences, then you won't have the opportunity to correct any misconceptions he may have formed.

➤ In any discussion of race or gender or other differences, you'll need to begin by acknowledging difference(s). Your child notices differences in gender, skin color, physical abilities, and accent, so you can't just pretend they don't exist. But at the same time, help your child notice the similarities: Okay, her skin is not the same color as yours, but she's your age. You both like to swing on the swings, you both like peanut-butter-and-jelly sandwiches, you both have a baby brother. Help your child make connections and then point out that skin color really doesn't matter all that much, does it?

When you respond to your child's questions about differences, try to provide answers that are as simple and accurate as possible. Some examples:

➤ Nana needs a wheelchair because her legs are no longer strong enough to hold her up when she tries to walk. The wheelchair helps her get around.

➤ Your skin is dark because Mommy's skin and Daddy's skin are both dark brown.

➤ No, her skin color won't come off. Skin color is not dirt; it does not wash away. Skin color is like the different colors of your shirts. When I throw your red shirt and your blue shirt in the wash, they still come out red and blue. The color doesn't wash away.

➤ People are called white or black even though they have many different skin colors. But you're right, neither is truly white or black.

➤ Adriana doesn't sound funny, she just sounds different. You might hurt her feelings if you say she sounds funny. She and her family came from Guatemala. She still speaks Spanish at home and speaks English as her second language. Do you think you could learn two languages?

➤ You don't have a penis because you don't need a penis. You have a vulva. All girls and women have vulvas. Boys and men have penises.

These kinds of simple but direct answers advance your child's understanding of difference without imposing value judgments on those differences.

Airing Differences

Toddlers are not known for their tact. At some point, you can expect your toddler to ask you a question that may embarrass you or make you feel otherwise uncomfortable. Yet your child is not trying to hurt anyone's feelings. She wants an honest explanation of the differences that she's observed. And your child deserves straightforward answers to her questions about gender, race, and disability.

Try not to suppress the subject by offering non-answers. Your child will learn very little if you respond to her questions by:

➤ Chastising: "Shhh, it's not nice to ask."

➤ Evading: "I'll tell you some other time."

➤ Avoiding: Pretending you didn't hear the question.

➤ Changing the subject: "Skin color doesn't matter. We're all the same underneath." (This is a fine sentiment and a message that you should try to communicate to your child, but it doesn't answer "why" questions about skin color or about racial labels.)

➤ Laughing it off: "You say the funniest things."

➤ Implicitly agreeing with a stereotype: "Adriana can't help the way she speaks." (This implies that she does sound funny.)

In candidly answering your child's questions about differences, the idea to convey is not that differences do not exist. They do, and your toddler plainly sees that they do. Instead, try to communicate the idea that though such differences do exist, they should not have any effect on the way we treat people. In fact, they enrich the world, making life more interesting and fun. If you want your child to grow up free of bias, you need to instill the fundamental notion that people should be regarded as individuals and valued for who they are and what they do, rather than for their sex, skin color, physical appearance, or country of origin. (Later, you can add religion and sexual orientation to this list. Toddlers and preschoolers rarely notice these more subtle distinctions.)

Many parents think that they're doing their child a favor by protecting her from the knowledge that prejudice and injustice exist in the world. Indeed, it's a natural parental instinct to want to protect your child not only from evil, but from the knowledge of evil. Yet ultimately, it will not help your child if you try to avoid unpleasant issues. It will only make your child more vulnerable to hurt when these issues come up on their own. In fact, your child will gain a better understanding of differences and bias if you address the subject in a calm and everyday setting, rather than in the emotionally overcharged atmosphere that sometimes envelops an incident involving racism or sexism—an event that forces you to deal with the issue.

Open and honest discussion of differences and unfair biases is the single best way to combat prejudice. Yes, you may end up "putting ideas into your child's head," but isn't that part of your job as a parent? Better that you put ideas about refusing to accept prejudice in your child's head than to leave it to others to put ideas in her head or to ignore ideas that are prejudiced.

The Trouble with TV

Television is fascinating for toddlers. It opens up new worlds for them. Unfortunately, your child would probably be better off not visiting some of these worlds.

Even today, most television programs—especially on commercial stations—tend to create or perpetuate stereotypical images of both men and women, as well as African Americans, Asian Americans, Native Americans, and other ethnic Americans. Television not only significantly underrepresents these groups—as well as children, the elderly, and homosexuals—but usually stereotypes them when it features them at all.

Almost no TV shows feature female heroes or even strong female leads. (Sadly, this applies to public television as well as commercial TV.)

Why does TV ignore strong female characters? Because the money made by TV stations depends on the size of the audience. Programmers naturally want to maximize their audience. And their research tells them that while girls will watch programs with either male or female leads, boys are less willing to watch shows that highlight female characters. Likewise, racial minorities will apparently watch programs with predominantly white characters much more readily than whites will watch shows featuring characters of different races or ethnicity.

Reruns of "classic" TV may be even worse. Cartoons and other programs from the 1960s and 1970s or even earlier, currently rerun on many cable stations, present worlds that are almost exclusively white and male. Many feature the stereotypical image of the stay-at-home, full-time mom. Others present stereotypical images and racial caricatures that could not even get produced today.

To find programs with female or nonwhite heroes, you may need to rely on videotapes. Yet you'll have to screen these carefully, too. Compilations of old cartoons, for example, often feature painful images of slow-talking, shuffling, large-lipped blacks or of slow, shifty Mexicans. And female characters are almost entirely absent in the cartoon world of yesteryear. (How many good mothers can you think of that have appeared in Disney's animated movies? Evil stepmothers or entirely absent mothers abound. Good, caring, knowledgeable mothers are few and far between.)

So if you want your child to avoid absorbing stereotypical images that you would not teach him yourself, you may be wise to limit your child's access to commercial TV and its biases. And when you do see stereotypes, whether in TV, videos, movies, or books, don't hesitate to challenge them. (See Chapter 14 for more on TV and your toddler.)

Creating an Environment that Rejects Prejudice

You can take positive steps to help your toddler (and later your preschooler) to resist and reject prejudice. With a little effort, you can create an environment that encourages and assists the development of anti-bias attitudes.

Start by taking a look at yourself. Remember that prejudice (negative or positive values attached to race, gender, ethnicity, and so on) is learned. So if you have negative attitudes toward other ethnic groups or toward the opposite sex (or even toward your own race or sex), then children will begin absorbing these attitudes in their preschool years.

Creating an environment that rejects bias must therefore begin in the home—with an examination of your own attitudes. Only after dealing with your own biases can you effectively deal with the biases of the larger culture.

I'm Unique

You can begin to battle the influence of bias in our culture by teaching your toddler to value differences. One way to start is by encouraging your child to appreciate her own uniqueness.

How is your child special? She's two years old. She has a particular hair color, eye color, and skin color. Her ancestors have a specific cultural heritage. (Sharing stories of people—family members, historical figures, or contemporary role models—from your ethnic group of whom you feel proud can also build an appreciation of your child's cultural heritage.) Your toddler also has a distinctive name, which may reflect some family history or cultural background.

Defining the ways in which your child is unique or special is a great way to encourage her to value differences because toddlers love talking and learning about themselves. By talking in a positive way about your toddler's physical characteristics and cultural heritage, you will help her build a positive sense of self. And if she learns to value what makes her different from others, your toddler will be more open to the notion of appreciating the differences of others as well.

> **Q-Tip**
> You can introduce your child to the notion of differences by starting within your own family. Do different members of your family have different color hair (black, brown, blonde, red, grey, white)? Different texture of hair (curly, straight, thick, wispy)? Different color eyes (brown, blue, hazel)? Acknowledging and valuing the diverse physical traits within your family can help your child appreciate diversity outside the family, too.

No Teasing or Insults

If you want to nip prejudice in the bud, don't let your child ever insult, tease, or reject another person because of race, gender, or ethnicity. Make it a family rule—one that you, of course, observe as well as your child—that you cannot tease, insult, or reject other people for who they are. Attacks on another person's identity simply cannot be allowed.

If you do hear your toddler tease or insult someone because of their gender or race (or if you hear another child teasing or insulting your toddler), step in immediately. Remaining silent will only give your child (or the other child) permission to repeat it and to go on hurting others. Just as you would if your toddler had physically hurt another child (see Chapter 11), comfort and reassure the injured child first. While doing so, make sure your child knows that you disapprove of what he did. You may choose to discipline such bias attacks just the way you would discipline violence or physical attacks.

At the same time, however, try to find out what underlies the insult. Chances are it didn't come out of the blue. If another problem, like having trouble sharing or difficulty taking turns, underlies the slur, then teach your child to address the problem directly, rather than attacking the person's race or gender. Help your toddler see that the other child's gender or skin color or ethnic background has nothing to do with the sharing problem. If fear of people who are different is an underlying factor, then you'll need to come up with some activities that will increase your child's opportunity to interact with other children who are racially or culturally different.

Seeking Out Difference

Start by trying to expose your child to a variety of influences in your community. Get to know people of different races, religions, and cultural backgrounds. Then let your toddler get to know their children. After all, you can't expect your child to make friends with people of different races and cultures if you don't do the same.

If you live in a largely homogenous community, you can expose your child to different races and cultures by stocking up on books, videos, dolls, toys, and posters or photos that show people of different races, genders, and physical abilities engaged in a variety of activities. A diversity of images of males and females, whites and blacks, and people of all races will broaden your child's appreciation of both similarities and differences without glossing over the subject.

You also can expose your child to people of different races and cultures by carefully choosing television programs that present characters with different backgrounds. Like all toddlers, your child will enjoy watching kids like her on TV. Unless you're white, how-

Q-Tip
Your local children's librarian can probably help you find a good selection of multicultural books (and perhaps videos, too).

ever, this may be difficult on most shows—especially shows on commercial television. Though many children's television programs do offer either stereotypes or limited diversity, if you look, you will find several good programs (mostly on public television) that do present differences in a positive light. Shows like *Sesame Street*, *Barney & Friends*, and *Reading Rainbow*, for example, feature multicultural casts and features that will expose your child to many different cultures.

Playing with Gender Roles

You also can help build resistance to bias by encouraging your child to engage in activities that go beyond or go against traditional sex-role stereotyping. Sex-role stereotyping often begins with the purchase of toys for toddlers. When you buy a push toy to help steady your toddler's walking, do you automatically gravitate toward the shopping cart or vacuum if you have a girl or the truck or lawn mower if you have a boy? Why not try buying the reverse? Boys can enjoy shopping too; and girls can have fun mowing the lawn.

Similarly, both boys and girls can both take care of "babies" (dolls), "cook a meal" (with a toy kitchen), and "fix things" (with a toy tool box). Encourage your child to explore all the opportunities open to her or him. Remember that you're teaching the future mothers and fathers of the world. Don't you want your son as much as your daughter to grow up to be a nurturing parent? Likewise, as he or she grows older, won't you want your child to be independent enough to cook a meal for himself or fix a broken bicycle herself? You can nurture interest in these activities by deliberately rejecting gender stereotypes in choosing toys and play for your toddler or preschooler—and in the roles you play in your own home.

Don't Let Them Get Away with It

If you want to raise a bias-free child, you will need to do more than opening your child up to an appreciation of different cultures and races and genders. You will also need to confront and challenge the biases that appear throughout our popular culture. Do not stand silently by and tacitly approve of the subtle and more overt biases in our society. Your child will interpret silence to mean support. So point out biases, prejudice, and injustice to your child whenever you see them—and note that they are wrong.

It's also not enough simply to reject negative values attached to certain people; you'll need to attach positive values to them, too. That's why it will help to introduce your child to multicultural books, movies, music and, of course, people. Through these influences, your child will form positive associations with people of different races, cultures, and gender.

Don't just ignore prejudice and hope that it will go away by the time your toddler grows up. If you do, you're leaving it to the dominant culture to teach your child what differences mean. And though our culture does now send out messages on tolerance and the value of diversity, it also still broadcasts many stereotypes and biased images.

Find a Positive Use for Biased Materials

The most prejudiced portrayal of stereotyped characters can be a positive learning tool—if you put it to good use. Even if your child is just two or three years old, you can use biased books, movies, videos, and TV shows as a touchstone for discussions of fair and unfair portrayals of certain types of characters.

Start by sharing your opinions of characters and stories with your child. By challenging bias when you see it in fictional or real-life situations, you can teach your child to do the same. Through your modeling, your toddler (and later your preschooler) will learn to recognize stereotypes and unfair caricatures. If you prefer the aspiring, active, intellectual, and courageous Belle in Walt Disney's *Beauty and the Beast* to the passive, dumb-as-a-doorpost Snow White (or *Aladdin's* Jasmine, who is nearly as passive and serves as little more than a door prize in the struggle between Aladdin and Jafar), talk to your child about why you feel that way. Even at ages two or three your child can understand such distinctions and your example will encourage her to think critically about what she reads or sees.

Give Characters a Sex-Change Operation

The world of children's books is still largely a male universe. Characters, especially in children's classics like the works of Dr. Seuss, Maurice Sendak, Crockett Johnson, and many others, are almost exclusively male. (To his credit, Dr. Seuss also wrote one of the classic works of children's literature that expressly teaches tolerance: *The Sneetches*.) These are all wonderful stories and should not be rejected wholesale just because the lead characters are all male. But there's also no reason why you can't change the gender of some of these characters as you read these books to your toddler—whether your child is a girl or a boy. With very few exceptions (Mickey in Sendak's *In the Night Kitchen*), none of these characters is drawn with a penis. Harold (with his purple crayon) could be a girl; so could Little Bear or Max, ruler of the Wild Things.

In reading a book based on Disney's *The Jungle Book*, for example, you can make Mowgli a girl. Baloo the bear or Bagheera the panther also can be female. And for balance, you can make one of the story's two villains, Kaa the snake or Shere Khan the tiger, a female, too. Alternatively, you could refer to all of the animal characters using the word "it" rather than "he."

Rewrite the Story

Encourage your child to think about how a story might have unfolded differently—especially if you notice bias in the storytelling. When watching *The Lion King*, for example, you might ask your three- or four-year-old whether things might not have happened differently after Simba exiled himself from the land around Pride Rock. Question why Nala and Simba's mother and the rest of the lionesses allowed the evil Scar to continue to rule over them once he'd shown his true colors.

Then suggest alternatives or tell a story that counteracts the movie's or book's stereotypical image of females or minorities. For instance, once the land began to go to ruin, couldn't the lionesses have overthrown Scar and restored the land themselves? Then when Simba grows up and returns to Pride Rock, the pride might still welcome him back—not necessarily as their ruler, but rather as just another contributing member of the pride. If you have a little imagination and the inclination to do so, you can retell familiar stories in a way that more accurately reflects your own values.

What your child learns now, when he is two, three, and four years old, will have an enormous influence on the attitudes he will have later in life. So don't let prejudices take firm root in your child. Teach your child that it's not necessary to fear the "other" or refuse to associate with the "other." Indeed, if your child learns to open himself up to others, his life will be richer because of it.

Baby Talk
"What its children become, that will the community become."
—Suzanne LaFollette

The Least You Need to Know

> ➤ Discrimination is natural: Toddlers notice differences in gender, race, skin color, and ethnicity just as they notice differences in noses or other features.

> ➤ Prejudice (assigning values to these differences) is learned—from parents, peers, and popular culture.

> ➤ Don't avoid talking to your toddler about bias. Your silence signals your assent.

> ➤ Helping your child appreciate the ways in which she is unique will also make her more tolerant of the differences of others.

> ➤ Emphasize that differences *enrich* the world.

Chapter 14

The Twilight Zone—and Beyond: TV and Toys For Toddlers

In This Chapter

➤ What TV can do *for* your child—and what it can do *to* your child

➤ How to exercise greater control over your child's television watching habits

➤ Encouraging reading and the love of books

➤ Appropriate toys and games for your two-year-old

Your toddler's physical and intellectual skills take a remarkable leap forward during the third year. New worlds open up to her. At one, your child probably had little interest in the TV. Now she wants to watch it all the time. Just a year ago, you and your baby read only picture books with little or no text. Now your toddler has an insatiable thirst to know what will happen next in a story. A year ago, your child had trouble fitting the lid of a baby food jar into a flexible slot. But this year, she will master jigsaw puzzles, shape boxes, and even begin threading beads onto a shoelace. Your child is quickly becoming her own person. And the growing number of things your toddler can think and see and do are helping her on her way.

The Boob Tube

TV offers an easy target for the ills of contemporary society—including the difficulties of childrearing. After all, look what television does to us. It has turned us into a nation of mind-numbed couch potatoes—and it threatens to do the same to our children. The remote control and MTV-style editing have left us with attention spans that even a flea wouldn't envy. Hypnotized by the idiot box, we have abandoned reading altogether—except maybe *TV Guide.*

Our educational system—once among the finest in the world—has literally gone down the tube. Television robs our children of their youth by introducing them to an array of scenes and subjects that they're not mature enough to handle. It breaks into our homes with a barrage of real and fictional violence, terrifying our children and convincing adults and children alike that the world is a much more dangerous place than it really is.

So we should all throw open our windows, shout, "I'm mad as hell and I'm not going to take it anymore!" and toss our TV sets out onto the street, right? Well, not exactly. If you want to take that tack, more power to you. But it's probably unrealistic to expect any parents to throw away the TV. After all, 98 percent of American homes have at least one, while 69 percent have two or more. Besides, do you really want to throw out the baby with the bath water? TV can offer specific benefits to toddlers and preschoolers. In moderation, TV can encourage the development and advancement of reading skills and promote further learning.

Baby Talk
"Once I thought the most important political statement we could make about television was to turn it off. But television can instruct, inform, and inspire, as well as distract, distort, and demean. And turning it off rejects the good with the bad."
—Bill Moyers

In addition, from a practical standpoint, the TV is often indispensable when you have to make dinner or clean the house or take a shower. Most parents today use television as a "babysitter" for at least a little time almost every day. It's perfectly understandable: You need to do a few chores or maybe return some phone calls. If you turn on the TV and find a show that engages your child—or if you pop in a favorite video—you'll know exactly where your toddler will be while you finish up your chores.

As a practical reality, TV is here to stay for most of us. So maybe instead of trashing it completely, we just need to find new and different ways of using it—and monitoring how our children use it.

The Good, the Bad, and the Ugly

Television is not automatically bad for us or for our children. Indeed, although much of it could still be described as a "vast wasteland," television also can educate and inspire your child. At its best, TV can:

➤ introduce your child to people and places from all over the world, people and places he might never visit otherwise (including, of course, some whom you'd rather he didn't meet);

➤ give your toddler a jump-start on building number skills, recognizing colors and shapes, increasing his vocabulary and language skills—and even motivate your child to want to read or read more;

➤ demonstrate healthy ways of expressing emotions and the consequences of expressing emotions in more harmful ways; and

➤ reinforce values that you are teaching in the home such as kindness, manners, taking turns, respecting differences, and sharing.

Unfortunately, not every TV program—nor even every children's program—represents television at its finest. Much of television (or too much television) also can:

➤ circumscribe your child's imagination and creativity;

➤ suggest that some of life's most complex problems can be solved in 30 or 60 minutes—often through violence; and

➤ eat up time that might otherwise be spent reading, learning, playing, getting exercise, or developing hobbies or other interests.

Okay, here's the ugly part. American children watch an average of 28 hours of TV a week (that's four hours a day). Yet studies have shown that children who watch four or more hours of TV a day develop poorer reading skills, do not get along as well with other children, develop fewer interests and hobbies, and are less likely to be physically active. What's worse, kids who watch four or more hours of TV also swallow the claims of advertisers more readily.

The average American child today will spend 18,000 hours watching TV by the time he graduates from high school. That's 5,000 more hours than kids spend in school from kindergarten through graduation!

TV Control (Not Remote Control)

As much as you can, you decide when your toddler goes to bed. You choose what toys to buy your child—and therefore what toys she plays with. You decide what foods your child will eat—or at least you provide a choice of good foods from which she can choose. So why wouldn't you choose to do the same with the amount and type of television your child watches?

As a parent, you have a responsibility to take control of the TV. Not remote control, but active, involved, participatory control.

Beat the Clock! How Much Is Too Much?

The average child watches too much TV. The problem is not just that the hours your toddler spends glued in front of the tube are hours she's not spending exploring or reading or creating worlds of her own. Just as troublesome is the fact that the more TV your child watches, the higher the chances that she'll be watching junk at least some of the time.

Q-Tip

Most of us underestimate the amount of TV we—and our children—watch. Try keeping a log for two weeks or a month. Write down the exact time you turn on the TV, when you turn it off, and what programs or videos your child watched during that time. You may be surprised at how much time your child spends in front of the TV.

The American Academy of Pediatrics, the National Parent Teacher Association, the National Education Association and others all agree that parents should limit the amount of time that their kids spend watching TV. The cap recommended by most of these organizations is about 10 to 15 hours a week. (That's a maximum of about two hours a day.)

If your child watches more than 15 hours of TV per week, you can try one of three strategies to try to cut down. You can:

➤ gradually cut back, reducing the amount of time in front of the set by a few hours every week until you reach your target;

➤ immediately cut down to two hours (or less) a day;

➤ quit cold turkey, declaring a moratorium on the TV for a week and then allowing your child to watch a limited amount of TV after that. (Play fair: If your child quits TV for a week, you should, too.)

Of course, if you cut out ten or fifteen hours of TV watching from your toddler's routine, you'll need to engage or entertain her yourself. Suggest other activities that will occupy her time. This means more playtime together, more playdates with friends, more art projects, and more reading together. If you don't make the effort to involve your child in other enjoyable activities, you have only yourself to blame when she starts begging, whining, or issuing demands for more TV.

Remember also to model good TV-watching habits yourself. You can't reasonably expect your child to limit herself to two hours a day if you're watching five to six hours yourself. That's hypocritical—and kids will catch you up in your inconsistency. So when you have some free time, don't just plop down in front of the TV (even if you're sitting with your child). Instead, spend it playing with your toddler. Do some art projects together or go on a "field trip" to a library, park, or museum.

Watch What Your Child Watches

Limiting the amount of time your toddler (or preschooler) spends watching TV is important. But just as important, and perhaps even more important, is placing limits on what your child can watch. There's a significant difference between *Sesame Street* and *Road Rovers*, between *Barney & Friends* and *The Flintstones*, between *Little Bear* and the *Big Bad BeetleBorgs*. But your child doesn't know what's junk and what's not. You do. Yet surprisingly, nearly six out of seven parents (of children aged three to eight) do not help their children select the programs they watch on TV.

If you don't watch out for what your child watches, you leave your child prey to such shows as the *Mighty Morphin Power Rangers* and Saturday morning TV programs. In addition to offering virtually no educational value, these shows average about two dozen acts of violence per hour. What's even worse, most of this violence has virtually no consequences. After all, how many times can Wile E. Coyote ("Super Genius") be blown up or crushed by an anvil and still bounce back?

But there's really no reason for you to let this happen. You can get the idea of what any series is like by watching two or three episodes. You can prescreen videos—and you can even prescreen TV shows by taping them and reviewing them before letting your child watch them. But you can't properly monitor children's TV programs unless you at least occasionally watch the same TV shows or videos that your toddler watches.

> **Childproofing**
> The same concerns about violence in children's TV programs also apply, of course, to many children's video games. So if you have introduced your child to the wonders of Nintendo, be sure to prescreen all games that to make sure that you approve of their action.

Quality Programming

If you look for them, you can find creative, entertaining, and even (gasp) educational TV shows for toddlers and preschoolers. Some of the quality TV series for toddlers and preschoolers include:

➤ *Arthur* (PBS)

➤ *The Busy World of Richard Scarry* (NICK)

➤ *Lamb Chop's Play-Along* (PBS)

➤ *Madeline* (FAM)

➤ *Maurice Sendak's Little Bear* (NICK)

➤ *Mister Rogers' Neighborhood* (PBS)

> **Childproofing**
> Research has shown that viewing TV violence may be linked to increased aggression, decreased sensitivity, and less tolerance toward others. TV violence is definitely linked to increased acceptance of violence as an appropriate and effective way to solve problems and to heightened distrust and fear of the world in general.

➤ *Papa Beaver's Storytime* (NICK)

➤ *Rory's Place* (TLC)

➤ *Sesame Street* (PBS)

➤ *Shining Time Station* (PBS)

➤ *Storytime* (PBS)

➤ *The Magic School Bus* (PBS)

➤ *Reading Rainbow* (PBS)

➤ *Wishbone* (PBS)

As an added bonus, almost all of these shows are shown without commercials.

You Are the TV Guide

Besides guiding your child's selection of what to watch on TV, you also can teach her how to watch. Television can be a passive medium, encouraging viewers just to sit back and watch—but it doesn't have to be. Good programs, educational programs, can actively engage your child's—and your own—intelligence.

Good children's programs promote both physical and intellectual activity. Shows like *Barney & Friends* and *Rory's Place* can prompt your child to get up and jump, clap, dance, and sing. Children—and especially toddlers and preschoolers— also are intellectually active when they watch TV. Your child strives for increased understanding. And just trying to make sense of what she's seeing on the screen takes a lot of intellectual activity.

You can help your child become an active TV watcher by nurturing critical viewing skills. At least on occasion, watch TV with your child. Don't talk through the entire program, but every few minutes, while you're watching:

➤ Comment on what you're seeing

➤ Ask questions about the content to make sure your child understands what she's seeing

➤ Encourage your child to ask questions about anything she doesn't understand

➤ Ask your child to guess what will happen next

➤ Try to connect what you're seeing with something from your own or your child's experience and comment on that

After you turn off the TV, talk more about what your child watched. A television program can serve as an excellent starting point for further learning, discussion, and activities, yet less than one-third of all parents take advantage of this opportunity.

If, for example, your child seemed fascinated by a show on dinosaurs, you can try your hand at drawing pictures of dinosaurs. You might want to get a set of toy dinosaurs that you can use to help your child create prehistoric worlds. You can see if a natural history museum in the area has a dinosaur exhibit and take your toddler to see it. You can even go to the library or bookstore and pick out some books about dinosaurs.

Baby Talk
"Television may be the only electrical appliance that's more useful after it's turned off."
—Mr. (Fred) Rogers

Believe it or not, good children's TV shows can foster a love of reading. Children's book publishers, who originally feared the opposite, now recognize the advantages of being featured on *Reading Rainbow* or *Storytime*. (A reading on these shows—or even just a mention—can boost the sales figures for a children's book 400 percent or more.) Even if a TV show's format does not involve explicit storytelling or the reading of books, it can still promote reading. If your child wants to know more about what she has seen, books are the place to go.

You Are the TV Programmer

Now that 78 percent of American homes have a VCR, most parents have little excuse for letting their children watch a lot of commercial TV. Video allows you (with some input from your child, of course) to be your toddler's television programmer.

Of course you have to be just as selective in choosing videos as you would be in choosing broadcast shows. Children's videos can provide quality alternatives to network or even public broadcasting stations. But videos also can offer little more than junk food for the mind. For this reason, videos demand parental monitoring, too.

Videos give you a tremendous amount of influence over what your child watches on TV. Until your toddler or preschooler figures out the mechanics of inserting a tape and working the remote, he can't watch TV without your help. You (and your child) get to choose exactly what he will watch. And you don't even have to depend on quixotic TV schedules. Your child can watch whatever he wants to watch whenever it's most convenient for him—and you.

Children's videos are often a bargain. Almost all sell for under $20 and many good ones can be found for less than $10. In addition, you can tape episodes of your toddler's favorite shows to create your own personal video library. Best of all, you can even avoid commercials—by skipping the commercials when you make a tape or by zapping through them when you watch it.

I Want That! Combatting Kids' Commercials

The average American child sees an astonishing ten to twenty thousand commercials every year. Advertisers are no fools: They don't spend $700 million a year aiming advertising toward kids without expecting a return on their investment. Commercials create a desire in children—and in many adults—so strong that it approaches an absolute need.

Yet almost none of the products advertised on children's television come close to being necessities. For example, 96 percent of food ads featured on children's programs are for junk food, cookies, sugared cereals, and candy—nice treats for sure, but not exactly representative of the four basic food groups.

> **Q-Tip**
>
> *Consumer Reports* and HBO have produced a video series called *Buy Me That: A Kids' Survival Guide to Advertising*. The videos teach your toddler some of the tricks of the advertising trade (manipulative film editing, pouring glue instead of milk on cereals so that the flakes won't get soggy, and so on). The first and third videos in the series can be ordered by calling 1-800-343-4312; the second is available at 1-800-526-4663.

If you're going to let your toddler or preschooler watch commercial television at all, help your child become more savvy about advertising. Watch some commercials together. Ask your toddler what they are trying to sell and talk about what they do to make the product appealing. If you actually own a product that you see advertised on TV, compare what you can do with it to what you see people doing with it on TV.

You also can educate your child about advertising by playing games with the commercials. Time them and see how much of a half hour (or hour) is devoted to commercials and how much to programming. Or make a list of commercials that you see on a certain show. Based on your list, can you describe the audience (young children, boys, girls, older kids) that advertisers expect to be watching the show?

Better yet, try to avoid commercials as much as you can. If your TV has a "Mute" button, silence the sales pitches. Make this a condition of watching commercial TV.

Sharing Adventures: Reading to Your Toddler

Two is a terrific age for reading to your child. Your toddler wants to build her vocabulary and will eagerly sit to hear stories that offer her new words to learn. But reading books to your toddler does much more than just build language skills. Storybooks transport your child into new worlds of imagination.

Although your two-year-old will still enjoy simple, single-picture-per-page books, she'll also welcome storybooks now. So you now can begin introducing some of the best-loved books from your own childhood.

The best way to nurture a love of books and reading in your child is to read to her every day. By introducing your toddler to a ridiculous character, fun and fascinating stories, and silly poems, the best children's books will encourage her to want to read more. At the same time, these books will help your child become better able to express herself.

> **Baby Talk**
> "The memory of having been read to is a solace one carries through adulthood. It can wash over a multitude of parental sins."
> —Kathleen Rockwell Lawrence

Good Books

Ask your local children's librarian for help in choosing books and authors appropriate for your two-year-old. Chances are, your toddler will love books by any of the following authors:

Frank Asch (*Bear*)	Kevin Henkes
Ludwig Bemelmans (*Madeline*)	Crockett Johnson (*Harold and the Purple Crayon*)
Eric Carle	Else Holmelund Minarik (*Little Bear*)
David A. Carter	Beatrix Potter (*Peter Rabbit*)
Tomie dePaola	Dr. Seuss
P.D. Eastman	Maurice Sendak
Marjorie Flack	Esphyr Slobodkina
Don Freeman (*Corduroy*)	Martin Waddell

Choosing Appropriate Toys and Games

Your child will, of course, not spend all of his time watching television and reading books. If you decide to limit your child's TV time, you will need to engage him with other toys and activities. Here are some ideas:

➤ Many of the toys, games, and fun activities that your child enjoyed as a one-year-old (see Chapter 7, "Playtime!"), he will continue to love as a two-year-old. These include blocks, stacking cups, shape boxes, pull toys, and sand toys.

➤ Hands-on toys give your child a chance to practice and show off his rapidly improving hand-eye coordination. Any toy that requires your child to turn his wrist to fit pieces together

> **Baby Talk**
> "Child! do not throw this book about; Refrain from the unholy pleasure of cutting all the pictures out! Preserve it as your chiefest treasure."—Hilaire Belloc

(jigsaw puzzles, LEGOS, Lincoln Logs, and so on) will keep him busy for many hours. So will any toys that involve building or constructing (including interlocking blocks and sand toys).

Childproofing
Whenever your toddler rides a tricycle or any other vehicle that tips easily, make sure that he wears a safety helmet.

➤ Your child also will love toys and games that involve sorting or matching skills. Anything that helps to order his world is always welcome at this age.

➤ Wheeled ride-on toys, which you may have introduced in your child's second year, will become even more popular in his third. Toward the end of the year, you might even want to spring for your toddler's first tricycle and/or wagon.

➤ You also can keep your child physically active with lots of games that involve jumping, climbing, or hopping. Give your toddler every opportunity to jump, roll, run, and climb. Games like ring-around-a-rosy, Simon Says, follow the leader, or musical chairs—or just finding a hill and rolling down it—will give your toddler practice at making his body move the way he wants it to.

➤ In addition, games and play that involve creative movement—for instance, pretending to be an animal—will help him discover new ways to make his body move.

Welcome to My Fantasy

Your two-year-old will probably engage in lots of fantasy role playing. Role playing usually centers around the roles your child observes the most: family roles. Your toddler will cook imaginary meals, care for her "babies," and go off to her "work."

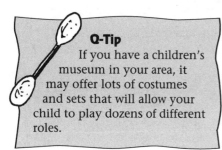

Q-Tip
If you have a children's museum in your area, it may offer lots of costumes and sets that will allow your child to play dozens of different roles.

Dolls provide handy babies in games of make-believe. But make sure that any doll highchairs, doll strollers, and doll beds are sturdy, because you can be sure that your child will use these for herself as well as for her dolls.

To assist your child's imaginative play, supply plenty of costumes and dress-up clothes. Check your closets for old, worn, or outmoded shirts, scarves, purses, hats, and so on. Your child will find hats especially useful in helping to transform into someone else.

Add a few role-playing toys—a doctor's bag, a tool box, or a play kitchen—and your child will have everything she needs for a trip to the land of make-believe. Your toddler will love pretending that she's engaged in an adult occupation (almost anything that she's observed, she'll try to copy): a teacher, a nurse, a doctor, a police officer, a fire fighter, a librarian, a truck driver, a grocery store clerk, a ballerina, and of course, a mommy or a daddy. The more realistic the fantasy toy, the more your child will use it to help pretend.

Your toddler's love for fantasy play will merge with other kinds of play as well. While riding about on a tricycle or other wheeled toy, your child will probably begin to make motorcycle noises, "drive" trucks, or take the "family car" to the library or day-care center.

The Budding Artist

Arts and crafts are especially good activities for 2 ½- to 3-year-olds. Projects like stringing beads on a piece of yarn, a shoelace, or some other thick string fit well with the rapid development of your child's manipulative skills. Modeling clay and play dough provide the sensual experience of sculpting and shaping something out of a lump—even if that something turns out to be just another lump. And though your two-year-old will still find scissors difficult to manipulate, safety scissors can be introduced toward the end of the year to cut shapes for collages, and so on.

Your child will enjoy working with different colors and a variety of media. So give him an array of crayons, water colors, washable markers, finger paints, and colored chalk. Help him to tear pictures from magazines and make a collage. Or try an ink pad and stamps. Or cut a shape out of a potato or apple and use that as a stamp by dipping it in paint.

Paints and paste provide sensual pleasures for toddlers, too. They delight not only the sense of sight, but also the senses of touch and smell—and taste. Most children's art supplies are delicious. You'd sure think so if you've ever seen your toddler playing with them.

Most importantly, art projects help to improve your toddler's manipulative abilities. Don't expect your child to produce anything particularly recognizable, because that's really not the point at all. Like so much of 20th-century art, the process of creation is far more important than the product created.

Art projects provide a fascinating illustration of the principles of "cause and effect"— because your child is the cause and his creation is the effect. In scribbling out a "picture," your child learns to coordinate both of his hands toward a single goal. At two, your toddler will start out making zigzag lines across the page—probably horizontally. A few months later, he will add some vertical "lines" to the horizontals. Later in the year, he'll practice swirling spirals. And by his third birthday, your child may begin to notice that the type of line he produces with a crayon changes depending on how hard he presses down on the paper. But it all began with the realization that a stroke of your toddler's crayon produced a line. And really, that's an amazing enough discovery in itself.

The Least You Need to Know

➤ Television can be very good or very bad. It all depends on how much your child watches, what she watches, and how she watches.

➤ There's really no reason not to exercise control over what your child watches.

➤ Building a video library can help you avoid commercial TV and TV commercials.

➤ There is life beyond TV: Books, fantasy, and art all offer your toddler new worlds to explore.

Part 3
A Real Person: The Three-Year-Old

Wow! You made it through the terrible twos. Now you have at least a brief break before the ferocious fours. Three is a terrific age. Your child now has the language skills to express most of his thoughts, needs, and desires. He also has the physical strength and coordination needed to take care of many of his most simple needs and desires.

At three, your child will burst out of his cocoon to become a social butterfly. If you allow and encourage it, his social circle will expand beyond your own household to include virtually everyone he meets. So wave goodbye to the years in which you had almost exclusive influence over your toddler. He's a preschooler now. So watch out world, here he comes.

Chapter 15

You're a Big Girl (Or Boy) Now: Preschool Development

In This Chapter

➤ Your child's increasing strength, agility, balance, and coordination

➤ The exciting expansion of your child's vocabulary and language skills

➤ The development of your child's rationalization and reasoning ability

➤ Your child's emergence as a social creature

➤ Your three-year-old's fragile independence

Three is a great age for children—and their parents. Energy and eagerness to please are no doubt the hallmarks of your three-year-old's personality. Because he wants so much to please you, your child is probably very cooperative, helpful, and sometimes even generous. He may have a tendency to show off both for adults and for other children as a way of courting approval. Your child probably even wants to help with simple chores around the house.

At this age, he wants very much to do things "right," and when his abilities fall short of his aspirations, he may get very frustrated. But because he is as easy to please as he is eager to please, your child is probably agreeable and has a generally sunny disposition.

I Can Do That

Your three-year-old has endless reserves of energy and could probably run, jump, climb, and dance all day. Throughout this fourth year, your child will become stronger, nimbler, more graceful, and more coordinated every day. Her walking and running (and trotting and galloping) will become more confident and agile. She will begin swinging her arms when she walks, just as an adult does, instead of leading with her belly the way a toddler walks.

Stairs? No problem now. Your child walks—or even runs—up stairs with great self-assurance, probably alternating feet, just one per step, while going upstairs. Coming down stairs—directly facing the potential of a long fall—may cause a little more nervousness. So your child will probably still take steps one at a time, always leading with the same foot and then bringing her trail leg down even with the first leg before continuing down to the next step. But when she gets to the bottom step (or even the second from the bottom), don't be surprised if your child suddenly takes a bold leap. Jumping is one of your child's favorite feats of daring: off the stairs, off the couch, off the bed, off the slide, and off the wall.

Balance and coordination show marked improvements. Your three-year-old can now manage the coordinated leg movements needed to ride a tricycle or a pedal car. And she can probably balance on one leg for one or two seconds—but she can't do (or even think of) anything else while doing it. Your child's improved balance and coordination make dancing a terrific activity (for a boy or a girl) at this age.

Of course, all three-year-olds are different. So if your child hasn't mastered one or more of these skills, don't worry. She will.

Take It to the Limit

Besides mastering these physical abilities, your preschooler will constantly set new challenges for himself. At three, your child's sense of his own strength and competence are important to him. He repeatedly needs to test and stretch the limits of his physical abilities:

➤ Can I stand on one leg?

➤ Can I stand on my head?

➤ How far can I walk?

➤ How fast can I run?

➤ Can I run faster than she can?

➤ How high can I climb?

➤ How far can I jump?

➤ Am I strong enough to move that chair?

➤ Am I strong enough to lift that baby?

Through success (or failure) at these challenges, your preschooler will learn about his body and what it can do—in other words, what he can do. Such useful skills as protecting his face with his arms and hands when he falls will become second nature. He'll discover that it's easier to run downhill than uphill. Most important, your preschooler will discover—and simultaneously expand—the limits of his own strength, balance, and agility.

Your preschooler's manual dexterity also continues to improve during this year. For much of the year, your child will hold crayons or paint brushes with his whole fist. But his ability to vary the pressure of the crayon on the paper or alter the brushstroke steadily improves. If he practices a little, your child will learn to roll and bounce balls with ease and may be able to throw a ball roughly toward a chosen target (probably you). Catching a ball is a more difficult skill for your three-year-old to master, but not an impossible one.

Besides becoming more adept physically, your three-year-old also gains a large degree of physical independence. More and more, he can attend to his own physical needs: dressing, getting out (and, in an ideal world, putting away) his own toys, eating, using the toilet, washing. This doesn't mean your preschooler doesn't need you any more. But as your child takes on more of the responsibility for his physical needs, you will have more time to spend stimulating ideas through play, books, and conversation.

Childproofing
Your heart may stop dozens of times as you watch your preschooler take on physical challenges with the daring of Indiana Jones. Yet try not to overprotect your child or you risk crushing his spirit and inhibiting his curiosity.

Try to trust your child's growing sense of himself and what he can and cannot do. The physical challenges he sets for himself will help him to form his own sense of physical safety. Unless egged on by others, your child's own fears are likely to keep him from attempting anything that seriously threatens his safety.

Wonderful Words

Perhaps the most dramatic change in the fourth year involves your child's mushrooming language skills. To your three-year-old, words are no longer used almost exclusively to label objects she can see, hear, touch, smell, or taste. Language becomes richer, more detailed, and conveys abstract ideas.

Your three-year-old will learn thousands of new words this year. But while your two-year-old focused on nouns, your child will now learn words that do more than label. In the course of this year, your preschooler will learn:

➤ her full name;

➤ specific nouns that allow for much more subtle distinctions (not just a dog, but a Dalmatian; a rock versus a stone; a hill versus a mountain);

➤ a variety of verbs that enable her to express complete ideas in short sentences;

➤ words that enable her to express her feelings (angry, happy, tired, cold, frustrated, sad, scared);

➤ prepositions that convey spatial relations (in, out, under, over, up, down, on, between, beside, by, near, to, from, back, front, upstairs, downstairs, inside, and outside); and

➤ adjectives that allow detailed description of size, shape, color, and other physical characteristics.

Q-Tip

After your child has mastered a handful of adjectives, you can reinforce her understanding as well as her observational skills by playing the "I See Something" game. Although usually played with colors (for example, "I see something red."), you also can play this game with shapes ("I see something round.") or size. ("I see something as big as my head.")

Your child may still have some difficulty with pronouns at age three and may quite sensibly choose to avoid using them altogether. Gradually, however, pronouns will begin to make sense to her. Just focus on using pronouns correctly yourself and let your child go on using proper names until she feels more comfortable with pronouns.

Can We Talk?

Your child's improving language skills, combined with his increased attention span, makes sustained conversations possible at age three. And the more conversation, the better. Your modeling of good language skills is more important than ever. So no matter how your child constructs a sentence or creates new words, try to respond with proper grammar and vocabulary.

You can talk about anything and everything with a three-year-old. You no longer need to confine yourself to talking about the immediate present. You also can now talk about the past, about the future, about things in the realm of the mind (yours or your child's). In short, you can talk not only about facts, but about ideas.

Your child needs you to hold real conversations with him, though. When your preschooler starts to talk a mile a minute—stuttering, stammering, and repeating himself again and again as he struggles to find the right words—it may be tempting to just nod and say, "Uh-huh." But if you do, your child will know that you're not really listening to him. Now that your child is three, conversation needs to be a two-way street.

Certainly, you will want to fill your preschooler's head with ideas and observations that are important to you. But at this age, your child wants to do the same thing to you. So try to avoid talking nonstop yourself and listen—really listen—to what your child is trying to tell you.

Instead of talking in simple shorthand, which may have been more appropriate for him when he was a toddler, you should now express complete ideas. Indeed, elaborate on the ideas that you might only have sketched at an earlier age. For example, instead of just saying, "I'll get it," say, "Let me help you get that box. It's on a high shelf and I can reach it more easily because I'm taller than you are."

> **Baby Talk**
> "Notoriously insensitive to subtle shifts in mood, children will persist in discussing the color of a recently sighted cement-mixer long after one's own interest in the topic has waned."
> —Fran Lebowitz

If you speak in shorthand, all the language you'll offer your child is the word "get." But if you take the time and make the effort to cover all the details, you'll provide words that convey the ideas "help," "get," "box," "high," "shelf," "reach," and "taller." If you speak this way throughout your day-to-day life together, you will introduce or familiarize your child with words that convey ideas about shape, size, color, number, and action.

Why? Why? WHY?!

You may not even need to make an effort to get a conversation started. All you have to do is respond to your three-year-old's endless stream of questions. At the beginning of the year, your child's questions will focus on words themselves. "What's that, Mommy?" Your child will want to know—or be reminded again—of the names of the objects in her world. If possible, she'd like to know the words for everything.

Toward the end of the year, your child's questions will move beyond expanding her vocabulary and begin to focus on expanding her understanding. Your preschooler will ask interminable "why?" questions:

➤ "Why is the sun in the sky?"

➤ "Why is the sky blue?"

➤ "Why is water wet?"

➤ "Why doesn't a dog talk?"

➤ "Why does Daddy have a penis?"

➤ "Why does Grandma live in Florida?"

Don't try to pretend you have all the answers. It's as important to show your child how to find out things as to give her the answers. So if you know the answer, respond as simply and clearly as possible. But if you don't know, admit it freely. Say something like, "I don't know. Let's find out." Then consult a book, an encyclopedia, your partner, your local children's librarian, or anyone else you know who might be able to answer. If you don't have the books you need, make a note to find an appropriate book the next time you go to the library. Doing research to find out what your preschooler wants to know will be fun for both of you and good training for when your child goes to school.

Tip of the Tongue and Other Troubles

You may be concerned if your preschooler starts to stutter and stammer a lot. Don't worry about it. Stuttering and stammering are common at this age due to the lag between a three-year-old's ability to think and his ability to form words. Especially when he's excited or upset, your child's ideas will probably out race his vocabulary.

In some ways, despite your child's improving vocabulary and language skills, language actually becomes more difficult at three. For one thing, your child now knows that there's a right word for everything, and he wants to use the right word all the time. For another, he can now talk about things that he's not observing directly; about ideas. This move toward greater and greater abstraction is also a challenge.

You can help your stammering child by listening carefully and patiently and trying your best to understand what he is trying to say. Try not to become impatient and finish sentences for him. You can also help your child feel more relaxed in conversation by showing him that you enjoy talking—and listening—to him. When your child is talking—and especially when he's struggling to get a word out—pay attention and try not to wander away (literally or figuratively). Give your child time. He will almost definitely grow out of his stammering and stuttering.

Another problem many three-year-olds have is mispronunciation. Again, don't worry about it. Don't make a point of correcting it, because this may make your child more self-conscious about speaking and worsen the tendency to stutter and stammer. Instead, merely pronounce the word the right way when you speak it and give your child the opportunity to correct himself. Like good wine, your child's pronunciation will improve with age.

Your preschooler may at some point revert to baby talk (or continue using it long after outgrowing the need to use it). If you have always indulged your child's baby talk, he may think that adults find it cute.

But if you want your preschooler to stop using baby language now, try to avoid doing an immediate about face. Don't suddenly refuse to acknowledge your child when he speaks in baby talk. Instead, if you answer your child's baby talk with baby talk of your own, first resolve to stop speaking any more baby talk yourself. Then, in responding to your preschooler, translate everything he says in baby talk into grown-up talk. Within a few months or so, he'll no doubt stop using baby talk entirely on his own.

Words of Wisdom

During this fourth year, your child's dramatic increase in language skills will move her along from toddler to preschooler. As a toddler, she was all action and little talk. As a preschooler, she no longer needs to express herself exclusively through her actions. Now she has talk—lots and lots and lots of talk.

As your child becomes more proficient and more comfortable with the use of language, she may begin to enjoy playing with language. She may try to invent new words—not so much because she doesn't know the "real" words (which prompts toddlers to make up words), but just because she likes the silly way they sound. Your preschooler may also like making funny mispronunciations of familiar words and will develop a real taste for nonsense rhymes.

The Unseen World of the Mind

As a toddler, what your child learned and thought was often right out there in the open. In the preschool years, nearly all of this takes place, literally, all in his head. Your child will think, create, imagine, play make-believe—and you won't know the half of it.

But you can still see your child's mental development through the ideas that he actualizes. An exciting development in the fourth year is your preschooler's blossoming ability to make what he imagines actually come true. In his mind's eye, perhaps he sees the color blue; then he puts a brush in the blue paint and applies it to paper. Voilá! Blue. Or he may come up with an elaborate game of make-believe. Then, on his own, he gathers all the props he needs to act it out. Indeed, your child may know what he wants so precisely that he will accept no substitutes and may get frustrated if he can't find the exact scarf or stick he's looking for.

What your preschooler imagines may become as real to him as anything he can perceive through his senses. For example, he may begin to create imaginary friends. If he does, he may insist that you recognize this "friend," too. He may ask you to set a place at the table for his friend, or to make sure his friend can see the book you're reading, too. Try to indulge (within reason) your child's insistence that the imagined is real. Having imaginary friends rarely indicates any underlying psychological disturbance. In fact, it's a great way for your child to exercise his creativity and imagination.

Despite spinning out elaborate worlds of imagination, your preschooler will become better able to distinguish between fantasy and reality. Increasing language skills play an important part in helping make this distinction clearer. Your three-year-old can now recognize the truth at least some of the time (although he may not always honor it).

Listen to Reason

Improving language skills also allow your preschooler to become more communicative and reasonable. You and your child can be mutually understood. For instance, she may begin to recognize the reasonableness of some of your demands and limits—though that doesn't mean she always abides by them.

Your child's increased understanding enables her to listen and respond to your words. Finally, explanation now works almost as well as demonstration. You no longer have to race after your preschooler and catch her before she walks into traffic. You can simply say, "Don't step into the street." You don't always have to remove her physically to stop her from doing herself or others harm. You can just say, "No!" Even when angry or frustrated, your preschooler may go to the time-out chair (okay, not always, but sometimes) without you picking her up bodily and depositing her there.

Your child's increasing rationality—and deep commitment to the principle of fairness—makes three (and four, too) the age of bargaining. Bargaining, of course, works both ways. Either you or your child can launch the negotiations by saying, "I'll do this if you'll do that." If you're willing to make a deal, your preschooler probably will be, too. This can make it much easier for either of you to negotiate your way out of potential battles.

Your preschooler's increasing rationality also may enable her to begin to see the unreality of some of her fears. You can now appeal to her reason to help deal with certain fears:

➤ Don't worry. That dog is on a leash.

➤ There are no monsters here. Monsters are only make-believe.

➤ I'll be just down the hall, so if you need me you can just call me.

The fear of separation, in particular, also can be eased by your child's newfound ability to think and talk in abstract terms. Your preschooler doesn't always need to be able to see, hear, and touch you to feel secure. She will probably become less dependent on you for constant physical comfort. Although at times your three-year-old will still need your hugs and caresses to feel calm and safe, in some cases reassuring words may provide all the comfort she needs.

Back to the Future

At three, your child begins to develop an understanding of past and future. He now remembers yesterday and can look forward to tomorrow. (This understanding lacks a certain amount of precision. For another year or so, for instance, your child may still refer to anything in the past as "yesterday" and anything in the future as "tomorrow.")

The development of your child's memory will foster a new ability to anticipate situations. Your three-year-old can now apply his experience and past learning to current situations. (Of course, he won't always do so, but he now has the ability.) In addition, your child's new capacity for anticipation will make him better able to wait for something he wants—though perhaps not for long—and therefore better able to take turns. He can understand, for example, that "not now" doesn't mean "no."

Your child's increasing grasp of the past and the future also will make him better able to understand and accept your promises (though not necessarily better able to keep his own). If you have established his trust by keeping the promises you've made in the past, he knows that such phrases as "after I've finished cleaning up the kitchen" or "I'll pick you up right after lunch" imply a definite end. He won't have to wait forever. Oh, he still may not like waiting or have much patience for it, but your child has now become capable of deferring certain pleasures—within reason, of course.

Body and Soul

Despite her dramatically improving verbal skills, your three-year-old will often still express her emotions physically—and histrionically. When angry, she'll hit, push, stomp, or yell. When sad or disappointed, she'll throw herself down on the floor and overact a protracted death scene. When happy, she'll squeal with delight.

Don't bother trying to tell your preschooler to control her emotional expression. First of all, she probably can't do it anyway. And second, if you forbid or attempt to curtail your child's physical expression of emotions, you may deny her the emotion itself.

Remember, your three-year-old probably doesn't have all the words she needs to express everything she feels. If you tell your excited preschooler to sit quietly or restrain herself, you can unwittingly transform her excitement into frustration and even sadness. So try to accept and even encourage the way your child expresses emotions. Support her feelings and any nonviolent way that she expresses them, whether that means tears, kicking the floor, or bouncing off the walls with joy.

> **Q-Tip**
> Remember that your child will look to you as a model of how to express emotions. So make a point of expressing your own emotions honestly.

> **Q-Tip**
> Try to encourage your preschooler's use of words to express emotions—especially anger and frustration. It can help to reduce conflict—or at least provide an alternative to physical attacks. Whenever you notice your child using words or some other means to avoid violent behavior, applaud him and let him know how proud you are.

As the year goes by, your three-year-old's expression of emotions will remain very physical, but she will acquire additional tools (words) that will enable her to express her feelings in other ways. Certainly tantrums and other dramatic displays of emotion won't disappear. But your child will begin to use words to voice her emotions, too.

A Person's a Person No Matter How Small

Your three-year-old wants desperately to expand his horizons. He wants to know how everything (machines, people, social relations) works. He wants to know more, to see more, to understand more, and to do more. In fact, your preschooler's insatiable desire to move beyond what he already knows may make him bored with the familiar surroundings of your home. He will want to read more and go on field trips to libraries, aquariums, museums, farms, zoos, and tourist attractions. And he will want to take part in both adult activities and play dates with other children. In short, he is becoming a social creature.

Throughout this fourth year, you will see your child's personality and social behavior mature. This doesn't mean he'll undergo a drastic personality change. He won't suddenly become daring if he's always been timid and picky. He won't suddenly relax if he's always been somewhat anxious. He won't withdraw into himself if he was outgoing. But more and more he will become his own person.

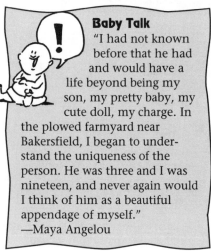

Baby Talk
"I had not known before that he had and would have a life beyond being my son, my pretty baby, my cute doll, my charge. In the plowed farmyard near Bakersfield, I began to understand the uniqueness of the person. He was three and I was nineteen, and never again would I think of him as a beautiful appendage of myself."
—Maya Angelou

What's better still, your child will begin to recognize you as a separate person, too. About midway through this year, your child will probably find separation from you somewhat easier, especially if he's used to relating to other adults and friends of his age. Don't worry, your child will still depend a great deal on you emotionally. But when you have to go away, he now understands—and trusts—that you will come back.

As part of this emergence of personality, your three-year-old may sometimes show a stubborn streak. This stubbornness will often come into play in arguments about "fairness" (as defined by him), about his "rights" (again, as he defines them), or about the "right" way to do things. Yet even at his most obstinate, your preschooler may respond to suggestions if they are worded positively: for example, "Let's try…" or "How about…?"

The Social Observer

Given the opportunity, your child will become a social creature this year. She now begins to see the value of having friends and playmates and has the motivation and attention span needed to play social games with other children. At this age, your child can sometimes empathize with others' feelings and recognize their rights. Not that she always respects the rights or feelings of others, but at least she now knows that they exist. This increase in empathy enables your child to offer genuine sympathy and concern to those she cares about. For the first time, your child is capable of genuine giving as well as taking.

As social relationships become more important to your preschooler, she will want to know as much as she can about social roles and social behavior. Guess who serves as the primary objects of her social studies? That's right. You (and your partner) now get the chance to find out what life in a fishbowl is like.

Baby Talk
"Children are made of eyes and ears, and nothing, however minute, escapes their microscopic observation."
—Fanny Kemble, 1839

Your preschooler will watch the two of you carefully: as a couple and in relation to other men, women, and children. Your three-year-old social scientist will observe, analyze, and copy the way you behave with each other and with other people. She will take note of:

➤ the ways you relate to your partner;

➤ the ways you relate to other adults of the same sex;

➤ the ways you treat children;

➤ the ways you relate to strangers and acquaintances;

➤ the ways you balance job and family responsibilities; and

➤ the ways you handle conflicts with others.

Your preschooler will not watch any of this with a critical eye, however. (That comes later.) Your preschooler will not pass judgment on the way you treat each other; she will observe and accept what she sees and hears. And invariably she will conclude that the way you behave toward each other is the "normal" way that adults treat each other.

Gender issues take on a particular importance at this age. Your child now recognizes himself as a boy or herself as a girl. And the differences between your preschooler and children of the other gender no doubt fascinate him or her. Your three-year-old may become intrigued by the different ways boys and girls urinate or by the differences in their genitalia. Again, you'll be Exhibit #1 under the microscope. Your preschooler will examine your behavior to find out how "women" and "men" act. This observation, analysis, and imitation is all part of the process of gender identification.

At three and four, your child strongly identifies with others. You can see this in her play, which probably involves lots of make-believe: pretending to be someone else. Your preschooler will pretend to be friends; characters seen in books, movies or TV shows; animals; people she meets; and especially, you and/or your partner. Despite your best efforts to avoid or overcome sexism, you will probably observe many sexual stereotypes in this kind of play. But don't blame your child. She plays only the cards she's dealt. And for the most part, what she sees—in the neighborhood, in the world at large, in books, in movies, on TV, and perhaps even in her own home—probably conforms to such sexual stereotypes.

Mother's Little Helper

Your child's desire to please you will probably make him increasingly "helpful" to have around. He will probably eagerly welcome your invitation to do simple tasks like:

➤ shopping (finding specific items, getting them for you, choosing what kind of fruit or juice or cookies to buy);

➤ cooking (shucking corn, tearing lettuce, peeling carrots, pouring ingredients into batters or sauces, whisking pancake batter or scrambled eggs);

➤ setting or clearing the dinner table;

➤ gardening (weeding or planting);

➤ washing the car;

➤ helping to make beds;

➤ helping with the laundry (sorting socks or helping to fold sheets);

➤ sweeping the floor (with a dustpan and brush while you use the broom); or even

➤ picking up after a mess, especially one that he created.

For you, of course, all these things are chores. But for your child, these chores can not only be fun, but help him feel useful as a contributing member of the family. Your preschooler will especially enjoy helping in ways that allow him to test and stretch his physical limits:

➤ climbing up on a stool or small stepladder to get out the cereal, bowl, and spoon;

➤ putting his muscles to work "helping" you carry groceries inside;

➤ raking leaves or shoveling snow.

Yes, you could probably do all of these things faster and more efficiently by yourself. But that's hardly the point. In assigning (or at least offering) your preschooler certain responsibilities and allowing him to help, you will help him to feel important and needed. A reward for your child's cooperation is nice, but probably not necessary: His heightened sense of importance and usefulness are probably reward enough.

Hugs and Kisses

With improved coordination, balance and strength, rapid intellectual development, growing language skills, and greater emotional stability, your preschooler will become more independent throughout the year. She can do many things for herself: dressing, eating, using the toilet, washing, or bathing. Your preschooler's thriving imagination and creativity may even enable her to entertain and amuse herself for extended periods of time.

However, take care not to push too much independence on your child too soon. Your preschooler still needs you to provide fundamental emotional and physical security. She depends on your watchful eye to judge what she can handle on her own. The conflict between your child's need for independence and her need for safety puts you in a difficult spot: straddling the fence between neglect and overprotectiveness.

No matter how independent your three-year-old seems, she still wants and needs you to provide signs of physical affection (though perhaps not as often as before). Yet many preschoolers—and especially boys—suffer from a lack of hugs and kisses as their parents try to condition them to be "grown up" or "masculine."

> **Q-Tip**
> Even if your child begins to resist your hugs and kisses, you can still offer her plenty of physical signs of affection. Let your child use you as a jungle gym or bounce on your legs and knees. Play chasing games that end with you scooping her up in your arms. Or curl up together with a good book.

If you believe that a person can still be physically affectionate despite being grown up or masculine, then why would you stop giving your preschooler hugs and kisses? Even if you believe that being grown up and/or masculine means reining in your emotions and avoiding any physical demonstrativeness, try not to be in such a hurry. Your child has plenty of time to grow up. But right now, your child needs signs of your love and affection.

Continue to offer your child the warmth of your touch. Offer hugs and kisses to congratulate your preschooler for completing a difficult task, to console her when she cries, to comfort her when something (a scrape, a bump, a shot) hurts, or to show your love when she's going to bed, when you're parting, or when you're reunited.

Of course, if your child doesn't want a kiss, then don't force it on her. Even at the tender age of three, some children become self-conscious about signs of affection in public. If your child balks at public hugs and kisses, spare her any embarrassment by choosing more private situations (bedtime, for example) in which to kiss her.

If your preschooler seems wary of signs of affection whether offered in public or in private, then let her know how much it means to you to hug or kiss her. But if your arguments don't convince her, then honor her wishes.

The Least You Need to Know

> ➤ Don't overprotect your child. Setting physical challenges enables him to test and stretch his limits and build confidence.

> ➤ Your child desperately wants to share his thoughts, feelings, observations, and experiences. So despite the stuttering and stammering, listen carefully to him.

> ➤ Have patience with your three-year-old's emotional explosiveness. He's still learning to use words to express emotions.

> ➤ Your preschooler will model his use of language, his expression of emotions, the way he relates to others, and his notions of gender primarily on what he sees at home. So think before you speak or act.

> ➤ No matter how independent your three-year-old seems, he's still only three. He needs your support, guidance, and most of all, your love and affection.

Chapter 16

An Apple a Day: Preventive Medicine for Preschoolers

In This Chapter

➤ How to nurture hygienic habits in your child

➤ Hair care that won't work you (or your child) into a lather

➤ How to handle toilet-training derailments

➤ Proper dental care now that your child has a full set of teeth

At three, your child may come into contact with more germs than in the previous three years combined. If your child starts day care or preschool, for instance, she will suddenly come into close contact with up to a dozen or more disease-carrying agents (known as other children).

Even if your child is a day-care veteran, she may become ill more often in her fourth year. Your child will become more socially oriented as the year goes on. And as she shifts her behavior with other children from parallel play to more interactive play, your three-year-old and her playmates will not only start to share toys, crayons, and activities, but bacteria and viruses as well.

Your child's increased exposure to germs makes the development of good hygiene habits important over the next two years. If you want to curb the spread of bacteria, viruses, and other disease-causing agents, you will need to nurture good hygiene habits. This will benefit your child well beyond the preschool years: If she forms good habits of hygiene at age three and four, your child will probably maintain them throughout childhood.

At this age, your child wants and needs to do more to take care of herself. So it's the perfect time to begin encouraging her to tend to her own washing, brushing, and toilet habits.

The Age of Reasons

With his improved language skills, your three-year-old can now understand why he needs to:

➤ bathe and shampoo regularly;

➤ brush his teeth at least twice a day;

➤ use a tissue to blow his nose;

➤ cover his mouth when he coughs or sneezes;

➤ change his clothes every once in a while; and even

➤ comb or brush his hair.

In fact, not only is your child capable of understanding the reasons behind these practices, it will become increasingly important to him to know the underlying rationale behind certain actions. (Just think how many times your child asks, "Why?" about every little thing.)

So take the time to explain hygiene to your preschooler. You will probably get more cooperation in bathing, brushing, and cutting down on the spread of germs if you explain your reasoning than if you just say, "Because I said so!"

> **Q-Tip**
> In explaining why your child needs to stay clean, try not to exaggerate the power that germs have to make him sick. Some preschoolers (and five- and six-year-olds as well) get obsessive about hand washing because they become so afraid of the germs that might make them sick. Remember, what you're trying to nurture here is good hygiene, not obsessive cleanliness.

Let your child know, for example, that germs can make him sick, but that hand-washing or bathing will help kill the germs. Let him know that food left in the teeth and gums will eat away at the enamel coating and allow germs to take up residence in his teeth. (If this rational explanation doesn't work, try telling him that the tooth fairy prefers clean, white teeth with no cavities.)

After your child understands the rationale behind hygienic practices, make sure you stick to routines. Your three-year-old will wonder just how important it really is if you consistently forget to help him wash his hands before dinner or after using the toilet or if you neglect to brush his teeth after a meal or before bed.

At the same time, recognize that kids do get dirty. Yes, it's important that your child wash hands before eating and after using the toilet. But don't drive yourself crazy trying to keep your preschooler clean. With many kids this age, it just can't be done. And even if it can, you will inhibit your preschooler's inclination to explore and develop his physical potential if you're constantly urging him to stay clean.

Rub-a-Dub-Dub, Your Kid in a Tub

If you've consistently made bathtime a fun time, your preschooler will probably still look forward to bathtime. But at three, your child may begin to resist taking baths. Even if she usually enjoys herself in the bathtub, she may sometimes balk because the bath may not seem as fun as whatever she's doing right before bathtime. If you've fallen into an "efficient" bathtime routine, with little time for play or bath toys, try to open it up to a little more fun. Face it: If you make bathing (or anything else) fun, your child will want to do it. So add bath toys, washing games, and, once in a while, lots of bubbles.

Remember, your preschooler does not need to bathe every day. So try not to make bathing a chore; instead, turn it into a treat.

Try to make your child's bathtime at least an hour before bedtime. That way you won't need to rush and your child won't be too tired, and perhaps too edgy, to enjoy the bath. Don't hurry your child through the bath. Your three-year-old will enjoy baths much more if you relax and encourage her to have fun. Of course, if your child starts to turn into a prune or the water gets ice cold, then you'll have to put a stop to it. To make the transition easier when your preschooler doesn't want to get out of the tub, just pull the plug. She'll probably get out soon after the water's gone.

> **Childproofing**
> Although a bubble bath can add some fun to your bathtime routine, try to make bubble baths a special treat rather than an everyday event. Many bubble baths are hard on the skin, especially if used night after night. Also avoid bubble baths if your doctor advises against them due to urinary tract infections.

> **Childproofing**
> The bathtub—slippery when wet—can be a dangerous place for a child even after the water has drained. So never leave your child (even a three- or four-year-old) unsupervised while in the tub.

Hands Up!

At age three, it's important to begin establishing good hand washing habits. Your child needs to make it second nature to wash his hands whenever he goes to the bathroom or gets ready for a meal. If your child remembers to wash his hands when he blows his nose, too, he can cut down on the spread of his germs to others.

If your child can't reach the sink on his own, make sure that you provide a stool so that he can turn the water on and off by himself. At three, your child may enjoy pumping liquid antibacterial soap into his hands. To ensure a thorough cleaning, you might find it easiest to give your child some soap and a bath toy that "needs" washing. Your three-year-old will probably welcome the chance to "help out." And by the time the toy is clean, his hands will be, too.

Hair Dos—and Don'ts

At three, your child probably needs to shampoo just once or twice a week. This may come as a great relief because your preschooler—like many others—may hate washing her hair.

If your child hates shampooing, try adopting one of the following strategies:

➤ When you absolutely have to shampoo her hair, get it over with as fast as possible. Do it almost immediately after your child gets in the tub. In fact, you might even want to try shampooing before you have filled the tub more than a couple of inches. This way, your child can lay down in the tub and can avoid getting water on her face (which is what most preschoolers find so upsetting). Unless shampooing makes your child so unhappy that she wants to get out of the tub right after you're done, shampooing first will give you a chance to end the bath on a happier note.

➤ Turn shampooing into a game. Let your child work up a lather herself. Then encourage her to "style" her hair with the shampoo. Give her a mirror so that she can see how silly she looks with her hair sticking up with lather.

➤ Use bath toys (bottles, watering cans, and so on) for rinsing. This won't stop your child from getting lots of water on her face, but may make it more fun.

➤ Ask your child to hold a washcloth or folded hand towel over her face while you wash and rinse. This minimizes the amount of water that pours over her face. A special bathtub visor, available in many baby-product catalogs, also may deflect water from your child's face—if you can get her to wear it.

➤ Ask your child to check how well you have rinsed her hair by rubbing a few hairs between her fingers. The hair should be literally squeaky clean.

➤ Give up shampooing in the tub. If your kitchen sink has a sprayer attachment, wash your child's hair there. Your three-year-old can lie down on her back on the kitchen counter with her head over the sink. Support your child's head with one hand while managing the sprayer and shampoo with the other. (The sprayer will give you more control of how much water gets on your child's face.)

Despite all your best efforts to make shampooing as pleasant and fun as possible, your preschooler may still loathe hair washing. If so, keep her hair short. The shorter your child's hair, the easier it will be to shampoo without creating a big fuss.

Hair Today, Gone Tomorrow

Every so often, you're going to need your child to sit still long enough to get his hair cut. This can present quite a challenge when you're dealing with a three-year-old.

If you want to take your child to a barber or professional hair stylist, take him to your own (if he or she cuts children's hair). Your child may feel more relaxed and put up with the "ordeal" more readily if he sees you getting your hair cut first. Remember to bring crayons or puzzles or some other activity that will keep your child busy long enough to get your own hair done. Then let your child hop up into the chair and get his hair cut. (Some savvy professionals who cut children's hair have now equipped their shops with TV sets and children's videos in an attempt to keep their customers still.)

> **Q-Tip**
> If your child objects to the term "haircut," which sounds painful, use the term "trim" instead.

If you're cutting your child's hair yourself, you'll have to do it fast unless you want to end up with the job half done. You can probably keep him still for half an hour or so by:

> **Childproofing**
> Make sure your preschooler knows that hair cutting is not one of the responsibilities you want him to take on himself. Despite your words of warning, your child will most likely give himself at least one haircut before kindergarten.

➤ letting him watch in the mirror;

➤ trimming his hair outside when weather permits;

➤ cutting hair in the bathtub; or

➤ cutting in front of the TV while letting him watch a favorite video.

Toilet Troubles

If you haven't yet started—or are just starting—to teach your preschooler to use the toilet or potty, that's okay. Some children don't begin showing any interest in toilet training until age three. If your child seems ready to start now, see Chapter 9, "Disposing of Diapers: Toilet Training" for pointers.

Even if your child has been trained for a year, however, accidents will still happen at age three (and four and five and six…). Accidents are especially likely:

➤ if she's away from home and reluctant to use a "strange" toilet;

➤ if your child attends a birthday party or other public affair, where she gets highly excited or nervous; or

Childproofing

Regression in toilet training may signal that your child is feeling anxiety. Talk to your child to find out if something is worrying her. Common causes of anxiety include: the arrival of a new baby; the need for more attention; the death of someone close; moving to a new home; and starting a new day care or preschool. If frequent accidents persist long after your child seemed to have mastered toilet training, she may have a urinary tract infection. In this case, consult your pediatrician so that it can be evaluated.

➤ if your child gets so caught up in playing, reading, watching television, or some other activity that she ignores her body's signals.

To reduce the number of accidents:

➤ Suggest that your child use the bathroom at home *before* you go anywhere that might be unfamiliar to your child.

➤ Offer to go with your child when she needs to use an unfamiliar bathroom. You should have no qualms about taking your preschooler into a public restroom designated for the opposite sex. At this age, your child probably doesn't care.

➤ Ask your child if she needs to go the bathroom if she hasn't in two or three hours. Don't nag or force her to go, just offer a helpful reminder.

Your child may feel embarrassed and will definitely feel uncomfortable after an accident. So try not to make it worse by heaping on your own load of shame (or even overconcern). Sympathize with your preschooler and treat it as matter-of-factly as you can.

Practical Matters

Some time during this year, you will find it convenient to encourage your child to switch from a potty (if that's what he uses) to a toilet. A stepstool and a child-size toilet seat that fits over the standard toilet seat will help. (If the stepstool is light enough, your child can move it over to the sink afterward and wash up all by himself.) Getting your child accustomed to using a toilet will free you of the need to lug a potty seat around with you wherever you go.

Try not to become overconcerned with the frequency of your three-year-old's bowel movements. (In fact, pay as little attention as you possibly can.) Of course, if you do have concerns regarding the frequency of your child's bowel movements, consult your pediatrician. But the normal range for preschoolers runs anywhere from two or three times a day to once every two or three days.

After using the toilet, your child may need some encouragement to wipe his own bottom (if his arms are even long enough to do so at age three). Remember to teach your daughter to wipe from front to back to avoid urinary infections. (Your son also will get cleaner if he wipes from front to back.) Even if your child is willing to wipe himself, you will probably also need to wipe his bottom after a bowel movement. Continue to do a once-over after your child has "finished" wiping until you are confident that he consistently does a thorough job.

When first learning to use the toilet, some boys urinate while sitting down (so make sure he points his penis down). But at some point during the fourth or fifth year, as gender identification becomes increasingly important, your son is likely to want to start urinating like his daddy: standing up. Your son will find this method quicker and easier. But especially at this age, try to avoid zippers. Zippers can be difficult to get down (causing accidents) and difficult to get up (causing painful accidents).

Indeed, whether your three-year-old is a boy or a girl, you should continue to dress your preschooler in a way that makes it easiest to go to the bathroom on his or her own. Help to cultivate your child's independence in going to the bathroom. Pants with neither zippers nor buttons will be easiest for your child.

> **Q-Tip**
> Despite your child's best efforts, accidents will continue to happen throughout the preschool years. So always carry an extra pair of underwear and pants for your child whenever you're away from home. (A small box of diaper wipes also may come in handy on such occasions.) And keep extra clothes and under-wear for your child at day care or preschool, too.

You're On Your Own (Well, Almost)

The more you teach your child to take care of her own day-to-day needs, the less you'll have to do for her. But it's not just a matter of selfishly easing your own load. Your child's ability to take care of bathing, brushing, going to the bathroom, and dressing on her own will give her a greater sense of independence and confidence. And learning these every-day skills also will prepare your preschooler for the upcoming school years, when you won't be with her every moment of the day to make sure she wipes her bottom and washes her hands.

So do everything you can to encourage your child's independence in hygienic practices. Provide a footstool so that your child can reach the toilet and sink. Put soap and towels where your child can reach them safely. (Your preschooler will find it especially easy to use a pump-bottle filled with liquid soap.) If you haven't already done so, adjust the water temperature in your home so that your child doesn't risk scalding herself. To help her dress herself, make sure her dresser drawers are neither too heavy nor jammed so full that she can't open them. And install clothes hooks low enough so that she can reach them.

To increase her sense of independence, offer your child choices. But at the same time, limit the available alternatives so that she chooses something that you want her to do.

You might, for instance, tell your child that she can brush her teeth before or after a story. Give her a choice between taking a bath tonight or tomorrow morning. Suggest that she go to the bathroom now, but offer the option of going later. Let her pick out the comb or hairbrush she wants to use.

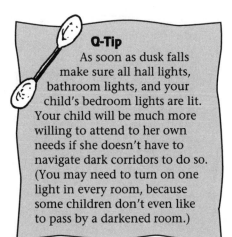

Q-Tip

As soon as dusk falls make sure all hall lights, bathroom lights, and your child's bedroom lights are lit. Your child will be much more willing to attend to her own needs if she doesn't have to navigate dark corridors to do so. (You may need to turn on one light in every room, because some children don't even like to pass by a darkened room.)

Throughout the year, try to give your child more and more responsibility for her own daily care. First demonstrate what you want your child to do. (Be patient. You may need to show your child many times.) Show her how to wash herself and brush her teeth and brush her hair and wipe her bottom.

Then step back and let her do it herself. Make sure to supervise your preschooler, at least until you're confident that she knows roughly what to do. You always can follow up with a "tooth check" or "clean check" after she's finished. But if you do, make it a habit, rather than a critical exercise. Try not to diminish your child's sense of competence by harping on what she did wrong. Instead, when doing a follow-up check, praise your three-year-old for everything she did right.

Common Contagions

Preschoolers who attend day care pass germs around as if they were crayons. Certain conditions are therefore more common among children in day care. Although most of the following conditions might be avoided through good hygienic practices, don't be surprised if your child brings one of these home from day care along with his valentines and other school projects:

➤ **Head Lice (Nits)**   These hard-to-see parasites attach pale gray or white oval eggs (called nits) to the hair, especially at the base of the scalp. They may make your preschooler's head itchy, especially during hot weather. Contracting head lice is not a sign of poor hygiene: Any self-respecting louse actually prefers clean hair to dirty hair.

To reduce the risk of contracting head lice, discourage your child from sharing hats, combs, hair bands, barrettes, and hair ribbons with other children.

If your preschooler comes home with head lice, call your pediatrician. He or she will probably recommend a shampoo that should quickly take care of the problem. (You should probably treat every member of the household.) After shampooing, comb the hair out with a fine-toothed comb to remove the dead eggs. (Rinsing the hair with diluted vinegar may make it easier to get the nits out.) You also should use the shampoo to wash all combs, hairbrushes, hats, and other headwear. Because the treatment is so effective, your child may return to day care immediately after beginning the prescription.

➤ **Ringworm**   A highly contagious and itchy fungal infection, ringworm produces scaly, red or gray patches on the skin or small bald areas on the scalp. The center of the round or oval patch may clear, but the outside ring will remain scaly (hence the name).

If your child contracts ringworm, call your pediatrician. If the ringworm is in your child's scalp, your doctor will prescribe an oral medication. Otherwise, he or she will probably prescribe an antifungal cream. Because ringworm is highly contagious and spread through direct contact, have your child wash his hands with an antibacterial soap whenever he touches the area (even to put on his medication). If you apply the medication for him, wash your hands immediately afterward, too.

➤ **Pinworms**   These worms lay eggs around the anus. The eggs can cause irritation (an itching or tickling sensation) around the anus, especially at night. You might notice the little white worms in your preschooler's bowel movements. Pinworms pass from child to child. The worm eggs may be ingested by a child who eats with his hands after washing his hands poorly (or not at all). The eggs then hatch, producing larvae inside the intestines.

If your child has pinworms, your whole family may need to take medication prescribed by your pediatrician. Wash often and thoroughly with an antibacterial soap. Have your child wear underwear when in bed to discourage scratching, and keep your child's fingernails short.

The Tooth, the Whole Tooth, and Nothing but the Tooth

By age three, your child should have a full set of 20 "baby teeth." Now that your child's mouth is full of teeth, food particles easily get stuck between them. Your child (with your supervision and help) should brush with a soft-bristled toothbrush at least twice a day: after breakfast and before bedtime. An up-and-down motion will dislodge most food particles.

> **Q-Tip**
> Try to get your preschooler to drink some water after snacks and lunch. This helps rinse her mouth between brushings.

Choose a fluoride toothpaste that your child enjoys. Fluoride strengthens tooth enamel, which will reduce decay. If your pediatrician prescribes it, have your child take fluoride supplements once a day. (But don't automatically give your child supplements, because too much fluoride can later lead to the development of mottled adult teeth.) See Chapter 2 for toothbrushing tips for toddlers, many of which can be applied to preschoolers as well.

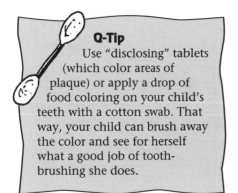

Q-Tip
Use "disclosing" tablets (which color areas of plaque) or apply a drop of food coloring on your child's teeth with a cotton swab. That way, your child can brush away the color and see for herself what a good job of tooth-brushing she does.

At three, your child will prefer to brush her own teeth most of the time. Still, stick around to supervise and do a quick follow-up brushing if necessary. (Most children cannot manage a thorough toothbrushing until the first or second grade.)

Don't discount the importance of dental care for your preschooler's "baby teeth." If a tooth decays so much that it requires removal, this could adversely affect the positioning of your child's permanent teeth.

An Apple A Day? No, Make It Cheese!

The best way to avoid cavities involves a combination of daily brushing and watching what your child eats. Sugar, in particular, produces an acid that removes calcium from the teeth, thereby damaging the enamel coating. This damage causes bacterial tooth decay and the formation of cavities.

Childproofing
Alkaline and acid neutralize each other. Eating some cheese at the end of a meal will produce alkaline saliva, which can counteract (at least in part) the corrosive effect of acids produced by sugar.

So try to limit your preschooler's intake of sugar. If you never bring sugary foods and candy into your home except on special occasions, then you won't need to face the awkward situation of denying your child food that he knows you have. But if you do keep sweets in your house, try to offer only candy that your child can eat quickly and all at once. (When your child eats a lollipop or a hard candy that sits in his mouth for a long while, it's like bathing his teeth in sugar.) You might consider some sort of trade-off: Your child can have occasional candy treats, but must always brush his teeth soon afterward. Or give sweets only as part of a meal and require your preschooler to brush his teeth after eating.

Besides candy and presweetened foods, fruit juice also causes a lot of tooth decay. So after your preschooler's teeth have been brushed for the night, offer him only water to drink. Otherwise, your three-year-old's teeth will remain coated with sugar all night.

Open Wide

Your preschooler should visit the dentist twice a year. If you do not have a dentist of your own with whom you feel comfortable, you may want to look for a pedodontist, a dentist who specializes in children's teeth. Although your own dentist might be just fine for your child, a pedodontist may have a bigger bag of tricks to ease your young child's anxieties and to relieve or eliminate pain.

Though cavities are relatively rare among preschoolers, regular dental visits will allow your dentist to make sure your child's teeth are coming in correctly. They will also allow your child to get accustomed to the idea of going to the dentist. (Take care to avoid transferring any negative feelings you may have about visiting the dentist to your child.) At every visit, stay with your child to talk to her and to hold her hand if she needs it.

Besides regular visits every six months, schedule extra visits if your child complains of tooth pain or if you notice any unusual discoloration. (Discoloration may be caused by decay that has deadened the tooth.) A chipped tooth, which can leave dangerously sharp edges, also should be seen by a dentist.

Of course, cavities are no fun. If your preschooler has a deep cavity, it will hurt when drilled. Yet even with a surface cavity, your child will have to endure the water pressure and the frightening and annoying whirr of the dentist's drill.

Q-Tip
Show your child just how benign a visit to the dentist can be. Let her accompany you on one or two routine visits before her own first appointment. Just make sure she doesn't come along if you're having root canal work!

If your preschooler needs a cavity filled, it may help if you give her at least a small degree of information and control. Ask your dentist to use a mirror to show your child her cavity both before and after the filling. Then let your preschooler signal the dentist whenever she needs to take a break, and make sure you have a dentist who will honor such requests. If your child has no control over the process and feels overwhelmed and tortured, good luck getting her back in the chair for her next visit, cavities or no cavities.

The Least You Need to Know

➤ Be consistent about maintaining and enforcing good hygiene habits. If you don't make them routine activities, they won't become habits.

➤ Make it as easy as possible for your child to take care of his own hygienic needs. A footstool will make the toilet and sink accessible. Keep soap, towels, toothbrushes, toothpaste, brushes, and combs all safely within your child's reach.

➤ Even three-year-olds have accidents. Try to accept them with good grace and a pleasant face.

➤ Dental care does matter, even with baby teeth. So brush your child's teeth at least twice a day and visit the dentist twice a year.

Chapter 17

Playmates and Playdates

Now it's time for your child to start making friends. At one or two, your child may have had playdates, may have had contact with other children in day-care settings, and may even have formed some attachments with other children. But really, little social interaction goes on between children before age three. Both playdates and day care for toddlers centered around parallel play (playing next to each other, but not necessarily *with* each other—or perhaps not even engaged in the same activity) rather than anything truly interactive.

At three and four, however, your preschooler should begin to play with others—not just next to them. Your child has become increasingly aware of other children as people with rights and feelings of their own. In addition, your three-year-old's improved language skills allow him to communicate with other children his age (and vice versa). For the first time, your child—if given the opportunity—will direct as much or even more of his conversation to other children as to you or to other adults. Your three-year-old can talk to other children, share knowledge, issue invitations, bark out orders, and ask questions.

Yes, your three-year-old will often still engage in little more than parallel play. But he is now capable of sustained, interactive play, too. Your preschooler has become a much more social creature.

Can't We Get Along?

If you have given your toddler ample opportunity to play alongside other children, as a preschooler she may shift over to playing with them relatively easily. But even if your child has had little experience playing next to other children, she will almost definitely become interested in playing with others and forming friendships at this age.

Even if your child has had lots of playdates in the past, but especially if she hasn't, she may have some trouble getting along with others. Indeed, until your child appreciates the benefits of playing with others, she will probably put little effort into adopting prosocial behavior. Yet even after she learns to value playing with other children, your child will probably still need to learn how to:

➤ take turns;

➤ share; and

➤ cope with conflict without biting, hitting, kicking, or other violence.

Baby Talk
"The law of grab is the primary law of infancy."
—Antoinette Brown Blackwell

In encouraging your preschooler to share and take turns, try to give her some control (within reasonable limits, of course) over when she hands over the mutually desired toy. You might find it effective to say something like, "You can play with that for a few more minutes, but please let Ryan know as soon as you're done so that he can have a turn, too." You may be surprised to see your child willingly give the toy up after just a minute or two.

Of course, if you give your three-year-old a fair chance to share and she still seems to be hogging the desired toy, then you may need to step in. Suggest that it's time for your preschooler's playmate to have a turn and, if possible, have something else ready for your child to do to induce (that is, bribe) her cooperation. (See Chapter 10 for additional tips on promoting prosocial behavior.)

Three is a great age for learning such social behavior. Your preschooler's new interest in other children—in what they can do, in how they do things, and in what ideas they have—will make it more and more important for her to figure out how to get along with others and to win their approval.

Three-year-olds have a keen sense of justice, fairness, and "right" behavior. If your child does not behave according to social mores—if she grabs toys or treats from other children, for example, or if she knocks down or breaks their projects— other children may (justifiably) be very hard on her. This may be equally hard for you to witness. But instead of rushing to knee-jerk defenses of your child, try to figure out what aspect of your darling's behavior the other children are objecting to. If you agree that it's unacceptable behavior, then work at teaching your preschooler other ways to cope or behave.

While teaching your child socially acceptable behavior, and especially while correcting unacceptable behavior, make sure that she knows that you love her. Try to get your preschooler to see that you want to make it easier for her to get along with others and that selfish or violent behavior will make it harder.

Q-Tip
You can cut down on violence toward other children by appealing to your child's growing sociability. Your three-year-old wants to get along with others, to make friends, have fun, and learn with other children. The importance of maintaining friendships with other children should increase your child's willingness to accept suggested solutions to conflict.

Everyone Has Feelings

Besides appealing to your preschooler's self-interest (the desire to play with others), you also can promote socially acceptable behavior through the development of empathy. Empathy begins with an understanding of one's own feelings. The more you help your child become aware of his own emotions and express them appropriately, the more he will begin to recognize these feelings in others as well.

You can help this fledgling development of empathy by:

➤ encouraging your child to talk about what he feels;

➤ asking questions about the feelings of characters in books, videos, and television shows;

➤ sharing your own feelings with your child (not in a confessional or confidential way, but openly and honestly); and

➤ pointing out and discussing the feelings of playmates.

Q-Tip
One of the best ways to encourage proper social behavior is to model it yourself whenever you play or interact with your child. Play games in which you take turns or share something you have with your child. If you do, she'll probably return the favor and this can provide good practice for when she's playing or interacting with other children.

When a playmate feels sad or angry, for example, remind your child of a similar situation in which he felt sad or angry. Through this kind of exposure to the emotions of others, your preschooler will begin to learn that what other people feel is not so different from what he feels. And that's what empathy is all about.

Your child needs to recognize that just as he doesn't want other children to bite him, they don't want him to bite them either. Just as he doesn't want others to grab a toy from him, they don't like it when he grabs either. Or, to put a more positive spin on it, just as he wants others to share their prized possessions with him, they would like it if he would share his with them.

It seems obvious to you, but until recently, your child has been almost entirely oblivious to the fact that other children even have feelings. By helping him to become aware of this fact, by nurturing your child's empathy for others, you will go a long way toward moving your child beyond the selfishness of toddlerhood. And once your child consistently recognizes that other people have feelings, too, then you can begin to preach the Golden Rule: Treat others the way you would like to be treated.

Opening Doors: Helping Your Child Make Friends

Preschoolers make friends quickly and intensely. To your three-year-old, a "friend" is anyone who is willing to play with her the way she wants to play at the moment. It could be someone she sees every day in the neighborhood or at day care. But it could just as well be someone she meets just once while playing in the park or playground or children's museum. (Even if she never sees that child again, your three-year-old may continue to refer to the child as "my friend.") Your preschooler's friends are just as likely to be boys as girls, because most three-year-olds play with either sex equally well and seldom have a preference for one or the other.

Because your three-year-old probably makes friends quickly, her relationships with other children are not necessarily long-term friendships. Your preschooler may move easily from friend to friend with each passing month (or week). You might hear her say that she has a "best friend," but the identity of this best friend may change monthly (or even daily). Although preserving a long-term special status for one friend comes more frequently at age five or six, your child may nonetheless develop a special relationship with one or two other children. (Holding hands and hugging are common among friends of this age.)

Friendships, no matter how fleeting, are important to preschoolers. Early childhood isolation—whether self-imposed, created by parental inattention, or caused by the rejection of other children—will not only be painful in the present, but may lead to emotional problems in the future as well. So encourage your child to form friendships.

Because most three-year-olds make friends so easily, you may not need to do that much to help other than offering her the opportunity to meet other children.

Who Are the People in Your Neighborhood?

It's important for your child to have friends who live in the same neighborhood and this importance will only grow as your child gets older. If your child has friends in the neighborhood, he can visit them on a moment's notice without needing a driver—perhaps without even needing to cross the street.

So if other preschoolers live in your neighborhood, try to begin with them. Try to find other kids who are roughly the same age as your child. Get to know the parents of other preschoolers in your neighborhood and then arrange some playdates or special outings that will bring your child and other three- or four-year-olds together. (Playdates will also give *you* the opportunity to spend time and share experiences with other adults.)

Q-Tip
At this age, you'd do well to give your preschooler the opportunity to make friends not just with children his own age, but with adults, too—in your presence of course. Your child will feel more comfortable dealing with adults in future situations if he has the chance to become friendly now with parents of friends, friends of parents, teachers, and so on.

Why Do You Think They Call Them Preschoolers?

If you have ever needed or wanted to put your child in group day care, three is a terrific age to introduce her to a preschool situation. Two or three mornings a week in a well-run preschool will not only provide your child with educational play, but also with the much-needed opportunity to make friends with many other children her own age.

Is Your Child Ready?

Some preschoolers who have only been exposed to in-home caregivers (parents, nannies, and sitters) have difficulty making the adjustment to organized day care. First of all, it means separating from you or other day-to-day caregivers for several hours. But it also means getting used to other adults feeding her, helping her in the bathroom, and changing her if she has an accident.

So before you place your child in preschool or day care for the first time, ask yourself these questions:

➤ Can she bear to be without you for more than a minute?

➤ Is she terribly shy?

➤ Can she talk freely to other adults or does she still depend on you to translate for her?

➤ Does she show interest in other children and what they are doing (in the park, in the library, and so on)?

The answers to these questions will help you judge if your child is ready for this radically new experience.

If preschool is a brand-new experience for your child—the first extended care that she's ever had outside of the home—you will probably need to ease her into it.

Q-Tip

Don't start your child in preschool just before or just after the arrival of a baby brother or sister. Your child will feel replaced and rejected if you push her out of the home just as the new baby arrives.

Q-Tip

A transition object (a blanket, a favorite stuffed animal, a photograph of you, and so on) can ease your preschooler's adjustment and help her feel more secure. She probably doesn't even need to hold it all the time. Try stowing it away in her cubby where it can be retrieved whenever necessary.

➤ Arrange to stay with your child for the first few sessions. This doesn't necessarily mean you have to stay all that time, but have the time available in case your child needs you to stay.

➤ Each day, let your child know in advance how long you intend to stay and then stick to it.

➤ During the sessions that you attend with your child, avoid being an overly active participant. Feel free to get out a toy or two to help your child get settled, but for the most part pretend you're not there. (Remember, eventually, you won't be.)

➤ Don't let your child avoid other children (and other adults) by taking refuge in your company. If your child keeps coming to you for help, steer her toward the teacher. Play dumb. Say things like, "I'm not sure where the bathroom is. Why don't you ask Therese?"

➤ At first, avoid making a big push to have your child "make friends" with other children (a concept totally foreign to your rookie preschooler). Focus on getting her to form a bond with the day-care provider or teacher first. After your child gets used to the same adult warmly welcoming her every day and helping her get settled, then she can move on to getting to know the other children.

➤ After a few days in preschool with your child, remind her that parents stay only with the new kids in the group and that she's no longer a new kid. Then turn her over directly to the adult in charge. That way, your child will know that an adult will be taking care of her every minute.

Parting From Your Preschooler

The actual moment of parting is often the most difficult. Your three-year-old may cry or make a fuss no matter how much he enjoys himself after you leave. So try not to make too much of your child's tears or let the tears dissuade you from leaving. When it's time for you to go, offer your child a hug and a warm goodbye.

Before leaving, let your preschooler know exactly when you'll be back. Of course, your three-year-old probably has no concept of clock time. So ask the teacher what the class will be doing in the half hour or so before you'll pick your child up. Then tell your child, "I'll be back a little after you have your lunch" (or naptime or free playtime).

Talk to your child's preschool teacher. Ask her (or him) whether your child stops and joins in with the group after you've left. Or stand outside the door and after a minute or two, peek in through a window to see how your child is doing. In all likelihood, you'll find that within a few minutes of your departure, your preschooler has started doing what the other children are doing. If he isn't, then talk to the teacher about getting your child more involved in a project or a group activity as soon as he arrives.

If things don't improve or the partings get worse, then consider taking your child out of the group for a little while. After a couple of weeks at home with you, he may get bored (not because you're boring, but because he needs additional stimulation) and want to go back to the group. (For more tips on handling separation anxiety, see Chapter 6.)

Make a point of picking your child up early or on time, especially during the first few weeks. If your preschooler starts to look for you when you're expected and you haven't arrived yet, he may fly off into a panic. Show interest in what your child did that morning. If you in turn tell him about your day, make it sound as boring as possible. Don't let your child think he's missed anything by being away from you.

> **Childproofing**
> Don't try to sneak away without letting your child know you're leaving just because he seems happy. Your preschooler will never get comfortable or really take part in the group if he's constantly checking to make sure you're still there.

Preschool Cliques, Preschool Tricks

Believe it or not, cliques begin to form even during the preschool years. The age at which your child begins including other children in her play is also, unfortunately, the age at which children begin excluding others from play. "You can't play here. Christina and I are playing and you can't play." If you overhear these painful comments, try to help the cliquish children find a role for the excluded child in their play. You might say something like, "Looks like you two need a real live patient. Oh, here's one. What's wrong? Are you sick?"

Cliques may sometimes make it difficult for your three-year-old to make friends in preschool. If your child feels rejected or friendless in preschool, first ask the teacher about your child's behavior in the group. Your child may be grabbing, hitting, kicking, biting, or behaving selfishly: All good reasons for judgmental three-year-olds to avoid her.

If the problem instead seems to be caused by your child's shyness, ask your preschool teacher to help. Preschool teachers and day-care providers can adopt a number of different strategies that can help your child fit in with other kids. The teacher may choose to:

➤ Help get your three-year-old accepted by one of the cliques in the day-care group.

➤ "Pair your child up" with another preschooler who is more outgoing, friendly, and popular. This raises your three-year-old's social standing in the group. (Sad but true, social status does exist even in preschool.)

➤ Pair up your child with a younger child. This increases your child's confidence, self-esteem, and assertiveness without putting any pressure on her to fit in with other kids her age. This may in turn boost her social skills among her peers.

➤ Assign your child important and helpful duties such as passing out napkins at snack- or lunchtime. Classroom responsibilities will simultaneously increase your child's self-assurance and boost her social standing.

➤ Break the group into smaller groups. Your child will find smaller groups of children less intimidating. In addition, small groups will almost force her to take part in social activities, because it's harder to fade into the background when you're not in a crowd.

➤ Suggest moving your child from a large day-care situation into family day care or a smaller class (for the same reasons mentioned earlier).

> **Q-Tip**
> You can help your child make friends at day-care, too. Arrange several playdates outside of the day-care setting. Your child may feel more comfortable getting to know her classmates one-on-one.

Preschoolers Who Aren't in Preschool

If you don't send your child to preschool, he will depend solely on you to make sure he has a social life (or indeed any kind of life outside the home). As your child's exclusive caregiver, you are entirely responsible for what he learns, does, and enjoys. You become the sole source of new experiences, field trips, playdates, and introducing new things and people to play with.

If you choose to keep your preschooler at home, you'll need to find alternative ways to give him the opportunity and the encouragement he needs to make friends. (You'd also be well advised to find ways that allow your three-year-old to spend at least a short time without you or his special caregiver so that he gets used to the care and company of other adults.)

Especially if your three-year-old has never experienced daycare, he will probably find it easier to make friends in small groups rather than in large ones. So try to find a playgroup, class, or activity that might both further your child's social contacts and give him the opportunity to experience small group activities.

> **Q-Tip**
> Having trouble finding an activity or playgroup that you and your preschooler might enjoy? Try forming a play co-op with other parents of preschoolers in your area. When you have the kids to your home, you'll have a mess to clean up but depending on how many parents and children you include, you'll then have two or three or more playdates that involve no clean-up at all.

Hosting Playdates

Besides finding group situations for your child, try to arrange for playdates and special outings with one or two other preschoolers. Encourage your child to feel free to ask friends over to your home (or to ask you to call their parents to invite them over).

When you're hosting a playdate, keep in mind that three- and four-year-old playmates still need at least some adult supervision. Tempers flare much too quickly among preschoolers to leave them alone safely for more than a few minutes at a time. If you're the responsible adult in charge, you have a duty to make sure all children in your care remain safe from themselves and from one another.

Fortunately, this doesn't mean you need to watch the children like a mother hen. Indeed, you may find that you can get more accomplished and have more time to yourself when your child has a friend over to play with than when you are her sole source of entertainment and companionship. But you do need to stay close enough to be able to step in whenever anything threatens your child's—or your guest's—safety.

> **Childproofing**
> If your child and her playmate are doing something unsafe or tempers flare, merely issuing a warning ("Be careful!" or "Calm down!") just doesn't cut it. Take a hands-on approach in enforcing such safety rules as "one at a time" on the swings or "no pushing" on the jungle gym. And whenever possible, separate and distract children before anger turns to aggression or violence.

Your Place or Mine?

If your child only wants to have friends to your home, he may be experiencing separation anxiety. If so, you can use some of the same techniques discussed earlier about introducing your child to day care. For instance, the first few times you have a playdate at a friend's home, stay there until your child feels comfortable with the place and his friend's parent(s). Before you go, tell him to have his friend's parent call you if he wants you to come back early.

If, on the other hand, your child always prefers visiting other children's homes to having his friends over to your home, try to figure out why this might be so:

Q-Tip

When your preschooler and a playmate are fighting, don't let either of them get you into the middle of an argument about who started it. It doesn't matter who started the fight; what matters is who ends it (and in all likelihood, that's you). Rather than letting the argument continue, quickly try to come up with a new activity that will divert attention from the altercation.

➤ Do you let your child know that you like having friends over?

➤ Do you make your child's friends feel welcome?

➤ Do you make the extra mess and noise seem like a bother when your child does have friends over?

➤ Do you do anything that might embarrass your child?

If you want to encourage your preschooler to form friendships by having playdates in your home, you'll need to create a truly welcoming and friendly atmosphere. In doing so, you'll make your child proud and eager to have friends over.

The Least You Need to Know

➤ Your three-year-old will need supervision when playing with others—and reminders on how to share, take turns, and handle conflict without violence.

➤ Appeal to your child's self-interest (her desire to play with others) and her growing capacity for empathy to encourage good social behavior.

➤ Some preschools can provide the opportunity to make friends and practice social behavior.

➤ Your three-year-old needs social contact with other kids her age. So if she doesn't go to preschool, make sure to arrange plenty of playdates and activities with other children.

Breaking Bad Habits

The bad habits of preschoolers—particularly those of your own child—are a great ice-breaker. Perfect strangers will come up to you on the street, in the library, and in department stores and offer you "helpful" advice on breaking what they see as your preschooler's bad habits. Of course, one person's advice may not agree with another's. You'll hear that:

➤ You need to impose harsher discipline.

➤ You should try not to be so strict.

➤ You should show your child more affection.

➤ You need to stop being so indulgent.

➤ You should try this therapy.

➤ You should try that therapy.

➤ You've got to nip that in the bud.

➤ You should just be patient because she'll grow out of it.

What's a parent to do? Well, here's some more advice. Trust your instincts. You know your own child better than anyone else does. So try what you think will work best.

Bad Habit? What Bad Habit?

This chapter focuses on bad habits rather than bad behavior, because behavior that troubles you becomes a problem only when it becomes habitual. All preschoolers behave in ways that parents wish they wouldn't, at least on occasion. Your child will be no different. But no matter how strongly you disapprove of certain aspects of your child's behavior, it should be cause for real concern only if it becomes persistent.

Before you resolve to go to any lengths to try to break one of your child's bad habits, take a good long look at the behavior—and at yourself:

➤ Why do you find the behavior so objectionable?

➤ Is this behavior really so different from the behavior of other kids your child's age?

➤ Is the behavior really something over which your child has control at this age?

➤ Will it harm your preschooler to let him continue behaving this way?

➤ What positive benefits, if any, does your child derive from the habit?

➤ What can you offer to replace the benefits your preschooler will give up by breaking this habit?

Bad habits are in the eye of the beholder. You may be tempted to define certain aspects of your child's behavior as "bad habits." But in reality, they may be little more than typical patterns of preschool behavior that you find bothersome, irritating, or even disgusting. Face it. Though preschoolers can be a great delight and source of joy, they also can be a real pain. Most three- and four-year-olds are by nature messy, careless, and noisy, for example. They demand instant gratification, forget what you told them just three minutes ago, and require an enormous amount of your time. What's more, they never, ever go away. But do any of these typical preschool behaviors deserve to be labeled as bad habits? It all depends on who's doing the labeling.

If, after examining your child's behavior and your own attitudes, you still regard something as a bad habit, then it deserves to be taken seriously.

Try to avoid automatically dismissing a bad habit as a "phase" your child is going through. Some habits may result from medical conditions (bedwetting, for example, which may be caused by a bladder abnormality). If so, the sooner you find out and treat them, the better. Other troublesome behavior patterns may refuse to go away if you ignore them. And while you're waiting for the phase to end, your child may suffer consequences that will persist much longer than the behavior itself. Your child may be shunned by other children—and by teachers, day-care providers, and other adults as well. And you may be shunned by other parents who hold you responsible for your child's bad habits.

Whose Fault Is It Anyway?

Despite what you might hear others say, don't take on all the blame for your child's bad habits. Bad habits are not necessarily a parent's fault—all or in part. Nor can you expect to cure some bad habits all by yourself. Persistent problem behaviors that seem different from those demonstrated by other preschoolers your child's age might best be discussed with your pediatrician. You might find out that the problem demands professional attention, but you could find out—much to your surprise—that your child is quite "normal."

Try to avoid blaming your child for bad habits. Bad habits are, after all, just habits. Most have their origin outside the realm of conscious intent. Bad habits among preschoolers may result from delayed development, from parenting mistakes, from emotional trauma or conflict, or from some physiological cause. But they are rarely if ever caused by a child's vindictiveness or conscious attempt to manipulate. Preschoolers simply aren't that calculating.

Attempts to blame yourself, your child, or anyone else will not help solve the problem. And imposing punishment for a troublesome habit doesn't really attack the root of the behavior. Instead, try to use positive reinforcement to change your preschooler's behavioral patterns. Rather than scolding or punishing your child's failures, focus on praising and rewarding her successes.

Baby Talk

"I must have been an insufferable child; all children are."—George Bernard Shaw

"My mother had a great deal of trouble with me, but I think she enjoyed it."—Mark Twain

Your Kid Sucks

Sucking is a basic and natural need for infants and toddlers. But when do children outgrow this basic need? Some adults—and a few children—may label preschoolers who suck their thumbs or still use pacifiers as "babies." But is it really a problem?

Thumbs Down

Some dentists insist that thumb sucking that continues beyond the age of four or so can damage the alignment of baby teeth. This can cause the adult teeth that replace them to be out of alignment, too. Yet others maintain that the need for orthodontia later in life has nothing to do with whether a child sucked his thumb when younger. So before you make a big deal about your child's thumb sucking, ask your dentist if it has started to affect the alignment of his teeth. If it hasn't, then there's no pressing need for your child to give up such a soothing habit.

If your child does suck his thumb, you know that he finds it comforting. When he's upset, it calms him; when he's hurt, it soothes him, when it's bedtime, it lulls him to sleep. Thumb sucking can continue to provide a sense of security, even for a preschooler. So gather more evidence from your doctor and think long and hard before deciding to wean your child from his thumb.

Childproofing
Bad-tasting solutions that you can apply to your preschooler's thumb have a serious drawback. If your child rubs his eyes, the solution may sting or irritate them.

All children eventually stop sucking their thumbs regardless of what their parents do. However, if you decide that it's time for your child to get his thumb out of his mouth, start by explaining your reasoning to him. Your preschooler wants to be agreeable, wants to understand, and wants to be as grown up as he can. If your arguments fail to convince your child, ask your family dentist to talk to him. The dentist may wield more authority as a detached professional than you can as an involved parent. If your child still needs a little push to give up the habit:

➤ Try restricting your child's thumb sucking to when he's in his own room. If that's the only place he can suck his thumb, your preschooler may willingly wean himself to spend more time with you and with his friends. (On the other hand, he may just lock himself in his room forever.)

➤ Have your child wear mittens for a week or so. Your preschooler will find thumb sucking much less appealing if it leaves fuzz in his mouth.

➤ Because your child will probably have the hardest time giving up thumb sucking at bedtime, have your child wear finger puppets or mittens to bed. Of course, he may want to put on a show before he settles down.

➤ Put some "pixie dust" in each of your child's hands before bed. Then tell him if he holds on to it tightly until morning, it will turn into a surprise. After your child falls asleep, leave a small gift next to the bed so that he'll find it in the morning.

➤ If all else fails, try applying a foul-tasting solution (available at most drugstores) on the thumb. Your child will probably not want to suck his thumb if it tastes horrible. On the other hand, he may actually develop a taste for it.

Putting the Pacifier in the Past

Most pacifiers are now designed with orthodontia in mind. They will not do any damage to the alignment of your child's teeth. So why make a point of asking your preschooler to stop using a pacifier? In time, your child will probably give it up on her own to avoid being labeled a "baby" by other children or by insensitive adults.

However, if you can't wait to wean your preschooler from her beloved pacifier:

➤ Give your child one last pacifier and let her know that when this one gets lost or worn out, you won't replace it. This will give her time to get used to the idea—and to guard that pacifier with her life.

➤ Lose it. Accidentally leave the pacifier behind somewhere and put off getting a new one. Your preschooler may find that she doesn't really need it anymore.

➤ Try soaking the pacifier in vinegar or something else that tastes sour or bitter.

➤ Give up television for a week, because most preschoolers who still use pacifiers use them primarily when watching TV and when going to sleep. Find more active ways to occupy your child's time—activities that require her to use both of her hands.

➤ If your child is ready to give up her afternoon nap, give up the pacifier at the same time. Your child will be much more tired at night, and may therefore fall asleep more easily without the pacifier.

Things That Go Bump (or Squish) in the Night

By the time your child is three, you'd probably do anything to get a solid night's sleep on a consistent basis. Unfortunately, through no fault of his own, your child may make that impossible. Bedwetting, nightmares, night terrors, and early rising will all conspire against your slumber. Because all of them occur during your child's sleep, he has no conscious control over these bad sleep habits.

In fact, although you may be able to take measures to cut down on their frequency, the best you can do with most of these problems is just try to cope with them until your child outgrows them. The good news: None of these sleep problems is likely to disturb your preschooler's sleep very much. The bad news: The same can't be said for your sleep.

Water, Water Everywhere (and Not a Drop to Drink)

Bedwetting is a common problem among preschoolers. Indeed, it should not even be considered a "bad habit," because your child cannot control it. Although bedwetting may persist through (or even beyond) your child's fifth year, most children grow out of it during the early years of school.

Childproofing
Bedwetting may require professional evaluation if it is associated with: fever, painful urination; excessive thirst, loss of bowel control, or sudden onset with great frequency.

If bedwetting occurs only occasionally, don't worry about it. In fact, consider yourself (and your child) blessed. But habitual bedwetting (which your pediatrician calls *enuresis*) is seldom a cause for concern. In nine out of ten cases, enuresis results from a delay or slowness in development. Only a handful of cases result from an emotional cause (pressure from parents to toilet train too early, for example) or a physical cause (a urinary infection or a bladder abnormality). If, despite these reassurances, you still have any concern about your child's bedwetting, you should, of course, discuss them with your pediatrician.

Whatever the cause of your preschooler's bedwetting—and no matter how frequent—it's certainly not her fault. So regardless of how tired you are or how angry and frustrated you feel at having to change the bed for the fifth time this week, try not to blame your child for her bedwetting. Have patience. Your child will probably stay dry both day and night by age five or six.

Childproofing
If your child is worried about her bedwetting, your pediatrician can probably reassure her. Consult your pediatrician in private first, without your child. That way you will spare your preschooler's feelings and you can let your doctor know that it's your child, not you, who is concerned about the problem.

A sudden rise in the frequency of bedwetting may indicate stress in your preschooler's daily life. The causes of a preschooler's stress are many: the arrival of a new baby, an extended or unanticipated separation from you or your partner, getting lost in the department store, an illness or hospital stay, a death in the family, and so on. If you recognize the source of stress, talk to your child about it as kindly and openly as possible. If you pamper your child for a while, chances are that the bedwetting frequency will revert to normal.

If you want to do what little you can to cut down on the frequency of bedwetting, try the following:

➤ Encourage your child to use the toilet right before she goes to sleep at night.

➤ Cut down on your child's fluid intake before bed. Although this may achieve some short-term success, it may have little or no long-term impact (besides being somewhat inhumane).

➤ Take your child to the bathroom before you go to bed yourself. Though this tactic may cut down on the times you have to change the bed, it will not in any way affect the overall problem of bedwetting. Nor does it really address the cause of bedwetting. Indeed, because taking your child to the bathroom at midnight may not even wake her up, this strategy might actually *encourage* her to urinate in her sleep.

The best approach to bedwetting is to treat it as no big deal. Accidents do happen, and habitual bedwetting usually signals late development, not illness. Your child will eventually outgrow it, but again, it might not be until she's six or seven years old.

So praise your child when she wakes up dry in the morning (without making too big a show of it), but don't chastise her for a nighttime accident (or a daytime accident for that matter). Strong parental disapproval only makes the problem worse.

Fright Night

Waking up (or at least waking you up) in the middle of the night is a common problem among three- and four-year-olds. Preschoolers walk or talk in their sleep or suffer from bad dreams or night terrors. All may result from nervousness or anxiety in your child's waking life, but they also may spring from unresolved questions that he has. Despite the rapid growth in his understanding, your preschooler still cannot make sense of everything in his world. His attempt to make sense of things may continue after he has fallen asleep. In addition, your child's increasing awareness of his fears and feelings may also come out more at night.

Some nighttime disturbances are, of course, less serious than others. If your child talks in his sleep, for instance, you probably shouldn't feel any concern. Likewise, sleepwalking should seldom raise alarm. Occasional nightmares, too, are generally not a cause for concern. If you get to your child and soothe him as quickly as you can, he will probably fall right back to sleep with no further disturbances.

> **Childproofing**
> If you do have a sleepwalker, make sure that you have put a secure gate at the top of the stairs before you go to bed—and cleared the floor of toys—to prevent serious falls during his midnight rambles.

Night terrors are somewhat more disturbing—at least for most parents. Although your child will likely grow out of them, when you first witness an episode of night terrors, you may become as terrified as your preschooler. If your child suffers from night terrors, you will hear a blood-curdling scream in the middle of the night. Rushing to his bed, you will find your child terrified, angry, and/or upset. He may be thrashing and screaming in bed or he may be sitting up, his eyes wide with horror, staring at some spot before him. Yet despite his apparent alertness, your child remains unconscious and will probably not respond to your desperate attempts to soothe him. No matter how intense his emotions become or how loudly he begins to scream, your child will remain asleep and unaware. (He won't remember the episode at all in the morning either.)

As long as your preschooler remains asleep and stays safe in bed, don't try to wake him. Just stay with him and wait for the terror to pass and his sleep to calm. (The episode may last for ten minutes or more.) Your child—unconscious and gripped by fear—cannot listen to reason, so don't bother trying to argue him out of his terror.

Instead try to soothe him with gestures: hugs, caresses, your arm around his shoulder, soft words in calming tones. Your preschooler may ignore your attempts to comfort him, seem totally unaffected by them, or may actively resist them, making you part of the terror. He may even shout something like, "Go away! I hate you!" But it's not really you he's shouting at. So though you may want to back off a little bit, don't leave until the terror is gone and your child seems to have returned to comfortable slumber.

A child in the grip of night terrors will very rarely leave his bed. However, if your child does start running around the room in a panic, then he may represent a danger to himself. Try to intercept him and pick him up unless that seems to increase his terror. If your child does try to fight you off, let him go but try to ward him away from such dangers as stairs, sharp dresser corners, and doors that are ajar. Just do your best to keep your preschooler safe until he will let you pick him up. Or try gently to wake your child. Let him know that he had a really bad dream, but reassure him that it's over now. Then offer a drink or take your child to the bathroom before returning him to his bed. You will probably sleep easier if you wait with your child until he has returned to a deep, peaceful sleep.

Do Not Go Gently into that Good Night

Your three-year-old needs less sleep than she did just a year (or even just six months) ago. This may wreak havoc with bedtime if you don't adjust accordingly. So if your child has difficulty dropping off to sleep, ask yourself: Does your child really need so much sleep or do you just need some time to yourself at night? If your child doesn't need as much sleep as you're trying to force on her, you might have more success if you either shorten (or even eliminate) her afternoon nap or move her bedtime back a half hour or so. After all, if your three-year-old isn't tired, you can't reasonably expect her to want to go to bed.

> **Q-Tip**
> You might want to establish a rule that your preschooler can't get out of bed except to go to the bathroom. But make sure that your child has a way to communicate with you if she needs a cup of water, and so on. Use an intercom or baby monitor. Or leave the door slightly ajar.

As with younger children (see Chapter 4), you will do best to establish a regular, soothing bedtime routine. Make it as pleasant as possible for both of you. Before starting the routine, alert your child that bedtime is approaching. You'll start off on the wrong foot if you try to pull her away from whatever she's doing because, "It's time for bed."

Make a bargain with your child instead: "Just one more puzzle now, and then it's time for bed." Then read or tell a bedtime story. You'll probably have more success in preserving a soothing atmosphere if you hold storytime in your child's bedroom rather than in another room. After storytime, your child might enjoy listening to music as she drifts off to sleep.

In leaving your three-year-old's bedroom, promise to return to make sure she doesn't need anything else in 10, 15, or 20 minutes—or as soon as you've finished up what you're doing. (Your child may be more willing to let you go if you let her know that you have dishes to wash or a shower to take or some other business that demands your attention.) Then follow up on your promise—or expect your child to come looking for you.

If you haven't yet done so, try to make your three-year-old's bed and bedroom as appealing as possible. If you make the bedroom a place where your child enjoys spending time, she will put up much less resistance when she has to go there. So put some effort into making the bedroom her special, private place and honor that privacy. One way to do this is to let your child help decorate. When your child switches from a crib to a big bed, for instance, let her help redecorate the room.

Your preschooler can do a lot to transform her room into her own special space:

➤ She can help pick out sheets that she likes.

➤ She can help rearrange the furniture to her liking.

➤ She can help pick out pictures, posters, and other ways to decorate the walls around her bed.

➤ If you put shelves next to your preschooler's bed, she can stock them with her favorite books, stuffed animals, toys, and a portable cassette player with plenty of tapes.

➤ To facilitate storytime (and "reading" by her-self), install a reading light above your child's bed.

Childproofing

If you or your child is uncomfortable with the drop from a big bed to the floor, invest in a removable safety rail—or just put the mattress directly on the floor. When you're both more comfortable that she won't fall out, then put the safety rail away (though not necessarily far away, because you or she might want it back at some point).

Q-Tip

Don't punish your child by sending her to her bedroom or by sending her—or even threatening to send her—to bed early. This will ruin all your efforts to make your preschooler's bed and bedroom and bed a soothing and pleasant place for her to be.

All of these will make your child's room a place she wants to be. And isn't that half the battle in getting her to go to bed?

Come Back at a Decent Hour!

Your child will wake up whenever he wakes up in the morning. He cannot help it if it's earlier than you would like. But by age three, he may be able to entertain himself for a while—especially if you've stocked his bedroom with easy-to-reach books, toys, puzzles, and music. Although it may take repeated lessons, you can teach your preschooler to respect your sleep. Try to get your child to agree not to wake mommy or daddy until he hears your alarm go off. Or try setting a clock radio just for him—to let him know when he can wake you.

Of course, your preschooler will probably still wake you if he's wet, hungry, thirsty, or needs to go to the bathroom. Though you shouldn't discourage your child from waking you when he has wet the bed or needs to use the toilet, you may be able to head off hunger and thirst. Try leaving some cereal or crackers and some water near your child's bed. When he wakes early in the morning, your preschooler will be happy—and proud—to help himself.

Finally, despite your best efforts to provide everything he needs to entertain and nourish himself, your child also may wake you up with loud play. At this point, throw up your hands in surrender. After all, you can't reasonably expect your three- or four-year-old to play by himself and do it quietly, too.

The Least You Need to Know

➤ What you call a bad habit may be normal behavior for a three-year-old. So be sure to ask yourself why you want your child to stop a habit and what harm the habit is doing her.

➤ Thumb sucking and sucking on a pacifier provide many positive benefits and few ill effects. So if you want your child to quit, you'd better have a good reason—and a substitute that will provide at least some of the same soothing benefits.

➤ Bedwetting and most sleep disturbances are not your child's fault and are not subject to her (or your) control. So let them slide for a while.

➤ Making your child's bedroom a place where she enjoys being can help make bedtime, naptime, and early mornings more pleasant for both of you.

Chapter 19

Welcoming (You Wish) a Baby Brother or Sister

In This Chapter

➤ Preparing your child for the arrival of a baby brother or sister

➤ Preparing your child for the time you may be away

➤ Smoothing things out between your children during the critical first six months

➤ Coping with your older child's regression

➤ Sharing parenting responsibilities

Believe it or not, there is a way to prevent sibling rivalry: Have only one child!

If you decide that you want to have more than one child, however, there's no escaping sibling rivalry. So reconcile yourself to the fact that there will be friction between your first child and your new baby. No matter how eagerly your child anticipates the baby before it arrives, her feelings may change rapidly when she sees how much of your time and attention the new baby is taking.

Let's face it. It's stressful and even painful for a child to have to share her parents with another child—especially after getting used to having their exclusive love and attention. So don't expect your child to be pleased with your decision. It doesn't matter whether your first child is a preschooler or a toddler or (yikes!) still not quite walking yet. She probably won't like the fact that you're having another baby. And she will definitely feel supplanted and jealous after the baby is born.

Baby Talk
"Reinhart was never his mother's favorite—and he was an only child."
—Thomas Berger

You can make things go a little smoother by planning ahead, by preparing your child in advance of the baby's arrival, by paying special attention to your older child after the baby's birth, and by juggling responsibilities with your partner. But no matter how much effort, care, and consideration you put into showing your child that you don't love her any less just because you're having another baby, your child will still feel hurt, angry, jealous, and resentful of that dreadful creature called the baby.

Family Planning

Time for some family planning decisions. When's the best time to have a second baby? Should you have your family all at once, spacing your children less than two and a half years apart? Or should you recover from the first before having the second, spacing them at least two and a half years apart? As the following table demonstrates, it all depends on your priorities.

Advantages of Having Children Close Together in Age

A child under two will quickly forget that he was once the only one.

If both you and your partner eventually want to get back to full-time work, you will be able to do so sooner.

If you make it through the first few years, your kids are more likely to have a close relationship, playing and sharing with each other.

Disadvantages of Having Children Close Together in Age

You may be nursing and pregnant at the same time—not always a pleasant combination.

You may suffer from morning sickness during the period when your toddler or pre-toddler becomes very clingy.

You will have two babies at the same time, which means double the diapers and balancing a child on each hip.

Advantages of Putting More Space Between Your Children

It will probably be easier on you both physically and mentally to have some breathing room between babies.

If both you and your partner want or need to work part-time during your children's early years, you'll find it much easier with a preschooler and a baby than with a toddler and a baby.

Your older child will probably be independent by the time the baby arrives, so you will have more time to devote to the new baby.

Disadvantages of Putting More Space Between Your Children

A child who can speak can tell you in no uncertain terms that he wants that *thing* out of here and he wants it out now!

No matter how close they get, your children will always be three (or four or more) years apart, which will make it harder for them to share and enjoy each other's company—at least during their childhood.

Fair Warning

No matter how you decide to space your children, do whatever you can to help prepare your two-, three-, or four-year-old for what's coming. (Unfortunately, you can't do much to prepare a one-year-old due to his limited verbal skills.)

Your child, especially if she's still a toddler, may not notice the dramatic increase in the size of your (or your partner's) belly. If you suddenly go away for a day or two and come back with a baby, your child will quite understandably have a fit. So give your child fair warning so that she has time to get used to the idea. This doesn't mean you need to break the news as soon as you find out that there's a baby on the way. But certainly your child should know about it by the sixth month of pregnancy.

Q-Tip
Especially if you have a young child, try to avoid telling her too early. By the time the baby comes, your older child may be totally bored with the whole idea.

Baby Talk

After you've broken the news, talk to your child about it often enough so that he can share new thoughts and concerns as they arise. But don't talk about the baby every day unless your child brings up the subject. (He needs to know that the baby isn't the only important thing in your life.) Talk about your reasons for wanting another child, about what babies are like, about how they grow inside a mother's belly.

If you don't know the sex of your baby, talk about that, too—but try not to build up expectations for one gender over the other. If you do know the sex, by all means let your child know, too (although you should keep in mind that methods of sex determination can sometimes be wrong). And ask your child's opinion about possible names you are considering.

>
>
> ### Kid Stuff
>
> A couple of months before the birth of her baby sister, three-and-a-half-year-old Emily was asked for her suggestions about first and middle names. After running through the names of all of her friends, Emily started looking around the house for more ideas. The name she finally settled on: Broccoli Nivea!

If your child wants to know why you want another baby, tell him as honestly as you can. But don't claim that you're doing it for your child's sake—so that he'll have someone to play with, for instance. In the first place, your child probably doesn't want what you're offering. He'd rather make friends and arrange playdates. In the second place, it's misleading, because your baby won't be able to do anything even approaching play with your child for many months after the birth. And in the final analysis, it's probably a lie. Though you certainly considered your child's welfare in choosing to have another baby, it probably wasn't the decisive factor. In the end you made your decision for your own reasons.

> **Q-Tip**
>
> In talking about the coming baby, try to give your child a sense of ownership. From the beginning of your discussions, refer to the new baby as "your brother" or "your sister" or "your brother or sister."

When you talk to your child about the baby during your pregnancy, help her to cultivate a sense of superiority. This helps build your child's self-esteem and may make him more tolerant of the baby's annoying presence when the baby does arrive. So let your child know how helpless the baby will be and how much the baby will need his help. Tell him that, unlike him, the baby won't be able to feed himself or wash himself or go to the bathroom by himself or even play by himself. Let your child know that the baby will cry whenever he needs something, but because the baby won't be able to talk, you'll just have to guess what that something is. Tell him that the baby will wet or dirty his diapers 10 or 15 times a day. (Depending on your child's age, he might find this last detail hilarious.)

Let your child know too that this helplessness will not last forever. It may help to begin telling him stories about things—especially funny things—that he did when he was "just a baby." Try to bring alive his own infancy for him. Pull out the photo albums and show him pictures of his first year. Get out the crib a little early and remind your child that he used to sleep there when he was little, but that now it's for the new baby.

Encourage your child to express any feelings he has about the new baby—including anxiety and even outright anger—even before the baby arrives. By giving your child permission to voice the unpleasant feelings he has about the baby, you may help him to "make room" for warmer feelings (excitement, pride, and so on), too.

You can also encourage the development of warm feelings for the coming sibling by including your child in the pregnancy (as much as he wants to be included). Give him the chance to feel the baby kicking. This will help the baby become real for your child even before he appears. Let him know what he can do to help during your pregnancy, but don't put pressure on him to help if he doesn't want to. (Your three- or four-year-old probably will.)

Smooth Sailing

Most importantly, do everything you can well before the baby is born to establish the routines that you will need to adopt after the baby arrives. Try to get your child's life going so smoothly that the arrival of the baby won't disrupt her routines. Some examples:

> ➤ If your child will be going to day care or preschool or if you will need to hire a new sitter, do it well in advance of the final months of pregnancy.

> ➤ If your child does not attend day care, be sure to establish regular playdates at some of her friends' homes months before the birth. You will really appreciate these playdates after the baby comes—and so will your child, if only because it gives her a break from obsessing about you and that bothersome baby.

> ➤ If you have a young child who still breastfeeds, wean her several months before the new baby arrives. Otherwise, your child may still remember breastfeeding, and whenever you nurse the baby, she'll feel, "Hey, that's mine!"

> ➤ If you plan to take time off from work after the baby is born, stop working well before the baby arrives (unless you cannot possibly afford to do so). Otherwise your child will feel (rightly so) that you're willing to stay home for the baby even though you never stayed home for her.

Q-Tip
If you have a young child who still sleeps in a crib and you don't plan to buy another, make sure to move him into a "big bed" well before the baby arrives. And do likewise if you'll be moving him into a new room. If he has to "give up" his space to make room for the baby, your child is sure to resent feeling supplanted in this way.

Q-Tip
You also can look to outside help to prepare your child for the arrival of a new sibling. Find out if your hospital or a local parents' group offers a class for expectant siblings. These usually provide a good introduction to infant behavior.

Oh, and Before You Go...

Even if you and your partner are planning a home birth, you may end up in a hospital or birthing center due to complications. So prepare your child for the time that you may—or definitely will—be away from home. Make sure to have some "dry runs" with your child's caregiver before the actual event. He and Grandma and Grandpa (or Aunt or Uncle) need some time to get comfortable with each other before the birth forces them together. Try to turn these practices into special events, making it a treat to have a sleepover at Grandma's house, for example.

If Daddy will be taking care of your child while Mommy's in the hospital, he may need some dry runs, too. Unless Daddy has shared equally in the child care, he should try to spend some extra time with your child in the final weeks of pregnancy.

With any new caregiver, run through all the routines that your child has developed, so that the caregiver will know exactly how you and he do things. Of course, the caregiver doesn't need to do everything exactly the way you do. But if you cut sandwiches into triangles and your stand-in cuts them into rectangles, your child may have a fit about it. Little things like these will matter a great deal when you are away.

Finally, avoid making promises unless you know that you can keep them. Complications do occur during childbirth and you can't anticipate all of them. So you can't guarantee your child that you'll stay home to have the baby. And if you're going to a hospital, you can't promise you'll be back in one or two days. You may be able to explain both what you plan and the fact that complications may change your plans to a four-year-old, who will probably understand this distinction. But if your child is three or younger, try to keep plans as vague as possible. This will allow you to maintain the trust of your child.

And Baby Makes Four

The onset of labor may throw all of your well-laid plans out the window. Your baby, of course, was not in on the plans and may not honor them. So it's important to have one (or more) people that you can call to help you out with child care as soon as labor begins.

Special Delivery—At Home

If you are having a home birth, you need to ask yourself an important question: How much do you want your child involved? Do you want her involved at all? (Your child, of course, needs to ask the same questions of herself.) Childbirth truly is a miraculous event. Depending on her age, interest, and temperament, your child may be fascinated. Even so, the sound of painful labor and the sight and smell of blood and other fluids may disturb your child. In addition, if she's constantly demanding your attention, your child will distract you from the important business at hand (which will be a blessing only at certain times during labor). So think carefully about whether she—and you—can handle her being there. And don't offer more participation than you think your child can handle.

If you and your child decide that she wants to stay close by, you'll need to prepare her thoroughly for what she might see and hear. No matter how well you have prepared your child and how eager she seems to participate in some way, plan for a change in plans. Have someone other than the birthing partner available to take your child away whenever necessary. (The birthing partner needs to be there for *the mother*.)

> **Q-Tip**
> If you are taking a refresher course in childbirth, explain your situation and ask the teacher if you can borrow a video on childbirth to show to your child. This may give her a good idea of what to expect.

Special Delivery—In the Hospital

If you plan to deliver your baby in a hospital or birthing center, you probably don't need to worry about whether to include your child. Most hospitals won't allow it.

Make sure to say goodbye to your child before you leave for the hospital. Even if you head out in the middle of the night or early in the morning, wake your child up to say goodbye. Your child may find it hard to say goodbye, but still it will be less upsetting to him than waking up to find you gone.

After the baby is born let your child visit you in the hospital (if he wants to) at the first convenient opportunity. Yes, your child might find it upsetting if Mommy is zonked out in bed, hardly able to sit up, and grimacing with pain at every movement. But a sensitive partner can prepare a child (especially a preschooler) for this sight. Comparing postpartum recovery to recovery from a cold or a stomach flu may help your child understand how Mommy might feel.

When your child comes to visit you in the hospital, it will help if neither you nor your partner is holding the baby. At some point during his visit, you can introduce your child to the new baby. But don't be surprised or disappointed if he takes no interest in his new sibling. Chances are, your child didn't come to the hospital to see the baby; he came to see you.

> **Q-Tip**
> Buy your child a small present beforehand and when he or she comes to see you after the birth of the baby, offer it as congratulations for becoming a big brother or sister. Many greeting card and party stores have buttons that read, "I'm the big sister!" or "I'm the big brother!" Your child may like this token of his or her importance.

The Arrival of a Rival

All the preparation in the world may not affect more than the first few days at home with the new baby. After your baby has been born, you, your partner, your child, and the baby will all have to make the best of the upheaval this arrival creates. There's no turning back now. And it will help enormously if you get off on the right foot.

If your baby is born in a hospital, have someone else carry him when you come home. You need to have your arms free and ready to give your child a big hug. (You also may want to give her a little present "from the baby.") Then try to spend at least a few minutes with your older child before rushing off to tend to the baby.

Q-Tip

If presents arrive for the new baby, let your older child open the packages. Many of your friends and relatives—especially those who are parents themselves—may be savvy enough to send small presents for your older child whenever they send something for a newborn. But just in case, you might want to keep some small presents for your older child on hand to minimize jealousy.

In your baby's first week or two at home, try to make your older child feel as loved and special as possible. Plan some special time alone with your older child. Or if, for example, your older child is more attached to one of you than the other, have the other hold the baby whenever possible. This will enable you to preserve your special bond with your oldest child.

If you breastfeed your baby, be discreet—at least at first. As you know from your first child, breastfeeding cements a special bond between mother and child. Your child will on some level recognize this. So it will only fan the flames of jealousy to nurse your baby in front of your older child. Try to give your child a few days or a week to get used to the idea that the baby is here to stay before letting her watch you nurse the baby. Enlist your partner or some other caregiver to do something special with her when the baby needs to eat.

When you decide it's time to let your older child watch you breastfeed, talk to her about it. Explain how the baby eats and what the baby eats. Remind your child that that's how she ate, too—before she got big enough to feed herself "real food." Be sure to ask if your child has any questions. Don't be surprised if her question is whether she can taste some breast milk. If it makes you uncomfortable to do so, gently refuse your child and tell her why. But if the idea doesn't repel you, then why not? Put a few drops on your finger and give your child a taste.

In explaining breastfeeding and talking to your child about other aspects of baby care, continue to cultivate an attitude of benign superiority. Repeatedly point out to your older child the many things she can do that the baby cannot, for example walking, talking, feeding herself, bathing, jumping, singing, and doing somersaults.

In extolling your older child's abilities, suggest that maybe she could teach the baby when she gets a little bit older, too. Even a patronizing attitude on your older child's part is better than out-and-out hostility.

Her sense of superiority may allow your older child to help you care for the baby. If she seems willing, ask your child to help in any small way she can. She can run and get you a diaper, hold a bottle for the baby, or gently stroke the baby's hand or cheek or tickle his toes. If your child refuses to help, don't insist on it or make a big deal of it. Instead, try to understand the difficult emotions that underlie her refusal.

Baby Love?

You can't force your older child to love (or even like) your baby, so don't even try. Because your child will feel jealous and resent the baby much of the time, it will be difficult for him to have many (if any) warm feelings toward the baby. Try to understand this and acknowledge your child's right to see the baby as a royal pain. But at the same time, suggest that some day (hopefully) your child and your baby may get along well enough to play with each other and, who knows, maybe even like each other.

If the baby already likes him, your child will find it much easier to like the baby. So try to help your child feel that the baby likes him. By the third month, it should be relatively easy for your child to get the baby to smile at him. Make a point of noticing and milk it for all it's worth.

No matter what he feels, give your child free rein to express his emotions, especially those regarding the baby. Try to avoid making him feel guilty about hating the baby. In fact, if he's three or older, your child may feel an excessive amount of guilt about hating the baby all on his own. So give him permission to say it out loud for all to hear, and let him

> **Childproofing**
> NEVER leave your baby alone or unwatched where your older child can reach her. Your baby's room should be not only babyproof, but childproof as well, preventing your older child from going into the room without adult supervision.

know that you understand his feelings and that he need not feel guilty. (Of course, you also might want to add that you hope those feelings will change as the two of them get to know each other better.) Your child has a right to his feelings and they should not be regarded as shameful. After all, they are perfectly normal and understandable. (Just think how you would feel if your partner brought a new spouse home.)

Of course, just because your child has leave to express his emotions in words doesn't mean you should allow him to act them out. Make it clear from the start that though you welcome his verbal expressions of feelings, your child is not allowed to harm the baby in any way. You can give him at least three good reasons:

➤ you won't like it and will certainly discipline him for it;

➤ your baby certainly won't like it and will cry, meaning you will need to pay even more attention to her; and

➤ your child won't like it, at least not for more than a moment. Even a toddler will feel guilty about hurting a baby

Try to do more than merely defusing tense situations that might cause your older child to strike out at the baby. Do your best to remove the opportunity for your child to hurt the baby. If possible, aim to prevent your child from inflicting even accidental harm on your baby. Toddlers and preschoolers still have a magical belief in wish-fulfillment. So even if your child hurts the baby by accident, he may feel a tremendous sense of guilt. After all, that may have been just what he was wishing for.

One Step Forward, Two Steps Back

Regression in certain abilities—or in the willingness to perform up to capabilities—is common among both toddlers and preschoolers when a new baby arrives. Just when you most need your child to dress herself or feed herself, she suddenly won't do it. The reasons are easy to understand. Consciously or unconsciously, your child decides that if she were a little baby, too, you'd pay more attention to her. So no matter how desperately she tried to prove that she was a big girl before the baby arrived, your child doesn't want to be a big girl anymore.

Q-Tip

Arrange special treats or special events that aren't appropriate for babies, but that your older child can enjoy. At least occasionally offer special foods, or special outings, like a trip to the movies or an indoor playspace. If you make a point of noting that your baby can't enjoy these pleasures yet, your child may appreciate being more grown up. (As a bonus, this may also relieve some of your child's anger toward the baby, replacing it with pity for the poor miserable thing.)

Try to handle regression with grace and good humor. Let it slide as much as you possibly can. Of course she doesn't need to act like a baby to win your affection. But what's obvious to you might not be so obvious to your child. So shower her with praise whenever your child helps out in any way—whether that's helping to care for the baby or helping to care for herself.

But at the same time, let your child know through both words and actions that she doesn't need to push herself to be grown up either. Avoid the odious phrase, "Act your age!" Make it clear to your child that you always will love her, no matter how she behaves.

Play along with your child when she plays at being a baby. Transform it into a game of make-believe that allows you to baby your older child a little. If she suddenly talks in baby talk, coo to her the way you do to the baby. If she crawls around on the floor, scoop her up and give her a big hug. If she insists, let her drink from a bottle for a while.

It's important to your child to know that whatever you give to the baby you'll give to her if that's what she wants. Let her know that the reason you stopped feeding her and dressing her and bathing her in the sink before the baby arrived was not that you no longer wanted to do these things, but that she had outgrown them. In taking this kind of approach, you give your child the power to make a choice about how to behave. If she knows that she can freely behave like a baby or get what the baby gets whenever she wants, chances are she'll soon stop doing it.

While allowing her to act like a baby, help your child recognize the advantages of being a big kid, too. Give her some new privileges and, if she's willing, offer her some new responsibilities. For instance, you may make a point of letting her stay up an hour or so after the baby goes to bed at night.

My Time Is Your Time (Well, Some of the Time)

In general, try to stick to activities and routines with your child similar to those you did before the baby arrived. Certainly you won't be able to do everything you did before or do it as much. But when you can't, try not to "blame" the baby—for instance, saying, "I can't because the baby needs…." Sometimes it will be unavoidable, of course. Your child will see that you are nursing or changing the baby and that's why you can't play with him. If so, own up to it, but promise your older child that he will get his turn with you soon.

Do everything you and your partner can do to set aside at least half an hour a day (each) to spend alone with your older child, giving him your full attention. Your special time can be after day care, at the breakfast table, at bathtime, before bedtime—or as often as you can when your baby's napping. Use these special times to shower your big boy or girl with love and affection.

Share Care

Especially during the first weeks of your baby's life, try to get some help from others. A helping hand will not just lighten your own load, but also will make your older child's life more enjoyable.

A supportive partner can make an enormous difference during this transition from one child to two. Ask and expect your partner to help more with the kids.

> **Q-Tip**
> If your child is in day care, alert your day-care providers that he may need special attention, a sympathetic ear, and pointed praise for a while as he adjusts to the new baby. And do the same for him at home.

The "natural" division of labor is for the mother (especially one who breastfeeds) to care more for the newborn and the father to take care of the older child. But you need not fall into such rigid patterns. In fact, if Mommy handled the bulk of child care before the new baby arrived, your older child may resist spending so much time just with Daddy. Even if she welcomes Daddy's attention as a rare and special treat, however, your older child will miss a Mommy who suddenly shifts all of her energies to baby care.

> **Q-Tip**
> Even though a father can't breastfeed, he can, of course, give the baby a bottle or two every day. Some babies do prefer to eat exclusively from the breast. But if the baby accepts a bottle of formula or expressed breast milk, it will allow Mommy more flexibility—and more chances to spend special time with the older child.

So try to divide the labor more evenly. With the sole exception of breastfeeding, a father can handle every aspect of baby care that a mother can. So try to balance the time each of you spends with each of your children. When Mommy is feeding the baby, Daddy should of course entertain the older child. But when the baby isn't eating, Daddy is just as capable of taking care of the baby, giving the older child a chance to spend some time with Mommy.

Life Goes On

The first six months of your second child's life can provide a good—or a poor—foundation for her older sibling's relationship with her. If hostility runs rampant, it will get even worse when your baby starts to crawl and get into your older child's things—or when your older child is forced to clean up his things to keep your baby away from them.

Certainly, all your problems won't disappear after the first six months. They will merely become different problems. For instance, regardless of how close in age they are, your children will always be on different developmental levels and have different needs, interests, and abilities. In arranging family activities, family vacations, and family outings, you will have to balance them as best you can.

> **Baby Talk**
> "Comparison is a death knell to sibling harmony."
> —Elizabeth Fishel

Because they're on different developmental levels and have different talents and personalities, avoid making comparisons between them. They may be as different from each other as two complete strangers. And if you point to one child as an "example" or "model," the other child will surely resent it.

Remember that some rivalry, jealousy, annoyance, and fighting is normal between siblings. So don't feel you have to mediate every dispute unless the threat of violence is imminent. Your children can learn important lessons about conflict resolution and getting along with others through their sibling relationship. So whenever possible, let them work things out themselves. (Naturally you will need to intervene sometimes to facilitate a resolution of conflict.)

Remember, too, that you can't force your children to love each other and you shouldn't force them to play together. But if you trust each of them and give them the opportunity, they will probably work things out on their own.

The Least You Need to Know

➤ There's no escaping sibling rivalry. Having another baby will invariably cause your older child to feel hurt, angry, jealous, and resentful. But with your help, she may eventually get over it.

➤ Let your child get used to the idea that you are having a baby before you actually bring one home.

➤ During the second half of pregnancy, establish enjoyable routines for your child that she will be able to continue without interruption after the birth.

➤ Encourage your child to express any feelings she has about the baby—but never in any way (whether hitting or shouting) that harms the baby.

➤ Expect regression in your older child's abilities and treat it as no big deal. Indulge your child for a while.

➤ Get help from your partner—or anyone else—in caring for your older child and in taking the baby so that you can spend some special time with your oldest.

Toy Story

Your preschooler has become a social being. He has friends of his own now and enjoys talking, joking, and playing with them. You may be somewhat surprised, relieved, or disconcerted at how quickly you fade into the background when your child's favorite playmate comes to visit. You have been supplanted (at least temporarily) as your child's first and best playmate.

That's all as it should be. Yet just because your preschooler has finally found other companions to share in his play doesn't mean that you should stop playing with him. Reduce your role as perennial playmate and unofficial camp counselor, but not so much so that the only time you spend together is occupied by chores. Your child still wants and needs you to play with him. Through play, you can add ideas and new language that will further enhance your child's play—with you, with others, and by himself.

Root, Root, Root for the Home Team

What should you do and how should you play with your child? Well, to some extent what you do at home depends on whether she attends preschool—and what she does when she's there.

Away Games

If your child does go to day care or preschool, try to complement whatever she does there with what you do at home. If your three-year-old spends a lot of time running around outside in the preschool playground, try to provide her with more contemplative activities (reading, sing-alongs, and just talking) at home. On the other hand, if her preschool day consists mostly of art projects and circle-time stories, reading, and music, then your child will welcome the opportunity to run around with you when she gets home.

At preschool, your three-year-old spends a lot of time in "learning play"—letter and number recognition, reading readiness, arts and crafts. At home, she may therefore prefer more relaxed play. It may still be educational, and it should certainly be fun, but it need not be "fun with a purpose"—that is, play aimed at teaching some new concept that will help prepare her for school.

> **Q-Tip**
> Because much of your child's time in preschool will be spent in group activities that her teachers choose for her, try to offer her a variety of alternatives at home and let *her* choose what she wants to do.

Most of all, your child needs—and wants—you to pay special attention to her, devoting time and energy to her needs and desires when she gets home. That seems only fair. After all, no matter how much time your preschooler spends in the care of others, she still needs you a lot. Indeed, she may only rarely want you to arrange any playdates for her at home. Instead, your child may want you all to herself.

Home Games

If your three-year-old does not go to preschool or day care, then he needs much more guidance from you in his choice of play activities. You will need to supply the structure, entertainment, and learning opportunities for your child's day. Everything your child learns is on your shoulders.

Children who go to preschool are introduced to many new experiences by their teachers. They have lots of different toys and art supplies. They learn to get along with groups of children. They go on field trips to farms and children's museums. But if your child doesn't go to preschool, you'll need to open these doors for him.

If you are your child's sole caregiver, try to vary your play activities. Orchestrate quiet times when you and your child can read, do puzzles, listen to music, or tell stories. But also arrange for some active play, outside if the weather allows; playing ball, tag, and other running-around games, taking a nature walk, visiting the nearest playground to use the slides, swings, and climbing apparatus.

You know your child better than anyone else does. So talk to him and explore his interests. If your child asks lots of questions about animals, borrow library books on animals and visit local zoos and nature centers. If he hears an ambulance or fire engine and wonders why it makes so much noise, talk to him about fires or medical emergencies. Then explore his interest further with books. You might even want to arrange a tour or visit of the local firehouse or your hospital. Whatever your child expresses interest in, encourage him to deepen his knowledge of the subject. You are still your child's first and best teacher.

Q-Tip

Your preschooler's mind, interests, needs, and energy are expanding. He needs much more physical and mental stimulation than any home can supply. So get out of the house and go someplace: Plan regular "field trips" to neighborhood parks, playgrounds, zoos, museums, libraries, beaches, and the countryside.

Are You Game?

Three is the perfect age to begin playing board games and card games with your child—especially if you like these kinds of games, too. Board and card games help teach your child about aspiration, success, and disappointment. She'll gain experience with both winning and losing—and learn that no matter what the result, next time she tries she'll begin again with a clean slate. Games also give you the opportunity to teach your preschooler about rules, about integrity and honesty, and about luck. Games also can help increase your child's ability to focus her attention.

Playing board or card games also is a very social occasion. Game playing enables and encourages your preschooler to practice important social skills that she will need to play well with other children. Nearly all games, for example, involve taking turns, sharing dice or a spinner, waiting for your turn, patience, and learning how to be a good sport. (When you play games with your child, try to emphasize the fun of game as much as possible, rather than focusing on "who's winning.")

Q-Tip

Picture lotto is a terrific game for three-year-olds. After your child has mastered simple matching skills, invent some variations. Divide the cards evenly and take turns being the "caller." The caller turns one card over and announces what card she has: "I have a bird. Does anyone have a bird on their board?" This allows your preschooler to practice her new vocabulary.

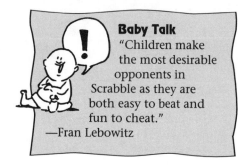

Besides helping to acquaint your child with "life lessons" and to practice valuable social skills, most good children's games also afford preschoolers the opportunity to sharpen certain academic skills. Most board games for preschoolers involve either counting or color matching, for instance. Similarly, most card games for preschoolers involve matching suits or numbers (Concentration, Go Fish, Old Maid, and Crazy Eights) or comparing numbers (War). Games like picture lotto can help expand your preschooler's vocabulary and give her practice at analyzing and matching pictures.

In introducing board and card games to your preschooler, choose the simplest ones first. If your child has to master a complicated set of rules before even playing the game, she—or you—will soon lose patience with it. Games that involve moving pieces around a board in a race to the finish, spinning a spinner or throwing dice, and counting up as high as six provide the perfect introduction to board games. Some classics include:

Candyland	Chutes and Ladders
Uncle Wiggly	Sorry
Hi-Ho Cherry-O	Trouble

Similarly, when you deal the cards to your child, start with simple games that involve matching pictures rather than skipping straight to Contract Bridge or even Hearts.

No Fair! I Never Win!

Should you let your preschooler win some games? That is, should you throw the game, take a dive, shave points, or lose on purpose?

Well, you might argue that intentionally losing a game patronizes your child. Rather than giving him a false sense of confidence, you should play as well as you can and let the chips fall where they may. If your child loses, so be it. After all, your preschooler needs to get to know both sides of competitive etiquette: how to lose gracefully as well as how to win without rubbing it in.

But then, you want your child to enjoy playing games. And if he loses all the time, chances are that rather than being motivated to try harder and win next time, he will lose interest in the game altogether. So if you want to maintain your preschooler's interest in games, he's going to have to win at least close to half the times he plays.

Of course, this still doesn't mean you necessarily have to throw a game. You can still take a hard line, refusing to take a dive to let your child win. But if you do, then you should probably confine your game-playing with him to games that are ruled strictly by luck or chance, games that involve little or no skill—in other words, games that your preschooler has an even chance to win. Most games for preschoolers—Chutes and Ladders, Hi-Ho Cherry-O, Candyland, and so on—are in fact ruled strictly by chance.

On the other hand, many card games appropriate for preschoolers—Concentration, Crazy Eights, even Go Fish—do involve at least an element of skill. In such games, you will (probably) be a superior player. If you still insist on playing your best and trying to win games that involve more skill and sophistication, then consider giving yourself some kind of a handicap. In Concentration, for instance, you might start your child out with six or eight pairs of cards before you lay out the rest on the floor. Trial and error will help you come up with an appropriate handicap: one that adds suspense (regarding who will win) to the game.

> ### Kid Stuff
>
> At age four, John became enamored with a Five-a-Side soccer game that he found in the basement. Of course, his hand-eye coordination was not quite as good as that of his father, who had become quite good at the game during hours he might otherwise have spent studying in college. After a few games in which John became increasingly frustrated, his father proposed a hefty handicap: He sat on his right hand, played only with his left hand, pulled his goalie off the board, and gave John nine goals in a game up to 15. After instituting the handicap, most games ended with 15–14 or 15–13 scores and John's love for the game returned.

Certainly your child needs to learn to lose gracefully. After all, other preschoolers are not likely to let him win when they play with him. So before he begins playing games with other children, your preschooler needs to understand that every child wants to win the game, but that only one can win.

But at the same time, the lessons of game playing should not revolve exclusively around losing gracefully. Winning a game, especially beating you (who are so much bigger and stronger and smarter, etc.), will give your preschooler great joy and an enormous boost of confidence. It also gives you an opportunity to model grace in defeat (if you can manage to do so).

> ### Q-Tip
> In certain games that seem to go on forever (War comes to mind), your child will probably not appreciate it if you just quit. In such cases, taking a dive may be the quickest and most painless way to end it.

By the Book

If you haven't yet gotten the message from Chapters 7 and 14 of this book, read often with your child.

Now that your child is a preschooler, choose picture books of increasing complexity. Instead of books with a single large illustration per page, try books with more complex and highly detailed illustrations. When you read with your child, explore the details of the illustrations. In this way, you can use the illustrations in your child's books to further her understanding of colors, shapes, and numbers.

> **Q-Tip**
> If you can, do more than just read books to your child. Give dramatic readings that bring the stories to life. Adopt distinctive voices for different characters and try to express some of the characters' emotions.

> **Q-Tip**
> If you've read a particular story many, many, times, ask your preschooler if she would like to "read" the lines for a particular character. Your child can probably remember the lines almost word for word. And if she misses a word or two, try not to correct her as long as she seems to get the gist of it.

Now also is the time to move beyond picture books. Longer stories can sustain your preschooler's interest now that she can follow a plot through a combination of words and pictures. Choose books that present comfortable and familiar stories about friendship, families, cars and trains, and animals who behave like people. (Try some books of children's poetry, too.) Books that tell stories, rather than just present objects or emotions, will provide many new words and new ideas for your preschooler and will heighten her understanding of real and imagined worlds.

You and your child will no doubt read the same storybooks again and again. Have patience. The repeated readings will help your preschooler begin to memorize books—and this also will help her when she begins trying to read the words.

Help further your preschooler's understanding by pausing for emphasis, talking about the picture, or asking questions like, "What do you think will happen next?" Encourage your child to ask questions about what she's seeing and hearing, too, even if it means interrupting the story.

If you read to your child before her bedtime, leave plenty of time so that you won't have to hurry through the book(s). That way you can read slowly and clearly so that your child can hear the words, and have time to understand them.

Your three-year-old will probably enjoy books by the following authors:

Anno	A.A. Milne (*Winnie the Pooh*)
Lillian and Russell Hoban (*Frances*)	H.A. Rey (*Curious George*)
Arnold Lobel (*Frog and Toad*)	David Wiesner
David McPhail	

Your local children's librarian can help you find many more books that your preschooler will love.

It also will help you nurture a love of reading in your child if you show her that you enjoy books, too. Your preschooler will be pleased to know that books are both fun and useful in the adult world, too. So read books for your own pleasure and/or use "adult" books (encyclopedias and other references) to help answer questions that she may pose.

Now I Know My ABCs (and Numbers, Too)

Reading often with your child will help him become familiar with the letters of the alphabet. And though you certainly don't need to put pressure on your three-year-old to begin reading, you can begin paving the way by teaching him the alphabet. So point out certain simple words as you read to your child—especially a word that will come up often in a particular book. Spell your child's name for him. And show him that the differently shaped letters correspond to certain sounds.

Take every opportunity to familiarize your child with numbers, too. Again, you don't need to teach him advanced calculus—or even basic arithmetic. But count with him while reading, cooking, eating, in the bath, dressing. How many dogs are on that page of *Go, Dog, Go*? How many eggs are you going to scramble for breakfast? How many pieces of hot dog does he have left on his plate? How many buttons are on his shirt?

Don't just teach your child a rote list of numbers to memorize. Mere counting for the sake of counting ("one, two, three, four….") will mean nothing to your preschooler. It won't teach him a thing about what numbers are and what they do. In fact, it's not really even counting, because counting involves finding out the number of some objects that you see.

After he grasps what numbers are, your child will soon move beyond just counting. He'll begin doing arithmetic: adding three books to two others, subtracting (taking away) one cookie from his pile of four, and even dividing his trains (three for you and three for me). And that's not only exciting for him; it's exciting for you, too.

All the World's a Stage

Your three-year-old will engage in more and more elaborate imaginative play. She will whip up entire make-believe scenarios with characters and events in abundance. Tricycles become cars, ambulances, motorcycles, and fire engines—complete with the appropriate noises. Simple cardboard boxes become cars, boats, trains, houses, tunnels, caves, puppet theaters, and castles. She will love it if you help her construct tents and playhouses by draping blankets over chairs or tables.

When your child gets together with one or more three-year-olds, chances are that they'll spend at least some of their time playing house: whipping up meals, putting the "baby" to bed, and so on. Playing house allows every child to play roles that they've observed a lot over the years. It also gives them a chance to rehearse social interaction in a cooperative way, practice that will enhance their building of "real" friendships outside the playhouse.

Q-Tip

Dressing up will enhance your child's fantasy play, but lots of fancy costumes, although fun, are not really necessary for an imaginative preschooler. Props are much more essential to her imaginative play. A fully equipped play kitchen, for example, or just some old pots and pans and cooking utensils that you seldom use for "real" cooking anymore, will probably get a lot of use this year.

Q-Tip

You can use the eagerness to play new roles to help your child express emotions. Take turns acting out the parts of a tired old man, a hungry baby, or a happy puppy. Role-playing that specifically encourages emotional expression helps your child use her body to better understand her own feelings (and the feelings of others). Through play, emotions can become more familiar—and safer.

In her play acting, your preschooler will imitate adult behavior, but you will notice a difference between this and her fantasy play at age two. Your child is no longer merely mimicking adults, but rather role-playing: inhabiting a persona and making it real. Play acting now is not just a matter of having the right props (although that is important), but of assuming the right attitude and saying the right words.

Most of your child's make-believe games will not require you to participate (or even listen). Indeed, it will probably expand your child's imagination more if you allow her to make up her own scenarios rather than offering your input. Let your preschooler create her own private world. If your child invites you to play a role, by all means join in. But take the role assigned to you and let your child control the unfolding of the plot.

Imaginative play also can help your preschooler sort out various anxieties or cope with approaching (or past) events that worry her. You may notice your child playing a lot of doctor games leading up to (or following) a stay in the hospital, for example. Or she may play more at being a parent in the wake of a new baby's arrival.

A word about war games: Most preschoolers do play such games no matter how much their parents try to dissuade them. By all means don't buy toy guns or war toys if they make you uncomfortable. But it's hard to get away from the violence in our society and culture. So don't be surprised if you see your child using a stick to "shoot" or "stab" or engage in "swordplay." Instead of wasting your energy in an attempt to ban certain games or toys, concentrate on teaching your child the value of nonviolence in reality. (Yes, your child does recognize a difference between fantasy and reality.)

Let's Get Physical

Physical play provides an important way for your child to test his limits. Activities such as climbing ladders, learning how to coordinate his body to get the swing going by himself (or keep it going once you get him started), and just running helter skelter will all help develop your preschooler's balance, strength, and agility. And as a bonus, physical play will help your child release some of his overabundant energy.

You can encourage the development of your child's muscles, coordination, and balance with games like hopscotch, Simon Says, follow the leader, and musical chairs—or just by jumping rope or holding hands with your child and each hopping on one foot. A backyard "playground" or the nearest public playground—complete with swings, slides, seesaws, and climbing apparatus—will boost your preschooler's confidence in his physical abilities and also provide lots of fun. And if you're planning on getting your child a tricycle, get it now. Even if at first your three-year-old only pushes along the ground with his feet instead of using the pedals, riding a tricycle will strengthen his calf muscles and build his confidence.

> **Childproofing**
> Obesity among children in the U.S. is on the rise. Especially if he watches a lot of television, your pre-schooler may have stopped running around like crazy. So turn the TV off once in a while and encourage your child to remain active by playing soccer, catch, or tag. Or explore creative movement—dancing or pretending to be various animals, trees, or clouds. Both of you will be healthier for it.

> **Childproofing**
> Make sure that any tricycle you buy for your child is the right size. This means that your preschooler should be able to remain in the seat and still reach the pedals (if and when he finally decides he wants to use them).

Art for Art's Sake

At around three, your child's artistic skills may improve dramatically. As your preschooler refines her hand-eye coordination and her artistry, her drawings may become more and more recognizable. She will probably still find it much easier to draw vertical lines than horizontal ones. But by now, your child may be able to make the ends meet to produce a closed circle—or at least an oval—with a crayon. After that, your preschooler will begin to notice that different strokes produce different lines and shapes.

A new artistic skill that your three-year-old will love practicing is cutting with scissors (safety scissors, of course). At first, your child will only cut a series of short snips to make a fringe on the edges of paper. But by the end of the year, she will be able to cut through an entire sheet of paper. So if she has access to scissors, make sure that your child has plenty of construction paper, old magazines, or scrap paper to cut. Otherwise you'll find snips taken out of new magazines, mail, the morning newspaper, telephone books, and so on.

Your preschooler will take great pride in making things by cutting, drawing, and painting. For a three-year-old, satisfaction comes simply by making something, anything, that

Q-Tip

Provide as much variety in art materials as you can afford. Also keep an eye out for throwaways that you can save and recycle as art materials. Your child can make creative use of paper towel tubes, empty egg cartons, and many other containers.

Childproofing

Remember the rules of scissor safety from when you were a child? They actually made a lot of sense. So don't let your child run with scissors. Teach your child to carry them closed, with the points down. Store them well out of reach and closely supervise any cutting activities. Otherwise, your child may injure herself— or at the very least give herself an entirely new hairstyle.

she herself has conceived. Don't force your child to define her creations by constantly asking, "What is it?" Your child may just be experimenting with various media and seeing what happens when she makes several different scissor-cuts in a piece of paper or perhaps exploring the varieties of line and color.

Try not to impose your own preconception on your preschooler's artwork. If your child proudly shows her art to you and you want to offer an encouraging word, try to talk only about what you see. Say things like:

➤ "You used a lot of blue in this drawing. I like blue, too."

➤ "I really like this swirl of lines down here."

➤ "Wow, you've covered every inch of the paper with color."

➤ "Gee, you're getting really good at cutting with those scissors."

This may come later in the year and will almost certainly come after she turns four. But if you suggest that your preschooler's art should represent something, you may unintentionally deflate the pride she feels in her work. And if your child actually did intend to represent something and you guess wrong, she may either feel that she let you down by not drawing what you suggested—or think you must be an idiot or a lunatic because you can't see what (to her eye) she has so clearly drawn.

The Least You Need to Know

➤ If your child attends preschool, find out exactly what he's doing there and try to provide complementary activities at home.

➤ Games allow your child to practice social skills (taking turns, winning and losing gracefully) and basic academic skills (counting, color recognition, vocabulary).

➤ If you refuse under any circumstances to "let" your child win, then play only games that give him an even chance to win.

➤ Bring storybooks to life for your child with dramatic readings.

➤ Avoid imposing your preconceptions about art on your child's creation of artwork.

Part 4

A Declaration of Independence: The Four-Year-Old

It's tough being a four-year-old. Your child is now bold and adventurous, but not yet big enough to cross the street by himself. A social creature, he wants to be cooperative and helpful, but he's still willful enough to be stubborn. He still could use a nap, but he's probably too wired all the time to take one. Your child is almost big enough for school now, but he still wants mama or daddy to stay close by.

For many parents, this is a tough year, too. You're excited that your child will soon be going out into the great big world, but you're not sure either of you is ready for it yet. You want to help him become more independent, but you're not sure you really want to give up control over him. You want to make this year a special one, but probably find your demanding, sometimes obnoxious child getting on your nerves.

You can—and will—make it through this year. If you can just help him find his own way—without actually getting in his way—you'll get along just fine.

Chapter 21

You Thought the Twos Were Terrible? Meet the Frightful, Fantastic Fours

In This Chapter

➤ The pros and cons of having a four-year-old in the house

➤ Channeling your preschooler's energy into physical activities

➤ Is your child hyperactive—even for a four-year-old?

➤ Your four-year-old's improving language skills

➤ Dealing with words of anger

Everyone's heard of the "terrible twos." And now that you've been through that year with your child, you know why two-year-olds got that reputation. Two is indeed a difficult year, marked by tantrums, the powerful discovery of the word "no," and repeated frustration over not knowing the right words to say or the right muscles to move. Yet because everyone anticipates trouble at age two, you probably found that the year wasn't nearly as terrible as you had expected it to be.

Not so with age four. Many parents find this age to be just as difficult as two, if not more so. Yet what makes it even worse is that it comes as a complete surprise: Four-year-olds don't come with an appropriate warning label. But they should.

Certainly not all four-year-olds are alike. With every year, your child becomes more of an individual and the developmental paths of different preschoolers begin to diverge sharply. Yet many parents do find four-year-olds difficult, and here's why.

At four, your child will probably display flashes of stubbornness and belligerence. While at three, your child almost always wanted to be helpful and cooperative, this year she may often be uncooperative, sassy, and perhaps even obnoxious. Misbehavior may increase. Your four-year-old will do little to conceal her misbehavior. But if you don't see what she's up to, your child may begin to add a new wrinkle after the fact: Covering up her misbehavior, refusing to admit it, or even lying about it.

At four, your child desperately wants to be grown up. She wants to be able to do what the big kids do—and what adults do, too. That's the source of much of the difficulty that you both will face this year. Your child, fiercely convinced that she knows how to do everything, will often resist your assistance, your suggestions, and your rules. She may become defiant and argumentative with you, your partner, siblings, and friends. She may demonstrate more impatience with others as well as herself, more selfishness, and even more violence than she did during her first four years.

The Good News

Although all of these aspects of your preschooler's personality add up to a difficult year, the pluses still outweigh the minuses (at least most of the time). Your four-year-old will be bold, exuberant, and full of life. He craves adventures and may be eager to go someplace or do something new. A real social butterfly now, he is likely to be outgoing and even polite (for the most part)—especially with other children that he's meeting for the first time. You and your child will laugh a lot this year, because your child will be silly and playful. Easily excitable, he won't have much interest in sitting down, at least not for very long. Four is a noisy age—but it can also be lots of fun.

Baby Talk
"Having children is like having a bowling alley installed in your brain."—Martin Mull

Your preschooler's sense of self expands dramatically this year. He will become much more independent and perhaps a little more self-centered. He clearly recognizes other children as other children now, rather than mere extensions of himself.

As a result, your child may put extra effort into trying to impress other children. Your preschooler will be eager to show off his talents and demonstrate his daring in front of his friends. You will probably overhear a great deal of boasting and bragging when your child plays with friends. You may even hear him boasting about how great you are. (Of course, just because your child, like most four-year-olds, feels proud of his parents doesn't necessarily mean he'll be any more compliant with you.)

Just as he did at age three, your four-year-old will enjoy feeling useful. A sense of his own worth is an important component of your child's rapidly growing ego. Your preschooler will enthusiastically welcome almost any independent responsibilities that you ask him to perform. He will gladly help out with some of your daily routines if you ask him—and he may even offer without prompting.

Q-Tip
Adding to your child's responsibilities in little ways helps to build his overall confidence. You might, for instance, give him small pitchers so that he can pour his own juice or pour milk on his cereal (after first practicing in the tub). If he spills a little—or even a lot—don't make a big deal of it. Just offer him a sponge and teach him how to clean it up.

The Active Life

Your four-year-old is no doubt active and energetic. She probably enjoys physical games and activities that involve a fast and frenetic pace. She runs fast, jumps, hops, and climbs to nerve-shattering heights with abandon (nerve-shattering for you, not for her). Your child has developed a great deal of coordination by now. She can walk in a straight line on the "balance beam" (which we adults call the roadside curb). She can race down a flight of stairs, landing with just one foot per step rather than leading with one foot and then following with the other. She can alternate feet in jumping rope. She can carry an open cup of water or juice without spilling it (most of the time, anyway). She may even be able to master the difficult art of skipping—or to move up from a tricycle to a bicycle (with training wheels, of course).

You can help put this new coordination to increasingly sophisticated use. If your child hasn't yet learned how to swim, her new coordination makes four a great age to start. You also can teach her how to jump rope. Another challenging physical activity you might want to introduce this year is roller skating.

Dance classes also are great fun at age four—for boys as well as girls. Dance classes give your child the chance to practice and perfect a variety of physical

Childproofing
Don't start your four-year-old out on roller blades—yet. Buy your child a pair "starter skates." Most have three settings: locked (the wheels won't turn at all), forward (the wheels will only roll forward), and full (the wheels roll at will). Start with the easiest setting and only switch to the next level after your child has mastered and become comfortable with the previous one.

skills (balance, movement, rhythm, and coordination) and also provide a terrific social opportunity. Other classes or activities that encourage both physical and social development include:

➤ Gymnastics

➤ Martial arts

➤ Soccer

➤ Horseback riding

If your child seems less coordinated than other children her age, offer some pointers. Show her how to climb a ladder safely or how to set her feet for the landing at the bottom of the slide. Teach her how to kick a soccer ball or throw a baseball or football. Consider enrolling her in one of the classes previously suggested. (Your town or city recreation department may sponsor preschool programs at low cost.) Activities like these will help her to put a variety of muscles to work, strengthen her muscles, and let her practice coordinating muscle movements.

Besides seeing improved coordination and balance as well as greater strength, speed, and overall agility, you will notice considerable refinement in your child's fine motor skills, too. Actions that mystified her less than a year ago will seem easy to your four-year-old—especially if you encourage her to practice these skills. At four, your child can probably button her own shirts and manage zippers (though she might need help getting started). She can pour cereal, milk, juice, and syrup if the containers aren't too heavy. She can cut skillfully and precisely with scissors and string beads no matter how small they are.

How Much Activity Is Too Much?

Almost all four-year-olds run around like crazy. They jump on beds and couches, throw themselves around like rag dolls, and literally bounce off the walls. They have an apparently endless supply of energy and exuberance. And they are very, very loud!

So just because your child can't sit still for more than a minute without jumping up and racing off somewhere (few four-year-olds can), don't jump to the conclusion that he must be hyperactive. In all likelihood, he's behaving perfectly normally for his age. Although rarely diagnosed before elementary school, Attention Deficit Hyperactivity Disorder (ADHD) is one of the fastest-growing diagnoses in American pediatrics today. But in the rush to label and treat genuine cases of ADHD among America's children, the disorder is now probably overdiagnosed.

Certainly, if you have genuine concerns about your child's "hyperactivity" and short attention span, you should consult your pediatrician. But unless your child finds himself unable to attend to *any* task, even one that he finds engaging, he almost definitely doesn't have ADHD. So before rushing to the doctor to see whether your preschooler has ADHD, first try to provide him with plenty of opportunities for active play (preferably outdoors): running, jumping, climbing, chasing, riding tricycles or pedal cars, circle games, tag, follow the leader, and general physical silliness.

Also try to orchestrate activities that involve shouting, screaming, and general loudness. Your preschooler may seem unusually fidgety only because he hasn't been given an outlet for all of his energy. Regular opportunities for physical release—shaking his sillies out—may make it easier for your child to enjoy quiet times, too. Who knows? You may even find some quiet time yourself.

Baby Talk
"Tomorrow, he knew...

...All the Who girls and boys

Would wake bright and early. They'd rush for their toys!

And then! Oh, the noise! Oh, the Noise! Noise! Noise! Noise!

That's one thing he hated! The NOISE! NOISE! NOISE! NOISE!"—Dr. Seuss

Q-Tip
Designate a space (outside or a particular room in the house, for example) where the "sillies" and unrestricted physical activity can be allowed without fear of breaking anything.

Down Time

At around four years old, your child may begin showing more resistance to settling down at naptime. Remember that sleep needs for all children, preschoolers included, vary widely. Your four-year-old may be one of those nightmarish creatures who actually don't need a nap in the middle of the day. If you insist that she take a nap anyway, you may undo all the work you've done to make your child's bed and bedroom an enjoyable place for her to be. And this may end up disrupting nighttime sleep routines as well. Unfortunately, if you cut naptime out of your preschooler's schedule entirely, you may end up with a tired, cranky, and accident-prone child all afternoon.

If naptime becomes increasingly difficult, work out a compromise. Your four-year-old may not want or need a nap, but she certainly still needs a rest. The nonstop outpouring of energy throughout the rest of the day makes it essential (for both of you) that she have some downtime, too.

Q-Tip

Your four-year-old may be much more willing to go along with the continuation of the naptime routine if you change the name of naptime to "quiet time."

So continue with your naptime routine (reading a story or otherwise helping her to calm down). Then pop in a 15- or 20-minute tape—or set a kitchen timer or clock-radio for 15 to 20 minutes—and tell your child that if she's still awake after that, she can engage in some quiet activities. Be sure to leave extra books, more music, puzzles, or other quiet toys where your preschooler can get them easily. If your child does end up giving up on her nap, try to make sure that she gets at least another 45 minutes of quiet time.

Watch Your Language

Talk, talk, talk. Your four-year-old has so much to say, so much to tell you (or almost anyone else who's willing to listen) that he's likely to be a chatterbox. He will tell and retell stories about his day or about memorable events from his past or about entirely imagined scenarios. Bragging is common at age four—or if not bragging, at least the attention-getting, "Look what I did."

And the questions. Your preschooler will ask endless questions, not just because he's curious (and he is), but just because he enjoys talking so much. Your four-year-old literally loves to hear the sound of his own voice. When your child's "whys" string on endlessly, it will sometimes be glaringly obvious that he's not as much interested in the knowledge and information you can impart as in just keeping the conversation going as long as possible:

➤ "Why does the elephant have such big ears?"

"Because they allow it to fan itself when it gets hot."

➤ "It's not hot here. Why does it have big ears if it's not hot?"

"Because it's hot in Africa and India. That's where elephants come from."

➤ "Why is it hot in Africa and India?"

"Because they're both near the Equator."

➤ "What's the Equator?"

"That's the circle that goes around the world in the middle."

➤ "Why is it hot there?"

"Because the Sun is closer to the Equator than any other place on Earth for the whole year round."

➤ "Why?"

Q-Tip
Don't feel as if you have to have all the answers to your preschooler's questions. If you don't know the answer, then say so—or better yet, say, "Let's find out." Then follow up by consulting an appropriate resource (a book, a video, or another person).

At this point, you may be ready to tear your hair out. But look at all the information you can offer in just such a brief conversation. And even if sometimes he's just talking to talk, at other times your child really does want to know the answers to his questions. So try to give him the benefit of the doubt. Until you've answered at least half a dozen or more "why" questions in a row, try to have patience and indulge his curiosity.

At age four, your child will direct her words even more toward other children (whenever they're around) than toward you. You will overhear both your preschooler and his friends whispering secrets, providing "useful" information, and issuing orders to one another. You may even hear them issuing threats to one another.

Your child also may begin talking to imaginary friends at this age. (After all, your four-year-old needs an audience. Other children aren't always around and you can only listen to so much yourself.) You may, for instance, hear your four-year-old "reading" books to his imaginary friends—or to his dolls or stuffed animals. You also may hear your child scolding his imaginary friends, dolls, animals, or even himself in tones and terms you recognize as your own. (See? He was listening.)

Favorite Words

Your four-year-old actually needs to talk a lot. Though she's become much more fluent in her use of language, your preschooler is still practicing with different sounds and words. During this year, she'll probably love words that exaggerate: enormous, tremendous, and emergency, for example.

Your child also will begin to pick up slang this year, including some "swear words" and mild "bathroom humor." Try not to appear shocked or scold or punish your child when she uses these words. Keep in mind that your preschooler is merely fooling around with

Q-Tip

If your child's swearing or "potty talk" bothers you, try offering a silly sounding substitute. Respond to her curses by making up a word that you'd prefer your child to say. Your preschooler will love it if you say something like, "You zoobaloo!"

vocal sounds and new language. If you ignore—or at least avoid overreacting—to her experiments with "impolite" words, she will probably lose interest in them after a while. (Of course, other children may reinforce her use of these words through their reactions.)

Your four-year-old may begin to love wordplay of all kinds. Of course, she's loved silly sounding words and made-up words for more than a year now. But now she will begin to laugh at puns and riddles (sometimes whether she gets the joke or not). She will play with rhyming words. She may even begin to appreciate the more sophisticated wordplay of Spoonerisms, in which you exchange the initial sounds of two adjacent words (for example, "brazen red" for "raisin bread"). Encourage your child to play with nonsense words and chants. If she can have fun with words, it will help build a love of language.

Kid Stuff

When Robert was four, he went on a Spoonerism kick. For days, he would spin out an endless stream of Spoonerisms (which his two-year-old sister Erica would then of course echo). "I want dot hogs (hot dogs)." "This is hi mouse (my house)." "Let's go to my red boom (bed room)."

One afternoon, Robert and Erica and their mother were heading into a department store when a fire truck drove through the parking lot. Robert instantly started chanting the Spoonerism for fire truck (which we won't print here) at the top of his lungs—with Erica quickly joining in. Despite her embarrassment, their mother recognized that they weren't trying to offend anyone. So she didn't try to silence them. But she did quickly steer them to other Spoonerisms ("copping sharts," "bum galls," and "gooing chum") to get them to take up a new chant.

Besides playing with words, your preschooler may begin to use them to talk about increasingly abstract ideas. Your child may, for instance, explore aloud her ideas about God, about love in general, about truth, about death, and so on. If she does, your four-year-old will want—and deserve—to be taken seriously.

Try to avoid laughing at her ideas or the way she expresses them. Don't be embarrassed if she says something in public you'd never say. And avoid quoting your child in a patronizing or even amused way within her earshot. (Of course, you will want to share some of these treasures—but be sensitive to your child's feelings.) Though her ideas—or the funny way she says them—may be amusing to you, your child is probably dead serious. So try to respond in kind—or you may inhibit her from speaking her mind and sharing her thoughts in the future.

Them's Fighting Words

Your preschooler's increasing facility with language will enable him to express anger and frustration—and, of course, happiness, excitement, sadness, disappointment, and so on—in words as well as actions. Though your child's physical aggression may diminish somewhat, verbal aggression will not yet replace it so much as provide a complementary alternative. Your child will still hit, kick, and bite—but now he can yell or scream at someone, too.

It's important at this age for your child to begin to understand that words have a limited power. Although your four-year-old will repeatedly explore and test the power of words, he probably doesn't understand their limits yet. So in the wake of one of his verbal barrages, you may need to reassure your child—and if he has directed his verbal attack at another child, his victim—that threats are only words. He needs to learn that though angry thoughts and harsh words can be powerful, they do not have the power to make themselves come true.

Similarly, you need to help your preschooler begin to understand that after he has hurt someone, simply saying, "I'm sorry," does not have the power to make everything right again. Though a good sign of wanting to get back in the good graces of someone he has hurt, apologizing in itself cannot always repair the damage.

You might want to introduce your four-year-old to the idea of making a conciliatory gesture. Offering something of value—sharing a favorite toy or giving up the last piece of candy, for example—can be a good way of showing how sorry he is.

Besides making an apology and some sort of gesture of reconciliation after hurting someone, your child also will need to resolve to try not to do it again. He'll need your help with this. Offer your child

> **Q-Tip**
> Try not to discourage your child from expressing his anger in words even if he goes overboard most of the time. It marks a developmental leap when he can start threatening you (or even another child) or calling you names instead of hitting or biting you. (If angry words merely serve as a prelude or accompaniment to violence, then your child needs a time out to cool down.)

alternatives to hitting, biting, or kicking someone who makes him angry: using words to express his anger, punching a pillow, and so on.

After your child grows more accustomed to expressing aggression, anger, and frustration in words, you may want to teach him more "appropriate" words to use. You can let your child know, for instance, that calling people nasty names and saying mean things about them do hurt—sometimes even more than a punch.

Build on your preschooler's growing empathy by asking him how he would feel if someone called him that name or said that mean thing about him. Then encourage him instead to concentrate on saying how *he* feels. Offer him words and phrases he may need to express his emotions:

➤ "That makes me so mad!"

➤ "Stop! That hurts and I don't like it!"

➤ "That's not fair!"

➤ "I'm so mad I could bite you!" (Even this is preferable to an actual bite.)

Keep in mind that emotions are extremely intense for a four-year-old. Your child loves and hates with great passion—and his feelings may change without a moment's notice. Though harsh words may seem rude or abrasive, your preschooler's use of them when he's in the grip of a powerful emotion actually demonstrates a great deal of self-control. So try not to be offended by his words. Instead, acknowledge your child's anger or frustration and commend him for expressing his emotion through words rather than through acts of violence. Now if only he could do it more often? (Don't worry. With your encouragement, he will.)

The Least You Need to Know

➤ Classes in athletics or movement provide your child with an outlet for her energy, a challenge to improve her physical coordination, and a social opportunity. Take advantage of them.

➤ Antsiness and boundless energy do not necessarily indicate hyperactivity in a four-year-old.

➤ Even if your child gives up on naptime, she'll still need quiet time or downtime.

➤ Try to answer as many of your child's questions as you can. Be patient and play along, even if you suspect that he's just trying to keep the conversation going.

➤ Don't discourage your child from using words aggressively—at least at this age. Harsh words provide a useful substitute for physical aggression.

Chapter 22

Safety First!

In This Chapter

➤ Teaching and explaining safety rules to your four-year-old

➤ The development of your child's conscience

➤ How to keep your child out of the street and safe on the playground

➤ How to keep your child safe from "strangers"

➤ How to keep your child safe from threats closer to home

Guarding your child's safety is your fundamental duty as a parent. If you don't protect your child's safety, the other joys and duties of parenting will matter little. Educational play, teaching responsibility, introducing moral values, all come second to keeping your child safe.

During the preschool years, you might think that you can relax some of your vigilance. And you can—but only to the extent that your child learns to avoid dangerous situations on her own. You are still ultimately responsible for your child's safety. But now, your child can begin to learn and absorb some steps that she can take to remain safe.

It's a Bird, It's a Plane... It's Superego!

Four is the age when conscience begins to develop (also see Chapter 23). When your child was younger, she did the right thing primarily because that's what you told her to do and she wanted to please you. You said not to cross the street without holding a grown-up's hand. So whenever she remembered what you said, she waited at the curb (most of the time). You told your child not to stick anything in the electrical outlet, so (hopefully) she didn't.

At four, your child still will stay safe because she wants to please you, but more indirectly. Your child will begin to absorb your safety rules and make them her own. This means that you probably don't need to tell her what to do as often or as urgently. She'll know what to do—and most of the time, she'll do it.

Going Over the Rules

When you teach safety rules to your preschooler, it will help if you provide clear reasons for the rule. "Because I said so" may win some degree of compliance, but will not convince your child to make it his own rule, too. Try to help your four-year-old understand that these rules are not intended to spoil his fun, only to keep him safe. The more fair and reasonable your rules seem to your child, the more likely he is to adhere to them and adopt them as his own.

Try to avoid resorting to scare tactics. The reason you don't want your child to climb to the top of the jungle gym is not "because you'll fall down and break your neck and die." It's that "if you do fall, you'll get hurt." If you overexaggerate possible dangers, one (or both) of two things will happen:

➤ You will lose your credibility. Your child will dismiss your rule because at some level he recognizes the unlikelihood of what you're saying.

➤ Your child will accept what you say, but grow up believing that the world is a scary place, with deadly dangers lurking everywhere.

When your preschooler disobeys your safety rules, you need to make him see that unsafe behavior has consequences. If your child runs out into the street you should immediately pull him back off the street, repeat your rule, explain your rationale (that drivers in cars may not be able to see him), and warn him not to do it again.

One warning is all you should issue. If your child then repeats the unsafe behavior, you'll need to enforce strict consequences. Whenever possible, try to make the consequence related to the unsafe behavior. In the example here, for instance, you might make him come inside right away. Help him make the connection between his action and the consequences. "I told you that you cannot run in the street. It's not safe. If you can't play outside safely, then you can't play outside."

If you teach your safety rules, if they seem fair and reasonable to your child, and if he recognizes that they are intended not to be mean to him, but to keep him safe, then he will probably be eager to obey them—and even adopt them as his own rules. What begins as obedience, in an attempt to please you, will gradually become identification with you and your rules, a critical part of his developing conscience.

Baby Talk
"Childhood is never troubled with foresight..."
—Fanny Burney

The Voice of Conscience

Keeping your preschooler safe requires more than just knowing the rules. Your child also needs to develop and trust her own instincts regarding what's safe and what's not. With your help, she needs to cultivate her own inner voice that warns her of possible danger. This voice keeps your child from climbing into a stranger's car or walking along the edge of a river. So teach your child to trust her instincts. Whenever she hears this voice, she needs to heed its warnings.

Safety Rehearsal

One way to hone your child's self-protective instincts is to rehearse safety situations with her. Use scenarios that allow you to turn these safety rehearsals into a game. Try to mix in some easy safety problems with the more challenging ones that you really want your child to master:

➤ What would you do if someone you didn't know came to your day care and told you to go home with him?

➤ What would you do if your ball rolled out into the street?

➤ What would you do if you couldn't find me in the supermarket?

➤ What would you do if you saw a three-year-old fall off the jungle gym?

➤ What would you do if another child sat at the top of the slide and refused to go down?

➤ What would you do if you dropped a glass of juice and the glass broke?

➤ What would you do if a friend asked you to do something you thought was unsafe?

➤ What would you do if the smoke detectors in your house went off?

If your child seems stumped for an answer, offer a suggestion—or allow your child to choose from two or three alternatives that you provide. Don't be surprised if your preschooler comes up with some wild answers:

➤ "I'd smear peanut butter on the man so he'd get all sticky and couldn't catch me!"

➤ "I'd wait for a car to kick the ball back to me!"

➤ "I'd put candy at the bottom of the slide so the child would come down."

Try not to laugh at your child's safety solution. She's probably not trying to be funny. Instead commend her for her ingenuity, offer a better alternative, and then ask the same question again the next time you play the game with her.

Accidents Will Happen

Of course, you want to keep your child safe from all harm. But the only way you can keep your child completely safe from any and all accidents is to lock him in a padded room and then cling to him whenever you take him out. So try not to make too much of a fuss and overprotect your child from testing his physical limits and learning from experience.

Baby Talk
"My father had always said that there are four things a child needs—plenty of love, nourishing food, regular sleep, and lots of soap and water—and after those, what he needs most is some intelligent neglect."
—Ivy Baker Priest

Accidents can help to make your preschooler wary of risky or dangerous situations. As long as they're not too serious, accidents help increase your preschooler's safety instincts. In addition, accidents further his understanding of his body and his abilities, which in the long run may lead to fewer accidents. So instead of aiming to prevent all accidents, the minor bumps and bruises of every preschooler's life, focus your safety efforts on protecting your child from serious accidents.

Playing Hard, Playing Fast

At the playground, your preschooler is safest when playing alone. She tests her physical limits, but for the most part stays within them. So let your four-year-old set her own challenges and try not to worry too much about her when she's playing by herself. Chances are, your child won't do anything that she really thinks is unsafe. She'll undoubtedly get hurt once in a while. But every challenge successfully mastered will build muscles, increase balance and self-confidence, and help your preschooler avoid further accidents in the future.

When your child is playing with other children, however, you probably need to be more vigilant. Many preschoolers will do anything to avoid being considered a "baby" by their peers. Other kids can talk your child (or your child can talk other kids) into unsafe behavior. So keep an eye out and don't let other kids dare your four-year-old into doing something she wouldn't normally do on her own (and vice versa). You may need to remind your preschooler and her friends that foolish daring is not the same as bravery.

You need to keep an especially keen watch if your preschooler is playing with older children. Older children may be even more likely to talk your child into accepting a challenge she's not capable of doing—just for the "fun" of seeing what they can talk her into doing. Even if older children don't tease or dare your child, they can unwittingly prompt foolish disregard for your child's safety. Your four-year-old is a mimic by nature. She may try to imitate the daring exploits of older children that she sees.

> **Childproofing**
> Pay special attention to ensure playground safety when your child is tired. Fatigue will make her more likely to have accidents. What's worse, because it will dull her safety instincts, fatigue also will make your preschooler more likely to take more dangerous risks as her frustration mounts.

Danger Is My Middle Name

What should you do if your child seems reckless? What if he seems to lack that inner voice that warns of danger? What if he doesn't have the sense to avoid risky adventures? Some preschoolers consistently climb too high, ride too fast, and jump too far. As a result, you will constantly be tending to scraped knees, bruised arms and foreheads, and perhaps even broken bones.

A reckless preschooler obviously still needs your help in setting limits. Try to devise interesting and fun physical challenges for him that are safe (like an obstacle course). At the same time, you'll need to continue to impose reasonable and consistent limits on the challenges he comes up with—just as you did when he was a toddler. As long as your limits remain reasonable and consistent, your child will likely accept them (perhaps even with some relief). In time, the development of your child's self-protective instincts may cause him to give up such reckless acts.

> **Childproofing**
> Never applaud your preschooler's exploits—even if he successfully completes his mission—if you regard them as dangerous. Your apparent approval will be taken as encouragement. If he escapes a stunt unscathed, let him know that you think he was lucky, not skillful, and that his daring was not brave, but foolish.

Street Smarts

You know that the street is a dangerous place for your preschooler to play. By now, she should know it, too. Drivers often cannot see small children over the hood of their cars—especially if children run out from between cars parked on the side of the road. And your preschooler cannot yet judge how fast a car is coming—or if it's a safe distance away.

Fortunately, many preschoolers who know about the dangers of cars are actually overcautious about crossing the street. If you've been stressing street safety since your child was a toddler, she probably won't step into the street if she sees a moving car anywhere within a mile of her.

Make sure that your preschooler knows to stay out of the street at all times and in all situations when she's not given permission by a responsible adult. By age four, your child's inner warning bells should go off whenever she gets within about six inches of the curb. If a ball, a Frisbee, or a Skydancer goes into the street while your preschooler is playing with it, her response should be automatic: Rather than running out into the street after it, she needs to call you to fetch it (and you need to come willingly).

Childproofing

Your child should still be strapped into a car seat, booster seat or buckled into a shoulder harness and seat belt whenever you go anywhere in a car. (You should be a good role model by wearing a seat belt yourself.) In addition, because the front passenger seat statistically suffers the worst damage in a car accident—and because the force of inflating passenger-side airbags has been known to kill small children—your preschooler should sit in the back seat whenever possible.

By age four, your child may balk at holding your hand while crossing the street. And as long as you have checked to make sure it's safe, your child can cross the street by herself. But no matter how much she wants to assert her independence at this age, you must never allow her to cross the street without your okay. You cannot depend on your four-year-old to check all ways before crossing the street. By all means, encourage your preschooler to look both ways (or all ways if she's anywhere near an intersection). It's a good idea to begin forming this habit now. But your child needs to understand that even after she checks, she has to wait for your okay before stepping into the street.

Your Worst Nightmare

One of the most troublesome safety concerns for parents is the issue of dealing with strangers. You certainly don't want to quash your child's friendliness if he is naturally outgoing. Nor do you want to terrorize your child, making him paranoid and scared of everyone by dwelling on such unpleasant possibilities as kidnapping, rape, and murder. Such horror stories make the evening news, but are thankfully uncommon.

As a preschooler, your child doesn't need to know the graphic and horrifying details that make you want to protect him against strangers. Your nightmares need not—and indeed should not—become his nightmares. Fortunately, you don't need to frighten your child to keep him safe. All he needs to know and follow is one fundamental rule:

> You (or whoever is entrusted with his care) need to know where he is at every moment.

266

Your child will appreciate the simplicity and reciprocity of this arrangement. After all, he probably always wants to know where you are (even if it's just in your bedroom or in the bathroom). So why wouldn't you feel exactly the same way about him?

Make sure that your child knows that this rule is absolute and unbreakable. If your neighbors want to take him out to the movies with their children, your child has to call or come home and ask you first. If he wants to look at the coloring books at the local drugstore while you pick out some Band-Aids, you need to know it first. Even if he just wants to go outside to play in the yard, your child needs to let you know. This simple rule, if strictly observed, will keep your child safe from other people.

Never (?) Talk to Strangers

On TV, Barney the dinosaur warns children, "Never talk to strangers!" But this tuneful advice is not only paranoid, but not very practical either. To your child, virtually everyone she meets is a stranger, at least at first: day-care providers and teachers, babysitters, the grocery store clerk, the bank teller, doctors and nurses and dentists, the mail carrier, even police officers. Most of them are probably friendly and kindly disposed toward children. "Never" is too extreme. If you're there, your child is safe talking to almost anyone. And if you're not there, if you've somehow become separated, then your child will need help from a stranger.

To protect your child from dangerous strangers, you'll first need to make clear to her what you mean when you use the word, "stranger." A stranger is not:

➤ merely someone your child doesn't know (because your child doesn't know many people, including most of your friends);

➤ someone who looks strange or mean (because many strangers look nice and normal); or

➤ someone who doesn't know your child's name (because strangers may overhear her name).

A stranger is anyone to whom your child has not been introduced by you (or your child's day-care provider, preschool teacher, or caregiver). After a responsible adult has introduced someone, that person is no longer a stranger.

Lost!

If your child is lost or separated from you, he will have no choice but to ask strangers for help. So if you have a hard and fast rule that forbids your child from talking to any strangers, he will be in quite a quandary.

> **Childproofing**
> Start to teach your child his phone number and address at an early age. By three, he should know, at the very least, his own full name and your full names. By three-and-a-half, he should have his address memorized, too. And by age four, your preschooler should know his phone number.

How will your preschooler know whom to ask? Again, rehearse the situation with your child before it happens. Teach him that when he absolutely must approach a stranger to ask for help, he should first look for uniforms. Your three- or four-year-old can probably tell the difference between a uniform and regular clothes. So your child should seek out someone in uniform: a police officer, a store security guard, a cashier, a waiter. This is the person to talk to if he's lost.

A Better Rule

"Never talk to strangers!" doesn't allow enough flexibility to be a viable rule for preschoolers. So what should you teach your child to keep her safe from other people? One simple rule:

> Never, ever go anywhere with a stranger (or for that matter, with a relative or friend) unless the people she knows and trusts best—that is, you or another of her caregivers—says it's okay.

Again, you or your child's caregiver needs to know where she is at all times.

Your child will remain safe as long as she observes this rule religiously. Make sure she understands that this is an absolute rule, and that she shouldn't listen to anyone who tries to persuade her to break this rule. (Indeed, she should notify you immediately if anyone does.) If she sticks to this rule, nobody—again, stranger, relative, or friend—will be able to lure your child into a car with promises of candy, ice cream, or a puppy, because she'll know she needs to ask permission first. No one can trick her into going away by saying that you're hurt or sick and need her, or that you're late and asked that person to pick her up from preschool, because she'll know that she must check with the babysitter or preschool teacher before going anywhere with anyone.

Just Say NO!

Unfortunately, your child may need to deal with dangers closer to home than strangers. The sad truth is that most forms of physical and sexual abuse are not inflicted by strangers, but by someone whom the abused child knows fairly well: parents, other relatives, friends of the family, neighbors. So you will need to teach your child to protect himself from the abuse of people he knows as well as from strangers.

The key to combating child abuse is to empower your child by giving him the right to say no. He needs to understand clearly that:

➤ His body is his own body and he has the right to keep it private.

➤ He has the right to refuse any kind of touch from another person.

➤ He has the right to say no to anyone who wants to keep something a "secret."

If he knows the names of all parts of the body, then you can clearly tell your child that no adult (or older child) other than a parent, doctor, or nurse has permission to touch his penis or bottom. (Of course, younger preschoolers may also need a caregiver or preschool teacher to help wipe them after using the toilet. Make sure that your child understands this exception to the rule.) You can also make it clear that no adult (or older child) has the right to force or ask your child to touch his penis or her vagina.

Emphasize your child's ownership over his own body. His body belongs to nobody else, not even to you. This means that he has the right to say no to any adult who wants to touch him in any way. Even if an uncomfortable touch seems accidental or the person who touches is a relative or someone whom your child trusts, he still has the right to say, "Don't touch me like that."

If you want your child to recognize, appreciate, and exercise his rights over his own body, you will have to respect those rights, too. Don't force physical signs of affection on your child. If you want a hug or a kiss, ask for one. But if he shies away or says no, as some preschoolers begin to do, respect that and back off a little. This same rule should of course be applied to all of your friends and relatives. When your sister comes to visit, you should never command your child, "Give your aunt a kiss." Rather, ask your child, "Do you want to give your aunt a kiss?" If he says no, don't apologize or make excuses. That's his right.

Finally, teach your child the difference between "good secrets" and "bad secrets." An adult who physically or sexually abuses a child will almost always insist that the child keep it a secret—and often threatens harm if he reveals it. So you'll need to give your child guidelines that let him know when to keep secrets—and when to tell them.

A good secret, one that's okay to keep, is usually exciting and fun (a birthday present, or a surprise party). A good secret almost always involves hiding knowledge from one or two special people for a short period of time (hardly ever longer than a month). But a bad secret probably won't make your child feel excited or happy. Instead, it feels like trouble—and

Childproofing
If you hit your child apologize as soon as possible. Explain that you lost your temper and admit that that's no excuse. Acknowledge that you have no right to hit him. Make it understood that you're sorry and will try never to do it again. If you hit your child regularly, seek professional help. The damage you're inflicting can hurt him for a long time.

Q-Tip
By age four, your child should know the names of most body parts. Many parents and teachers may be uncomfortable talking about genitalia, so preschoolers survey the body this way: "This is my head, neck, arms, hands, chest, stomach, legs, feet." What's missing? Your child needs to know that the penis, vagina, and bottom are parts of the body just like his arm or leg.

Q-Tip

Teach your child to distinguish between safe touch and unsafe touch: Safe touch (hugging, consoling, even mussing his hair) feels good. Unsafe touch (hitting, kicking, pinching, molesting) feels bad, uncomfortable, scary, or "funny" (weird).

Encourage your child to trust his instincts about which is which. Let your preschooler know that if he ever feels unsure he should come and ask you or another trusted adult.

no one is ever supposed to find out about it. This is the type of secret that your child should reveal to a responsible adult as soon as possible.

Your child needs to know that he can and should tell you or another trusted adult if anyone asks him to do something that makes him feel funny or uncomfortable or scared—or if anyone touches his genitalia. Encourage him to ask you about any adult behavior that confuses him or makes him uncomfortable. Most of all, your child needs to know that you'll listen to him if he does. So never punish him for revealing information to you. If you show that you are open to any and all questions and that you will listen if he tells you that something bad happened, then you'll go a long way toward protecting your preschooler from any potential abuse.

The Least You Need to Know

➤ Avoid using scare tactics to ensure compliance, but do explain the rationale behind your safety rules.

➤ Regularly rehearse situations in which your child may have to make safety decisions on her own.

➤ Focus on preventing serious accidents, not all accidents. Accidents that do little damage will teach your child about her body and increase her wariness of danger.

➤ To keep your child safe from abuse (from "friends" as well as strangers), teach one unbreakable rule: You or your child's caregiver MUST know where your child is at all times. Your child should therefore never go anywhere with anyone without coming to you for permission first.

➤ Teach your child that if she ever gets lost, she should look for someone in uniform to ask for help.

➤ Teach your child the differences between safe touch and unsafe touch and between good secrets and bad secrets. And let her know that when it comes to her body, she has a right to say no, even to an adult.

Do the Right Thing: Personal Responsibility

At one, your child depended on you to set limits, primarily designed to keep him safe from moment to moment. At two, he depended on you for control, for setting and enforcing rules that would keep him and others safe. At three, your child looked to you for discipline, for instruction not only on how to stay safe, but on fairness and consideration of others. Until now, in other words, you have played Jiminy Cricket to your child's Pinocchio. You have been your child's conscience, the voice in his ear that has told him how to behave.

...And Always Let Your Conscience Be Your Guide!

At four, it's time to begin moving from discipline to self-discipline. Now your child will begin to create his own conscience. Your preschooler will still depend on you to provide controls, limits, and rules, but as a four-year-old, he is now capable of absorbing and adopting your values and rules as his own.

Although still learning, your child now knows things he can do to keep safe and to get along well with others. Oh, he'll still need plenty of reminders. But at four he can apply the limits, moral lessons, and rules of behavior that you've taught him on his own.

In general, your preschooler now understands the concepts of right and wrong—though in particular situations he may become confused about which is which. (After all, he doesn't yet understand that the same action may be right in one situation but wrong in another setting.) He is now capable of choosing to do something because it's the right thing to do and not just to escape punishment. In short, your child is learning to control himself and take responsibility for his behavior. He is becoming self-disciplined.

Of course, your child still needs your discipline, too. Just because he can choose to do the right thing doesn't mean he always will. Temptations or sudden urges to break the rules often overcome your preschooler's conscience. For this reason, your child still needs you to remind him of rules and principles of moral behavior and to reinforce them in a consistent and evenhanded way.

I Know How You Feel

One of the keys to your preschooler's moral development is her growing capacity for empathy. As a toddler, your child was extremely egocentric. Whatever your toddler wanted to do she saw as the "right" thing to do. "Fairness" meant getting what she wanted. "Getting along with others" meant getting them to do what she wanted them to do.

But the preschool years mark your child's transition from egocentricity to empathy—or at least the potential for empathy. Your preschooler has probably become increasingly helpful and considerate of others over the last year. Of course, it's still a struggle for her. When forced to choose between her own self-interest and empathy, your four-year-old will still probably choose self-interest. Yet when her own self-interest is not threatened, your child may freely provide consideration and empathy to others.

You can help encourage the further development of your child's capacity for empathy by:

➤ Modeling helpfulness and empathy yourself.

➤ Paying attention to your child's feelings and encouraging her to talk about them. When you do, try to explore with your child what lies behind these feelings: why your child feels a certain way.

➤ Talking about your own feelings. Be honest and explain why you feel the way you do.

➤ Expressing concern for the feelings of others (including those of your child). If your child sees that you care about other's feelings, she will eventually absorb this same value.

➤ Citing empathy for or consideration of others as reasons for rules or moral decisions whenever you can. For example: "I know you want the last piece of cake, but Christopher will be sad if he doesn't get a piece."

➤ Making connections between your child's behavior and the feelings of others. Your preschooler won't always recognize how her behavior affects others. Clarify these connections for her. For example : "Did you see how the baby smiled when you gave her the rattle? That's her way of saying thank you." (For more on encouraging the development of empathy, see Chapter 17.)

➤ Emphasizing the Golden Rule: Treat others as you would want to be treated.

Model Behavior

The formation of conscience, which occurs during your child's fourth and fifth year, depends largely on identification with you and your rules. Your child wants to be like you. So he takes your values, rules, standards of conduct, and prohibitions and makes them his own. This becomes the foundation of your preschooler's growing conscience.

In trying to discern your values, standards, and rules, your child will not be listening to your words; he'll be watching every move you make. That's why modeling moral behavior yourself is so important to your child's moral development. Because inconsistency will confuse your child in his attempts to create a moral code, try to make your actions consistent with your words.

If you help him with projects, everyday tasks, and puzzles whenever he asks for your help, your preschooler is more likely to help you empty the wastebaskets or clean up his toys when you ask. If you treat your child with politeness and respect, he will gladly return the favor. And if he sees you trying to pass him off as a two-year-old to get into the zoo for free, he will not put a high premium on honesty.

> **Baby Talk**
> "Children have never been very good at listening to their elders, but they have never failed to imitate them. They must; they have no other models."—James Baldwin

Your preschooler also will look to you for clues on how to behave when he doesn't live up to his standards or goes against his conscience—in other words, how to handle guilt. So when you have done something wrong, admit it promptly and apologize. Admitting you have done wrong will not decrease your child's respect for you. Indeed, asking for forgiveness will actually increase his respect for you. It also will help him accept the fact that nobody (not even you) is perfect. Finally, it will demonstrate for your child how he should behave when he has done something wrong.

Judge, Jury, and Executioner

Another important element of your child's moral development, one that goes hand in hand with the growth of her conscience, is the onset of guilt feelings. You may be able to hear your child externalizing her guilt by scolding herself or her scapegoats: her dolls or stuffed animals. For instance, if your child spills some juice at a "tea party," you may hear her chastising or punishing her dolls (or herself). You may be surprised at how harshly your child speaks to her dolls on such occasions—certainly much more harshly than you would scold her.

In scolding or punishing herself or her animals or dolls, your child is clearly absorbing your rules and values and adopting them as her own. No matter how much your preschooler may rebel against your rules when you try to impose them on her, something is getting through to her.

As you can infer by listening to your child's harsh words of self-rebuke, preschoolers—confronting guilt for the first time—tend to feel too much guilt rather than too little. Be careful to watch your child for signs that she's going overboard, wracking herself with guilt for a relatively minor transgression.

Some preschoolers, for instance, punish themselves by pinching or biting themselves. If your child is being too hard on herself, she may need you to help let her off the hook.

Childproofing
Don't add to your child's overwhelming guilt feelings by referring to her as bad. Rather, label her behavior as bad (or good).

You can help your preschooler—and teach her—to relieve herself from overwhelming guilt feelings by suggesting appropriate ways to make amends. In some cases, encouraging your child to say, "I'm sorry" will be enough.

If you think your child needs to do more in a specific case, then help her come up with appropriate ways to show she's sorry. If she hits another preschooler and grabs her toy back from him, you might suggest (after a timeout, of course) that your child not only apologize, but give up the toy to her playmate for the rest of the afternoon.

At age four, most guilt comes after the fact. Occasionally, your child may anticipate guilty feelings (and possibly punishment) that will come if she does something that she knows you wouldn't sanction. This kind of guilt (or perhaps it's just fear of punishment) is very useful to your child's moral development, since it may stop her before she acts on her immediate urge. For perhaps the first time, your child may resist her urges, exercise self-control, and decide not to do something because it would be wrong.

> **Baby Talk**
> "Nature makes boys and girls lovely to look upon so they can be tolerated until they acquire some sense."
> —William Lyon Phelps

Moral Issues

During the preschool years, your child begins to identify with you and your rules and use this identification as the basis for his moral thinking: "I shouldn't do this because you wouldn't like it if I did." This represents a huge leap in moral thinking. It requires both:

➤ absorption or at least acknowledgment of your perspective on morality (a form of empathy); and

➤ anticipation of future consequences that will result from present acts.

Your preschooler's moral thinking is still probably simplistic. Moral issues must be clearly defined for him to understand them. Your child's thinking permits no moral ambiguities: An action is either right or wrong, good or bad. His conception of justice is also simplistic: Bad is always punished, while good is always rewarded.

In teaching your child how to think about moral issues, you will do well to appeal to his powerful sense of fairness. Your child's decision to do the right thing will often center on balancing his rights with the rights of others. This question of balancing rights is at the heart of such moral issues as:

➤ Whether to take turns when your child and another child want the same thing.

➤ Whether to take something because he wants it or not steal it because it belongs to someone else.

> **Q-Tip**
> Moral behavior involves not only avoiding the bad, but doing the good. So encourage your child to do good—to be kind and generous and considerate and to resolve conflicts peacefully—and praise him whenever he behaves this way. Be sure to issue moral instructions, as much as possible, in a positive light ("Do this") rather than a negative one ("Don't do that"). And define good behavior as specifically as possible. Avoid vague instructions like, "Be good," or "Behave yourself."

➤ Whether to hit someone when he's angry or respect the other person's right to safety and freedom from injury.

If you frame these as fairness issues, your child will probably distinguish right from wrong. (Of course, whether he'll actually do the right thing is another matter entirely.)

Don't expect your child to do something just because you "say so." Four-year-olds aren't inclined toward blind obedience. And although sometimes frustrating, your child's challenges to your authority will make him a better person. If your child obeys you just because you say so, he won't learn anything about moral principles or consideration of others. What's worse, if you fail to give him your reasons and then enforce obedience by punishing him for disobeying, you will raise a child whose moral sense is based almost entirely on fear. Though fear will sometimes keep your child in line, it also may prompt him to become deceitful, sneaky, and secretive to avoid your disapproval and punishment.

Baby Talk
"It seemed as if she had given these treasures and left him alone—to use them, or lose them, apply them, or misapply them, according to his own choice. That is all we can do with children, when they grow into big children, old enough to distinguish between right and wrong, and too old to be forced to do either."
—Dinah Mulock Craik

Love and understanding are much better motivators than fear. Your four-year-old wants to please you and win your approval. But he also wants to understand why certain actions meet with your approval while others don't. So reason with your child as much as possible. You might say something like, "Would you please move those cars into the corner? Somebody could fall and get hurt if you leave them at the bottom of the stairs." This lets your child know that you're not asking him to do this to be arbitrary or mean, but rather because you're concerned about everyone's safety. Besides, by telling your child why you want him to do (or not do) something, you will teach him moral principles that can guide his behavior not only in this specific instance, but in general as well.

House Rules

Just because your four-year-old has begun moving toward self-discipline doesn't mean she's there yet. She still needs you to set certain limits, remind her of rules, and correct misbehavior. Again, your child will be much more likely to honor house rules and limits if they are both fair and well-reasoned. So let your child in on the logic behind your rules.

In reminding your preschooler of the rules (or introducing new ones), try not to overuse the words "don't" and "no." Try to put a more positive spin on rules whenever possible. For example, instead of yelling, "No yelling!", you might want to try, "Would you please play quietly while the baby's sleeping?" Save "no" and "don't" only for behavior that you ban permanently:

➤ "No hitting (ever)!"

➤ "Don't (ever) cross the street without a grown-up."

➤ "No jumping in the bathtub (ever)!"

➤ "Don't (ever) stick anything into an electric outlet."

When you do establish rules with these words, it's important that you be consistent. Wavering from "Don't" or "No" rules for any reason will confuse your child and indirectly give her permission to bend the rules when it suits her.

In enforcing house rules, remember to reward good behavior rather than bad behavior. For instance, do you succumb to your child's whining requests just to shut her up? Do you ever reward her for not whining? Or is this the only way she ever gets a treat? If so, you are nurturing whining behavior. When your child hits a playmate or younger sibling, do you merely try to distract her with a new game or activity? If so, you're teaching her to hit to gain positive attention.

In general, you can probably trust in your child's good intentions. So as she grows older, give your preschooler more responsibility to regulate her own behavior. Let her know that you trust her to do the right thing. And remember to notice and praise her whenever she does behave well.

Rights and Responsibilities

As your child's moral conscience develops, you can introduce and nurture personal responsibility—that is, being responsible for his own actions. It won't do to say, "She made me hit her!" Nor will it work to blame the cat, the dog, the baby, or invisible monsters for damage he has done. (As if these ever worked!)

Q-Tip
Try to anticipate things that might tempt your child to break the rules. Just before your child will face one of these temptations, ask her to repeat your rule about this situation. This encourages your preschooler, by putting it into her own words, to make it her rule and to discipline herself.

Baby Talk
"If you would have your son to walk honourable through the world, you must not attempt to clear the stones from his path, but teach him to walk firmly over them—not insist upon leading him by the hand, but let him learn to go alone."
—Anne Brontë

In helping your preschooler to begin to accept personal responsibility for his behavior, you need to emphasize that actions have consequences—and not just that if he gets caught, he'll get punished. Preschoolers often don't see the connection between what they do and something else that happens as a result. But at four, your child can appreciate how his behavior affects others—especially if you make the connections clear: "You teased Sara and that made her feel bad. That's why she started to cry."

Baby Talk
"I'm going to stop punishing my children by saying, "Never mind! I'll do it myself."
—Erma Bombeck

Baby Talk
"What the vast majority of American children need is to stop being pampered, stop being indulged, stop being chauffeured, stop being catered to. In the final analysis it is not what you do for your children but what you have taught them to do for themselves that will make them successful human beings."—Ann Landers

Don't shield your child from the consequences of his actions by constantly doing things for him. Your child may learn a memorable lesson by suffering the consequences of his own actions. After reminding your child to bring in a book or painting that he left out in the yard, don't then run out when the first raindrops start falling to rescue it yourself. If the book or picture gets ruined, it may have a greater impact on your child's future behavior.

The notion of personal responsibility also implies that your preschooler needs to start to care for himself as much as he can. Of course, this doesn't mean your four-year-old needs to cook his own meals, put himself to bed, or give himself medicine when he's sick. But your child should really be doing many things for himself by now: getting dressed, picking up his own toys, and washing his hands after going to the toilet. Certainly you won't be there to wipe your child's bottom when he goes to kindergarten. So in this final year as a preschooler, your child needs to practice and master the kinds of things he'll need to be able to do in kindergarten. They're all a part of personal responsibility.

Have You Done Your Chores?

By the age of four, your child should be making at least a small contribution to the family as a whole. Assigning—or better yet, letting your child choose—a job to do around the house reinforces the value of cooperation: of working together to achieve common goals. Chores also help your child move beyond self-centeredness. Through doing chores or at least helping with them, your preschooler learns that personal responsibility means contributing to the "greater good," the welfare of the entire family. Finally, doing chores also adds to your child's sense of competence and self-confidence.

Preschoolers can do a lot to help around the house. Your child can now handle such jobs as:

➤ Setting or clearing the table

➤ Putting dishes in the sink or dishwasher

➤ Making her own bed

➤ Emptying wastebaskets

➤ Putting her dirty clothes in the laundry hamper or basket

➤ Sorting laundry into whites and colors

➤ Matching socks

➤ Bringing in the newspaper or the mail from the mailbox

Besides her assigned or chosen chore, let your preschooler do as much to help as she seems interested or willing to do. Encourage her to help. You will probably get more willing cooperation if you try to make the jobs as fun as you can. (Think of Tom Sawyer whitewashing Aunt Polly's fence.)

Kid Stuff

When two-and-a-half-year-old Leila offered to help around the house, she and her dad made a badge out of cardboard and a safety pin. Leila's dad wrote "WASTEBASKET MONITOR" and drew a picture of some overflowing wastebaskets. Leila wore her badge with pride and whenever she noticed a full wastebasket, she would bring it to the top of the stairs.

When her four-year-old brother Owen saw Leila's badge, he wanted a job (or at least a badge), too. Owen became the "LAUNDRY MONITOR," in charge of bringing laundry hampers to the top of the stairs and sorting them into whites and colors after one of his parents brought the heavy hamper to the basement.

Show Me the Money!

Before the age of four or five, most children have little concept of money and its function. Older preschoolers begin to understand its usefulness—and may want some of their own.

Giving your four-year-old a small weekly allowance can provide a helpful introduction to the idea of money management. Your preschooler does not need a lot of money, but that's not really the point.

If he has his own money, your child will begin to appreciate how much the things he wants cost. He will begin to make decisions as a consumer—whether to buy a candy bar or a coloring book. And if he wants something really badly, your child may even begin to save his money in anticipation of the future.

If you do decide to give your preschooler an allowance, try not to link it to doing his chores or helping around the house. Allowance, especially for preschoolers, is pocket money—nice to have but totally unnecessary. An allowance is not a payment for doing his chores. He should be encouraged and expected to help around the house not because he gets paid for it, but because he's a contributing member of the family.

Honesty: The Expected Policy

Until she reached age three or four, your child was not capable of lying—if by lying you mean intentionally distorting, concealing, or denying what she knows to be true. Apparent lies before age three or four most often result from forgetfulness or from a magical belief in wish fulfillment.

The belief in wish fulfillment remains strong in the preschool years. Your child desperately wants to be good, because she knows that will earn your approval. When your child does something that she knows she shouldn't have, her fantasies may be so strong that she can convince herself that she didn't really do it: "I really wish I hadn't broken that, so I didn't." But besides lies of wish fulfillment, your preschooler may now expand her repertoire, introducing an array of lies of all shapes and sizes.

I Cannot Tell a Lie (Yeah, Right)

By age four, your child has the ability to lie, to deliberately hide, distort, or deny the truth. Yet not all of her "lies" should bother you. Your child's tall tales about the invisible friends, fairies, and monsters with whom she shares her world, for example, aren't really lies at all. They're fantasies and fairy tales that demonstrate your preschooler's creativity.

Boasting and bragging probably shouldn't bother you too much either. Bragging—exaggerating the merits of something that belongs to your child (you, her toys, her house, her car, herself, and so on)—is common among four-year-olds. In bragging, your child may be attempting to bolster her self-esteem, to impress others, or to win someone's love or approval. If you think this might be the case with your child, put a little extra effort into praising your child's real accomplishments and demonstrating more affection.

On the other hand, your child also may be merely playing with words. (Preschoolers love words that convey bigness: "huge," "enormous," "tremendous," and so on.)

Your preschooler also may "try out" lies on you, just to see how you'll react. After spending four fun-filled hours with Grandma, your child may come back home and announce,

"I hate Grandma." If you look, you may catch her watching for your reaction. Try not to give your child the satisfaction she may be looking for. Don't overreact or make a big deal of these sorts of lies. Simply engage in some reality testing, offer a calm correction, and discourage her from this sort of lie. (In this case, appeal to your child's empathy by suggesting that it might hurt Grandma's feelings to hear this.)

While the lies discussed here are either harmless or minor transgressions, the lies that bother you the most are no doubt the ones your child tells in order to avoid responsibility or escape punishment. Indeed, these cover-up lies may make you angrier than the "crime" your child is attempting to conceal.

Q-Tip

If your child's bragging seems to be getting out of hand, you can take steps to curtail the habit. Start by confronting and correcting the exaggeration in "lie." Explain to your child the drawbacks of boasting. After her friends discover the truth that she's been exaggerating, they will doubt everything she says.

"Watergate Lies"

No child wants to be punished for his actions—even those that he knows are wrong. So as soon as your child becomes mentally capable of lying, he probably will figure out that lies can cover-up unpleasant truths (spills, broken things, acts of violence). If they're convincing, lies may even help him to avoid a scolding, punishment, or impeachment.

These "Watergate lies"—lies designed to avoid taking responsibility for his actions—must be nipped in the bud. For one thing, you don't want your child to get into the habit of telling cover-up lies. For another, his first attempts at covering up the truth probably will be the easiest to see through. As your preschooler gets older, his lies will become more believable and harder to penetrate.

So before your child gets into the habit of telling lies—or even worse, gets good at it—catch them and correct them. Confront cover-up lies right away. Let your child know that you regard lying as an offense that ranks right up there with violence. In confronting these lies, you can accomplish two goals important to your child's moral development:

Q-Tip

If your child confesses to doing something that would warrant disciplinary measures if you had seen it, don't let your admiration for his candor let him off the hook entirely. Let him know that although you are proud of him for his honesty—and for taking responsibility for his actions—you'll still need to put him in time-out for his misbehavior.

➤ You will make clear how much you value the habit of telling the truth.

➤ You will reinforce notions of personal responsibility, of owning up to behavior and its consequences.

Truth or Consequences

When you first realize that your preschooler is lying to you, you'll almost certainly find it disturbing. You may feel angry, saddened, disappointed, hurt, or offended—or all of these emotions at the same time. But don't punish yourself with thoughts that you've done something wrong. You haven't failed in your attempts to teach proper moral behavior. Indeed, you've just begun teaching moral behavior. Preschoolers don't yet have a firm sense of moral behavior. All preschoolers lie. It's your job to catch those lies, correct them, and in so doing, provide moral instruction.

Before responding in any way, make sure your child knows the difference between fantasy and reality. After all, if she doesn't realize that she's telling a lie, is it really a lie at all? If you determine that she did know the truth but lied anyway, then try to respond calmly.

First, try to find out why your child lied. Chances are it wasn't out of sheer ill will. In most cases, preschoolers tell cover-up lies for one of three reasons:

➤ They fear punishment for their misbehavior.

➤ They're afraid that their parents won't love them anymore.

➤ They feel overwhelmed by guilt.

Examine the way you usually respond when your child confesses to some misbehavior—or when you find out about it on your own. Do you have a tendency to get angry? Do you hurl accusations? Do you go ballistic? Or do you voice your disapproval calmly but firmly? If you throw a fit whenever your preschooler honestly tells you that she did something wrong (especially if she had been reluctant to tell you in the first place), then why would she ever willingly admit to something again?

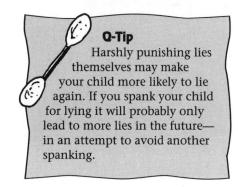

Q-Tip

Harshly punishing lies themselves may make your child more likely to lie again. If you spank your child for lying it will probably only lead to more lies in the future—in an attempt to avoid another spanking.

Also take a look at the way you impose disciplinary measures. Are your punishments too harsh? Why does your child want so much to avoid them? Certainly you need to correct misbehavior, but consider whether you may perhaps punish your preschooler too severely. Punishments for any misbehavior should be consistent and reasonable. Are yours?

Do you ever withdraw from your child or refuse to speak to her until she apologizes or atones for some transgression? If so, your child probably fears that you won't love her anymore if she behaves badly. Whenever you punish your child for lying or any other misbehavior, be sure to provide reassurance as well as discipline. Remind your child repeatedly that you love her even when you disapprove of her behavior or feel angry with or disappointed in her. Don't say, even in jest, "I don't love you anymore."

When you confront your child with one of her lies, frame it as a moral issue, a question of right and wrong. The most effective means of cutting down on lies is to explain clearly and forcefully to your child why dishonesty is wrong. Let your preschooler know the importance of truth to you, why it matters.

Explain the consequences of lying, too. If your child lies a lot, you won't know when she is really telling you something important and truthful. Tell stories or read books about lies and their consequences. (The classic story is, of course, "The Boy Who Cried Wolf," which teaches that habitual liars can't be believed about anything.)

Most importantly, model honesty yourself. Tell the truth (not necessarily the whole truth, merely what is appropriate to her age) to your child and to others. The more your preschooler sees you modeling honesty, the more she will want to be honest, too.

If your child observes you doing something dishonest it will confuse her. Even overhearing you do something as apparently innocuous as telling a "little white lie" or convincing a ticket seller that your child is under three in order to get into the museum for free will cause your preschooler to doubt your commitment to honesty. In the case of a white lie, explain to your child your reasons for lying (tact, sociability, and a desire to avoid hurting another person's feelings). In the case of buying tickets, pay your fair share. After all, if you lie whenever it's convenient, then why shouldn't your child?

Steal This Book

Stealing is not really a moral issue at this age. Your preschooler doesn't yet have a firm grasp of property rights. Everything seems so confusing. If he can take home an old ratty tennis ball that he finds at the park, then why can't he pocket a toy that he finds at a friend's house? If he sees you picking up tax forms at the library, then why can't he take a coloring book home from the drug store?

Even if your child does understand the concept of "stealing," his desires will often prove more powerful than his self-control. So try not to punish stealing too harshly. You'll need to begin by explaining why what your child did is considered stealing. Then go on to say why stealing is wrong, how it violates the owner's right to his or her own possessions. As to punishment, insist that your child return whatever he has taken to its rightful owner (or pay for it if he's already eaten or destroyed it) and apologize. This is probably punishment enough unless stealing becomes a recurrent problem.

> **Baby Talk**
> "Parents can only give good advice or put them on the right paths, but the final forming of a person's character lies in their own hands...."
> —Anne Frank

You and your partner are your child's first and best teachers, not only of academic skills, but of morality, too. Your own standards of behavior will serve as the foundation of your child's moral conscience. Yet the development of a moral conscience and the understanding of right and wrong takes time. So be patient with your preschooler. If you model moral behavior yourself, provide consistent instruction, and help your child work through the maze of defining right and wrong, you will be proud of his own moral development throughout his childhood.

The Least You Need to Know

➤ While teaching moral lessons and moral thinking, try to make your rules of conduct fair, reasonable, and consistent. And remember to model moral behavior yourself.

➤ Appeal to your preschooler's strong sense of fairness in steering her toward moral decisions.

➤ Don't just criticize bad behavior. Praise and reward moral behavior that makes you proud of your child.

➤ Encourage the development of personal responsibility by emphasizing that your child's actions affect others and by encouraging her to help around the house.

➤ Try to understand the motives underlying your child's lying. But at the same time, make it clear that lying is unacceptable behavior.

➤ Don't come down too hard on stealing. Simply explain why it's wrong and go with her when she returns the stolen object.

Chapter 24

Tackling Tough Questions About Sex and Death

In This Chapter

➤ How to talk to your preschooler about sex

➤ Handling issues of nudity, masturbation, and "playing doctor"

➤ What to do if your child sees you making love

➤ How to talk to your preschooler about death

➤ Helping your child through grief and mourning

Preschoolers are naturally curious about everything that goes on in their world. Yet many parents, mistakenly hoping to shield their children either from information that might "put ideas in their heads" or from "unnecessary pain and sorrow," never share the facts of life or the facts of death with their children. The subjects of sex and death make so many of us uncomfortable that we seldom talk about them with other adults, much less with children.

Children need to know about sex and death, however. Your child will have questions about them whether you discuss the subjects or not. And wouldn't you rather be the one to answer these questions?

Children whose parents try to repress their curiosity about sexuality may grow up thinking that sex is bad, that their bodies—especially "down there"—are dirty, and that they themselves are bad for having sexual thoughts, feelings, and urges, much less sexual behavior. Children whose parents deny their curiosity about death are less prepared to cope when tragedy strikes close to home.

Baby Talk
"Oh, what a tangled web do parents weave

When they think that their children are naive."—Ogden Nash

So if you want your child to grow up feeling good about her body and her sexuality, then you'll need to talk to her about sex. And if you want your preschooler better equipped to handle death when it inevitably makes its presence known, then you'll need to talk about death. The only question that remains, then, is *how?*

The Facts of Life

The best way to satisfy your preschooler's curiosity about sex and sexuality is to allow and encourage him to express it. Let your child take the lead and follow him as far as he wants to go.

Your talks with your child about sexuality will probably begin when your toddler or preschooler begins noticing differences between his own body and the bodies of others:

➤ Your son may notice that a girl's body doesn't have a penis like his does. He may wonder why daddy's penis has hair around it when his doesn't. Or he may want to know why a circumcised penis doesn't look the same as his uncircumcised penis (or vice versa).

➤ Your daughter may wonder about hair and why a boy has a penis—and why she doesn't have big breasts like mommy's.

➤ Your child may wonder why boys and girls urinate differently.

➤ Your child also may wonder where babies come from.

In whatever context he brings up the subject of sex, listen carefully to find out what your child really wants to know. Then answer as clearly, calmly, and simply as possible. You don't need to get encyclopedic or break out the sex manuals, because your preschooler probably doesn't want or need a lot of details. Just answer the specific question your child asks, and try not to succumb to the desire to get it all out at once. If you satisfy your child's sexual curiosity with simple, yet honest answers, he will trust you to answer other questions as he develops them.

Body Language

It's important to tell your child about all of the parts of the body—including the genitals. Don't be afraid that you might scare your child off if you use the real words for the genitals: penis for boys and vulva, vagina, urethra, and clitoris for girls. If your child knows the real names of all the other parts of the body, then referring to the genitals by cute nicknames or as "down there" sends a message that the genitals are bad—so bad you dare not speak their real name.

The questions will no doubt start off on a simple level:

"What's that?"

"That's called a penis. All boys and men have penises."

"And what do I have?"

"You have a vulva."

If your child indicates that she wants to know more, you can add, "Inside the vulva are the urethra, the vagina, and the clitoris."

Your child may simply be asking questions that will add new words to her vocabulary. But if you introduce words like these, be prepared for a follow-up question on function (which may come a minute later or a month later).

"What do they do?"

Again, answer as simply as you can. "The urethra is where your pee comes out. The vagina is where your own baby will come out when you're grown up. And the clitoris is for feeling good."

If your daughter wants to know why she doesn't have a penis, let her know that boys and girls have different parts. It's not that either boys or girls are missing something. True, a girl doesn't have a penis; but a boy doesn't have a vulva either. Help your child appreciate that every child, boy or girl, gets something special that's all his or her own.

> **Q-Tip**
> If your child asks pointed questions in public places about sex, let her know that you'd love to talk to her about the subject, but would prefer to do it in private rather than in the check-out line at the grocery store. Let her know that this talk might make others (not to mention you) uncomfortable or embarrassed.

> **Kid Stuff**
>
> The five-year-old niece of actress Betty Grable once asked her aunt if she could join her in the bathtub. When Grable agreed, the child climbed into the tub. Grable noticed that her niece was staring at her body and asked if anything was wrong. "No," the child answered, "I was just wondering why I'm so plain and you're so fancy."

Other common questions sparked by preschoolers' observations of anatomy include:

➤ **What's a belly button for?**   Answer: Before you were born, when you were still growing inside mama's belly, you got all your food through a tube called the umbilical cord. When you were born, you didn't need the tube anymore, so it was cut off (no, it didn't hurt) except for a little bit that fell off a few days later. Your belly button shows where the tube was.

➤ **Why can't girls pee standing up? Why don't boys pee sitting down?**   Answer: You can try the other way if you want, but it's easier the way you do it now. (If you make a mess, you'll have to clean it up.)

➤ **Why don't I have breasts?**   Answer: You do. Boys and girls both have breasts.

➤ **Why are your breasts so big?**   Answer: When girls get older, somewhere between the ages of ten and fourteen, their breasts grow larger. Yours will, too (if your child is a girl).

➤ **Why doesn't daddy have breasts?**   Answer: He does. But his didn't grow larger when he grew older. Men's breasts don't do that.

Baby Talk

Another common starting place for parent-child discussions of sex is the question of where babies come from. Especially if you're having a baby of your own, your preschooler will be curious about how, for example, the baby will get out of mama's belly. You can initiate these questions by pointing out women who are pregnant to your child.

In answering your preschooler's questions about where babies come from, remember to let your child lead the discussion and determine its direction. Provide the simplest possible answer first. If your child is satisfied with your answer, leave it at that. But if he asks more questions and shows he wants more information, then by all means go into more detail.

Try to avoid letting any embarrassment you may feel about the subject color the way you answer your child. All your preschooler wants is more knowledge. And there's really nothing unseemly about the knowledge he's asking for.

At three or four, your child is capable of understanding that a father provides the seeds or sperm and a mother provides the egg, and that when a seed and an egg join together, a baby starts to grow. This answer may be enough for your preschooler. But if he then asks where daddy and mommy keep their seeds and eggs, you can tell him about testicles and ovaries.

This anatomy lesson may prompt your child to ask how the sperm and egg get together. If he does, then there's no reason to avoid answering. Tell him that daddy has to put his penis in mommy's vagina so that sperm can (maybe) reach an egg. If you explain this as plainly and clearly as you can, your child will probably respond just as matter-of-factly: "Oh."

Other common questions that preschoolers have about babies and pregnancy include:

➤ **How does the baby get out of the mama's belly?** Answer: Most babies come out through the mother's vagina, which stretches to let the baby out. (Make it clear, if you haven't already, that the vagina is not the same as the urethra or the anus.) But if a baby has trouble getting out that way, a doctor can open up the belly and uterus, take the baby out, and then sew the mommy back up again.

➤ **When can I have a baby?** Answer: Girls and boys can make babies when their bodies start changing, usually at about twelve or thirteen years old. That's when boys start making sperm and girls' eggs are able to join with sperm. (Now comes the moral lesson.) But at this age, boys and girls still aren't grown up. So they really can't take care of a baby properly. That's why boys and girls should wait until they're grown up before having babies.

Fairy Tales
The story that the stork brings babies, common even in countries where storks have never lived, originated in Germany and the Netherlands. British children, even in this century, were told that doctors used golden spades to dig up newborns from under gooseberry bushes—or that girls came from under parsley beds, while boys came from under beds of nettles. How's that for quality sex education?

Q-Tip
You might want to scour the library or consult your children's librarian for age-appropriate books that can further your child's understanding of her body and the conception, development, and birth.

➤ **Can two women or two men have a baby?** Answer: They can raise a baby, but they can't make one. It takes a man and a woman to make a baby. But two women or two men can be parents if they adopt a baby or if one of them already has a baby when they decide to make a family together.

Don't be surprised if your child asks the same questions over and over again. This doesn't mean that you gave him a bad answer the first time. You don't need to change your story at all. Your child is just trying to satisfy his curiosity and further his understanding. He may need to hear the same thing more than once to absorb it.

The Naked Truth

Many preschoolers regularly see their parents completely or partially nude—either coming out of the shower, getting dressed, or using the toilet. Yet some parents feel uncomfortable about exposing their children to their naked bodies.

It won't do your child any harm to see you naked as long as you remain relaxed and comfortable about your nakedness. Modeling comfort with (or even pride in) your naked body is not at all a bad thing for your child. After all, you want her to feel comfortable and proud about her body too, don't you?

If you don't feel comfortable being naked in front of your preschooler then don't feel obligated to do so. In fact, if anyone in your household (you, your partner, or your child) feels uncomfortable with nudity, then it only makes sense to respect and consider his or her feelings and cover yourself up. Your child can find out about the differences between male and female anatomy or the anatomy of children and adults in many other ways.

If your nudity prompts your child to ask questions about the different size and shape and hairiness of his or her genitalia compared to yours, reassure your preschooler that all the parts of the body will grow and change as he or she does. A comparison with adult genitalia may make your child feel somewhat inadequate. To avoid this, you'll need to reassure your child that his or her genitalia are just the right size and shape for now—and will be just the right size and shape when he or she grows up, too.

Caught in the Act

If your preschooler witnesses you and your partner making love, try to stay calm. Talk to him about it. Let your child know what you were doing in as simple terms as possible. Tell your child that you were making love. What's that? It's a way for adults who care deeply for each other to express their love. Mommy and Daddy touch each other in ways that make both of us feel good. By touching our own and each other's bodies, we get to share in each other's pleasure and that makes us feel very close and loving. Keep in mind that your preschooler may think that whoever was on top was hurting the other. Make it clear to your child that that wasn't the case.

You might want to emphasize that making love is a private thing that you and your partner do, and that's why you close the door. Ask your child to knock the next time he sees the door closed, and then wait to be invited in. (Let your child know that you will respect his wish for privacy in the same way.)

In talking to your preschooler about sex with your partner, stress the loving, caring, and responsibility involved in an intimate sexual relationship. Make it clear to your child that:

➤ sexual intimacy is something very special;

➤ sexual intimacy is ideally loving and mutually satisfying; and

➤ sexual intimacy should be shared only by adults (never by children, whether with adults or with other children).

> **Baby Talk**
> "I married the first man I ever kissed. When I tell my children that, they just about throw up."
> —Barbara Bush

Handling Genital Handling

Whether you know about it or not, your preschooler will almost definitely play with her genitals from time to time. Masturbation is a perfectly natural way for your child to discover more about her body. What's more, children can get pleasure from masturbation just as adults can.

Nonetheless, it's somewhat disconcerting to see your little boy playing with his penis—and in a holdover from double-standard days, downright uncomfortable to see your little girl fondling her clitoris. And many preschoolers are not at all shy about playing with themselves in a room full of people.

When you notice your child playing with herself, try to avoid expressing shock—or, even worse, scolding or shaming her for this natural exploration of her body. Forbidding or repressing masturbation sends a very negative message about sex. Ignoring it can send a more subtle negative message, too: that sex is something people don't talk about. So try your best to provide a positive message about sex. Start by acknowledging to your child (and yourself) that masturbation feels good and that's how it's supposed to be.

After you've opened the discussion, your child may feel free to ask questions that may have been puzzling him or her for some time. Your son may want to

> **Childproofing**
> If your daughter asks whether she can put anything in her vagina, the answer is of course entirely up to you. It won't harm her to put her finger in her vagina gently, but other things might scratch or tear her vagina. If you give her permission, remind her to wash her hands first to avoid getting a vaginal infection.

know, for instance, why his penis gets hard. Let him know that when he gets excited or plays with his penis, blood, which normally runs through the penis, is blocked from leaving. The blood therefore collects in the penis, making it larger. Compare it to a balloon filling up with air or a hose filling up with water. Your daughter may want to know why she gets wet in and around her vulva. Let her know that the vagina produces something called lubrication—a slippery moistness. Compare it to saliva, which keeps her mouth from getting dry.

When you talk about masturbation, tell your preschooler that she should no longer play with herself in public, but rather only when she is alone. Let your child know that she should keep her masturbation private because it makes some grown-ups uncomfortable or embarrassed. It may help your preschooler's understanding if you compare it to picking her nose, which you have probably also urged her not to do in public—or to going to the bathroom, which all of us do in private.

Playing Doctor

At four, your child also may begin showing his genitals to others in play. Sexual play occurs between children of the same sex as well as children of opposite sexes. It's very common for preschoolers to engage in genital touching, hugging, and kissing, often accompanied by lots of tickling and giggling. For you, this activity may seem inappropriate. But for your child, it's a playful yet perfectly logical way to explore his natural curiosity about gender differences. What could make the physical differences between boys and girls clearer than a game of, "I'll show you mine if you show me yours." (Oh, sure, you'll think, now he learns to take turns and share!)

Childproofing

Whether or not you sanction playing doctor, make it clear to your child that young children and adults (or older children) should not touch each other's genitals. The only exceptions to this rule are: parents, who need to wash their child's genitals until he can do it himself; and doctors or other healthcare professionals, who sometimes need to examine children's genitals to check on a rash, for instance.

As with all matters of preschool sexuality, try not to overreact to sex play. Just because your child and his friend are exploring their genitals is no reason to panic. In talking to your child about it, let him know that lots of children do that when they're little. Acknowledge—and even applaud—the children's curiosity about each other's bodies. If you want them to stop, however, tell both children that certain parts of our bodies are private. Then try to steer them toward a book that might satisfy their curiosity about their bodies.

The Facts of Death

All life ends in death. But because our culture has difficulty accepting this fact, death has become an unspeakable terror. Death lurks in the shadows of our lives, ready to claim, at a moment's notice, someone we love.

Perhaps due to our own fears, speaking to preschoolers about death is an even greater taboo today than talking about sex. Adults try to justify their reticence by arguing that because young children can't possibly understand death, parents should spare their preschoolers the burden of thinking about it.

But this excuse for avoiding an unpleasant subject consigns young children to the darkness. If you don't discuss death at all with your child, she will be totally unprepared if someone close to her does die. Will you force your preschooler to deal with her grief and fears alone? Or will you help bear some of her burden by looking for answers together?

What Happens When Someone Dies?

Before a tragedy forces you and your preschooler to confront the specter of death together, try to bring it up in a neutral way. The opportunities to speak about death with your preschooler are endless, because death is literally all around us. Any of the following situations can provide you with the opening you need to bring up the subject of death in a nonthreatening, nonpersonal way:

➤ Your child notices a squashed squirrel in the middle of the road.

➤ One of your house plants slowly withers and dies.

➤ Leaves fall from the trees in autumn.

➤ Mufasa, the Lion King, gets trampled under a stampede of wildebeests while his son Simba watches helplessly.

➤ Your child delights in grinding an ant under his shoe.

➤ A family pet dies or is "put to sleep."

➤ A relative (one who was never close to your child) succumbs to a long illness or dies in a sudden accident.

Any of these scenarios can lead to a discussion that will allow you to explore your child's thoughts and feelings about death and to share your own thoughts with him. Indeed, your child will probably wonder about all of these events whether you talk to him about them or not. So take advantage of the opportunity they present.

If possible, focus your first discussion about death on one of these neutral scenarios. Try to steer this initial conversation away from acknowledging that eventually you, your child, or someone else he loves will die. Unless he has a context in which to fit this knowledge, it will damage your child's sense of safety and security.

Hopefully, you will have discussed death several times with your preschooler before he asks such painful personal questions as, "Will I die? Or will you die?" Of course, if your four-year-old does ask these questions, respond as honestly and reassuringly as possible.

You might want to tell your child, for instance, that most parents today live long after their children have grown and have their own children. Make it real for your child. If your parents (or better yet, your grandparents) are still alive, point to them as examples. Let your child know that you someday hope to enjoy your grandchildren just as your parents enjoy him. (Of course, if your child then responds with, "When will I have children?", you'll be right back into a discussion of sex again.)

Pointing to your own parents as examples of long lives may lead your child to ask, "Is Grandma going to die soon?" If this comes up, be honest. Unless your mother has a terminal illness, you can reasonably and truthfully say something like, "I don't know. Most people today live until they're 75 or 80 years old, but some people live as long as 100 years or even more."

Unless your discussion of death follows in the wake of a personal tragedy, the way you talk to your child about death should be similar to the way you talk about sex. Pay attention to avoiding the use of euphemisms for death, which can create misunderstandings and powerful fears among preschoolers. If you say that someone who died has "passed away," "passed on," or "gone to a better place," your child may think, "Oh, a better place. When's he coming back?" If you describe death as like "going to sleep and never waking up," your child will never want to go to sleep again. And if you describe it as "going away and never coming back," your child will never let you go on a trip without making a huge scene.

Preschoolers—perhaps influenced by adult euphemisms—most often associate death with going to sleep or taking a trip. Of course, this means that they consider it a temporary condition. They do not understand the permanence of death. They may want to know when a person who died will wake up or come back. If your child has this misconception, correct it as gently but as persistently as you can.

Most importantly, in all of your conversations with your child about death and dying, try to instill a reverence for life and an appreciation for the beauty of life along with an understanding of death. Try to place death in the context of the continuous cycle of change: the endless circle of life, death, and rebirth.

A Death in the Family

If you haven't brought it up before, you really must talk about death with your preschooler if someone your child loves dies. It might be painful for you to talk about it, but avoiding the subject won't make the pain go away for you—or for your child. Your child really needs your support as she grieves. So talk openly about your own feelings about the death and encourage your child to do the same. You may find that discussions with your child help you through your grieving process as well.

Even small children grieve over the death of someone they loved. Of course, children react to death in different ways, depending on their age, their relationship with the deceased, the circumstances surrounding the death, and the support they get from their family.

The death of a pet often provides a preschooler's first experience with death. If your pet dies, encourage your child to grieve over the loss. Let your child help you bury the pet, so that she has a chance to say goodbye.

Q-Tip
Make sure that you are the one who tells your child that someone close to her has died. Do it as soon as you can after the death. Otherwise, someone else might tell her in a way that you wouldn't.

Q-Tip
If your pet dies, don't run out and get a new pet right away. Give your child the time she needs to mourn before trying to fill the void in her life.

The death of one of her grandparents will affect your child unless she had little or no contact with them. The death may be somewhat easier for you to accept if your parents were old or sick before they died. But don't minimize your child's—or your own—need to mourn this death. Whether or not the deceased lived a long and happy life, his or her death still represents a significant loss to your child (and to you).

When a Young Person Dies

The death of a sibling (or a friend your child's age) is particularly painful for a preschooler. A sibling's death invariably brings on a wave of conflicting feelings in the surviving child. The elements of these feelings include:

➤ Relief that his rival is gone, coupled with guilt for feeling this way: guilt is a particularly strong emotion for a surviving sibling.

➤ Fear of his own vulnerability: Your child will feel that if his sibling died, then he can die, too. Your preschooler needs persistent reassurance from you that he is fine.

➤ Grief over his own loss of a sibling.

Children are of course supposed to outlive their parents. So if one of your children has died, you will be feeling profound and inconsolable grief. Yet so will your child. With all of your friends and family attending to your needs, ask yourself, is anyone attending to your child's? If your grief makes you unable to do it, make sure that someone whom your child loves is helping him through his painfully conflicted feelings.

Try to discourage anyone from comparing your surviving child to his sibling. This kind of comparison can put pressure on your surviving child to take the place of his sibling. He may feel as if it's up to him to make up for the loss of his brother or sister. And your child has enough to struggle through without having to worry about that, too.

Death of a Parent

Much of the same advice about helping your child through a sibling's death also applies if one of her parents dies. The elements of guilt and fear may be just as strong after a parent's death as they are after a sibling's. If your partner dies, your child will have a profound fear that you will die, too. She also will feel a tremendous sense of guilt over any of the conflicts she had with your partner.

The death of your partner may draw you and your child closer together. It will, of course, be difficult to cope with your own loss and at the same time help your child. But you may find that you depend on each other to get through this crisis. If you, your child's only surviving parent, openly show your grief, your child will be encouraged to do the same. If you can provide your child with love and reassurance, she will gain the confidence she needs to return love and reassurance to you. And if you talk about the death together, it might help both of you to make some sense of this senseless death.

Emotional Upheaval

Regardless of her relationship with the deceased, the emotions your child will feel after the death of someone close to her will cover a wide range. Your child may go through periods of endless crying, anger and irritability, self-blame, blaming others, and stoicism.

The most common emotional responses of preschoolers to the death of a relative or loved one include:

➤ **Denial**   Your child may refuse to believe it really happened. Denial may last just a few days or may stretch on for several months. If your preschooler is in denial, don't pressure her to accept the death. She'll do that when she's ready. Just try to provide your child with the understanding and patience she needs during this difficult time.

➤ **Anger and resentment**   Your preschooler may be enraged that the deceased abandoned her. This may lead to constant irritability. Try to be patient and understanding. Don't rebuke your child for her feelings, no matter how much it hurts you to hear her speak ill of the dead. Bottling these feelings up will only make them worse and might bring on a severe depression. So give your child the opportunity and permission she needs to let loose with her rage.

➤ **Sadness or loneliness**   Your child's sense of abandonment by the deceased may be compounded by the fact that you may be so involved in your own grief that you may unwittingly neglect her sadness. You need to move beyond your own grief and sadness, at least on occasion, to attend to hers. If you can't do it yourself, then ask another adult to whom your child feels close to help her through her sadness.

➤ **Depression**   Your preschooler may have trouble sleeping, lose interest in eating, and not even want to play anymore. In the wake of death, even a young life may seem somewhat empty and purposeless. Depression is a common response to the death of a loved one, but if it persists for more than a couple of months, your child may benefit from professional attention.

In the meantime, do what you can to bring some joy back into your child's life. Special treats, new games, and field trips may not remove your preschooler's underlying sadness, but they may give her a much-needed break from grief and help make life seem worth living again.

➤ **Guilt**   Your child may blame herself for the death. According to thinking common among preschoolers, misbehavior is punished. So if she's suffering such a severe punishment (the abandonment of a loved one), she must have done something terribly wrong (even if she doesn't know what it could be).

➤ **Fear**   Your child may go into a panic that she or you or someone else will die. She will likely suffer from severe separation anxiety. The fear may be tied to a particular condition or activity (sickness, driving) that parallels the circumstances surrounding the death. If your child is in a persistent panic state, she'll need repeated reassurances from you that you don't expect anyone else close to her to die.

> **Childproofing**
> Many grieving children now have access to support groups designed specifically for their needs. If you think your child might benefit from joining a support group, contact your local hospital—or better yet, your local children's hospital—to see if they can refer you to a group in your area.

> **Childproofing**
> Don't worry if your preschooler regresses somewhat after the death of a loved one. It's common for grieving young children to regress. You may see an increase in bedwetting or a return of thumb-sucking. She may understandably become extremely weepy and clingy. Be patient and understanding. Talking to your child and helping her through her grief will in time reverse this regression.

If any of these feelings persist—on a regular basis, not just recurring from time to time—beyond a few months, your child may need professional help.

Cause of Death

The way in which a person died also affects the way your preschooler will grieve. Unlike the images of death young children see on TV, natural death is usually not violent. The peacefulness of a natural death is useful for a preschooler to know. It can help not only in the child's anticipation of death, but also in dealing with the aftermath of the death of a pet or a loved one. Yes, it's still sad and your child will still miss the deceased, but he may be comforted by knowledge that death was not wrenching for the loved one.

Accidental death, on the other hand, can be particularly traumatic for a child (and for you, too). Everyone who loved the deceased is in shock. The lack of forewarning gives no one a chance to plan for death, and catches everyone unprepared. Your child may feel terribly guilty over the possibility that he might have done something to prevent the accident. You must help him see that attempting to change the past is futile—and that there was nothing he could have done.

Q-Tip
In the wake of the upheaval of death, try to maintain your child's routines as best you can. Your preschooler will benefit from the security of familiar surroundings, playmates, and activities.

To help your child through his grief, encourage him to talk with you about his feelings and his thoughts about death. Don't ever try to prevent your child from expressing his grief. Attempts to soothe and support your child by saying, "Don't cry" or "Be brave," will actually make it harder for him to mourn the deceased and get past a death, not easier.

Welcome and respond to any questions your preschooler has about death. When your child does want to talk, give him your undivided attention if possible. Besides providing a listening ear and an understanding heart, give as much of yourself to your child as you can. Hug him, caress him, read to him, talk to him.

Finally, try to give your preschooler all the time he needs to mourn. Don't try to rush your child through mourning, encouraging him to forget about it and move on. Rather, encourage your child to remember. Offer him pictures and small objects as keepsakes that will help him remember his loved one forever.

Should Your Child Go to the Funeral?

Your preschooler may have difficulty understanding and accepting the finality of death. You will need to help your child understand that the physical body never comes back to life (despite any ghost stories she might have heard)—and also that the body has no feelings after death.

If you believe your child is old enough and mature enough, attending a funeral can help with this understanding. A funeral can help make death "real" to your child. It will also give your preschooler the chance to say goodbye, which she needs just as much as you do.

If you are considering inviting your preschooler to come to a funeral with you, prepare her in advance for what she may see and hear there. Funeral rites (and funeral homes) can be strange and disconcerting to a child (or an adult). So talk beforehand about where it will be and what will happen. If there will be an open casket, let your child know that she can see her loved one's body, but that he will look different from the way she remembers him. Tell your child that the open casket gives her a chance to say goodbye if she wants, but that she doesn't have to approach the casket or look at the body unless she wants to.

If you do decide that your child can probably handle it, ask her whether she wants to go. If she says no, respect that decision. In this matter, your child truly may know best. So don't force or pressure her to go if she doesn't want to go. There are many other ways that your child can say goodbye to the deceased.

Explain what will happen at the cemetery, too. Again, ask whether your child wants to go to the cemetery, rather than compelling her to go. Allow your child to choose the way she will grieve.

What Happens After You Die?

When your preschooler asks you questions about the possibility of an afterlife, share with him what you believe. Many preschoolers have a difficult time understanding faith. Your child may be too grounded in reality (what he can observe and/or experience) to comprehend your ideas about religion and faith. Nonetheless, they may help him make peace with the death of a loved one.

You may find talking about your religious beliefs difficult, but it's an important way not only to help your child through his grief, but also to pass on your values. So explain to your preschooler as best you can what you believe. It's an essential part of who you are, and your child will benefit from knowing that part of you.

> ### Kid Stuff
>
> Young Charles and Mary Lamb, who would both grow up to become poets and writers, were taking a walk in a cemetery. Four-year-old Charles, an early reader, stopped to examine many of the words etched in the headstones: "loving," "caring," "beloved," "good," "virtuous," etc. "Mary," he asked, turning to his teenage sister, "where are all the naughty people buried?"

Religious faith and religious teachings help comfort your child in the wake of death. They also can help introduce and reinforce moral values that you want your child to honor. But when you talk about your beliefs, try to let your child know that they are not the gospel truth, but rather just that: what you believe. So explain that others have beliefs different from yours. For no matter how clear your beliefs, they are not the same as facts. Letting your child in on the distinction will help him to respect the beliefs of others.

If you have no strong religious beliefs, let your child know that, too. But try to stress the importance of respecting those who do.

Don't pretend that you know all the answers. Make it clear to your child that no one really knows what happens after someone dies. It might be useful to ask your child what he thinks might happen after death. Who knows? The answer he offers may end up helping both of you through your grief.

The Least You Need to Know

➤ Your child needs to know about both sex and death. This knowledge will add to her appreciation and understanding of life.

➤ Let your child lead any discussion of either sex or death through the questions she asks. Offer simple yet honest answers. Wait for follow-up questions before offering more details.

➤ Try to avoid making your child feel ashamed of her body or her sexuality.

➤ Emphasize loving, caring, and responsibility when talking about sex or making babies.

➤ Children need to grieve over the death of a loved one just as much as adults do. Encourage her to talk about whatever she feels.

➤ If you are so weighed down by your own grief that you can't help your child through hers, ask another adult whom your child loves and trusts to attend to her needs.

Chapter 25

Fun and Games

Four-year-olds are so active and playful that you will have a hard time keeping up with your child this year. Your four-year-old may make up games and activities, the rules of which only he knows. He may race back and forth from the kitchen, where he crashes into the refrigerator (on purpose, no less), to the living room, where he throws himself headfirst into the couch. A second later, he's back on his feet, racing toward the kitchen again. In fact, your four-year-old may be so energetic and full of life that you find it hard to get him to sit down for more than a minute or two.

You can use this abundant energy and your child's rapidly improving physical coordination to direct your child's play. Creative movement and dance are still fun at this age.

Despite his apparently inexhaustible supply of energy, your child does need to settle down every once in a while. Running around all the time will wear your child down, decreasing both his coordination and his tolerance for frustration. So especially if he's given up naps entirely, it will help his temperament (and your own sanity) if you can steer your four-year-old toward some quieter activities for an hour or two every day.

Of course, your child will probably be happy to sit down and watch TV. But you can also entice your preschooler to sit down with reading and storytelling, board and card games, and arts and crafts projects. And at four (or even earlier), your child will probably find it fun and fascinating to sit down and play on the computer.

Booting Up: Introducing Your Child to the Computer

If you haven't introduced your child to the computer, you really should this year. It doesn't matter if you don't know RAM from ROM. You don't need to know much about computers yourself to use most children's software. So even if you're a complete idiot where computers are concerned, you can still get your child started so that she won't be. (In fact, before long, she'll probably be teaching you a thing or two.)

Of course, computers (like television) should never be used as a substitute for reading, for hands-on science experiments, for art projects, for field trips to museums, zoos, or for time spent with you. But computers can be very useful, versatile, and entertaining learning tools, even for preschoolers. Quality software programs can supplement and even enhance your child's learning in a wide variety of areas.

Good software for preschoolers can help your child build such basic academic skills as:

➤ counting;

➤ addition and subtraction;

➤ telling time;

➤ letter recognition; and

➤ the association of sounds with letters.

In addition, the computer can bring worlds of knowledge into your home. It can introduce your child to various principles of music, art, and design. Children's design programs will allow your child to explore her creativity, exercise her imagination, and create her own works of art—with no messy cleanup required on your part. Besides, playing on the computer is a fun and educational way to spend your time together on a rainy afternoon.

Computer time with your preschooler is time that you spend with her. Although the software box may indicate that your child can run the program herself, don't believe it. She will almost definitely need your help. If your child is under the age of four, she may lack some of the motor coordination needed to use the mouse with any degree of accuracy. In addition, since most preschoolers can't yet read, your child may need help reading and following written instructions, no matter how simple they are. Finally, because her attention may wander, your preschooler may need your help remembering exactly where she is in a particular program.

Fortunately, the best children's computer programs are not only fun for your child to use, but at least somewhat entertaining for adults, too. So both of you can have fun using the computer together.

The computer has become so much a part of our everyday lives (and shows promise of having an even greater role in the future) that every child will benefit from learning how to use computers. Virtually every school and many preschools now have computers available for student use. So it will help if your child has at least some familiarity with computers by the time she enters school.

So don't force your child to hitchhike on the information superhighway. Give her a ride yourself.

Q-Tip

Limiting the amount of time your child spends on the computer at a single sitting helps to maintain her interest. Your preschooler will probably have the most fun and get the most out of a computer program if you limit sessions to 20 minutes or half an hour. With most programs, this will be plenty of time for your child to complete one or two learning activities.

Do You Have the Hardware?

Most children's computer programs now run on the same kind of computer that adults use. Because almost all children's software comes in both Macintosh and Windows versions, it doesn't matter whether you have an IBM-compatible personal computer (PC) with Windows or a Macintosh (Mac).

Because most children's software will run on the computer you already have, you probably don't need to buy a separate computer system for your child—unless you are always on the computer yourself. If you don't yet have a home computer, (and what planet have you been on anyway) you can buy or rent one.

Although you probably don't need an entirely new computer system, you still may need to make a few changes. (See the following list of features your computer should have to use most children's software.) In particular, you may have to upgrade the sound and graphic capabilities of your system.

What Your Computer System Needs to Make the Most of Children's Software

---

8 megabytes of memory (RAM)

At least 160 megabytes of storage space on your hard disk

A color monitor and VGA or SuperVGA display (to display multiple colors on screen)

Digitized sound—and if you want to run a program that replicates musical instruments, synthesized sound. (If your computer does not have digitized sound, you can buy a "sound card" that will upgrade your system. Your computer or software dealer will probably install this sound card at no extra charge.)

A mouse

A printer (preferably a color one)

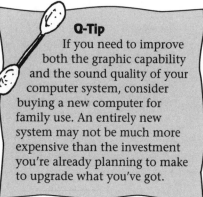

Q-Tip
If you need to improve both the graphic capability and the sound quality of your computer system, consider buying a new computer for family use. An entirely new system may not be much more expensive than the investment you're already planning to make to upgrade what you've got.

Q-Tip
If you plan to try out a software program in the store before buying it, be sure to bring your child with you. A program may seem cute, engaging and educational to you. But your child may be looking for different things than you are. If he thinks it's a bore, then you will have wasted your money.

Do you need to add a CD-ROM drive to your system (or buy a CD-ROM system)? Not really. True, CD-ROM offers terrific sound and graphic quality, which will enhance its usefulness and its ability to entertain your preschooler. However, most computer software for preschoolers that comes on CD-ROM format also comes on disk. They may not have as elaborate an array of sound and graphic features as their CD-ROM counterparts do, but these versions are engaging and entertaining enough in themselves. So if you already have CD-ROM, great. You'll use it. But if you don't yet have CD-ROM, you probably don't need to upgrade solely on your preschooler's account.

Before You Buy Software

Before you pay for any software program, read the box. Many software producers print the operating system a package will need on the outside of the box. Some even provide a helpful list of various brands and models of computers that will run the program. In addition, check to see whether color or enhanced sound are needed. Check also to make sure that the memory (RAM) and storage space (on hard disk) the program requires doesn't exceed your computer's capacity.

Also, do whatever you can to preview a computer software package before you buy it for your preschooler. Check with your local library to see if it has children's computer programs that you can either borrow or try out with your child on the library's computer. Borrow a copy from one of your neighbors. Or try it out in the computer store before making your purchase.

Also check your software dealer's return policy. If your store allows returns with "no questions asked," you can take the program home and try it out to see if your child likes it. If he doesn't, you can exchange it for store credit or a different software package (or occasionally, your money back).

Software Solutions

The best computer programs for preschoolers who can't read must feature bright and entertaining graphics, clear sound, and simple instructions. If your pre-reader has any chance of using them on her own, software programs should require no reading or minimal reading. Instructions should be rendered graphically or through spoken words that your child will be able to understand easily. The graphics and sound should not be just incidental, related only to non-essential parts of the program. Rather, they should be integrated into the activities to enhance the content and make it more engaging.

A good preschooler's program must also be "user friendly," requiring just the mouse or at most one or two keystrokes for your child to execute commands. Activities should be easy to get into and just as easy to get out of. Most good children's programs use a "menu" format. The program begins by presenting a list—or even better, a set of pictures (icons)— that allows your child to choose among a variety of activities. A click of the mouse on the appropriate icon begins the activity. Similarly, when your child wants to quit—or switch to another activity in the same software package—she should be able to do so with little more than a click or two of the mouse. Otherwise, your child may end up feeling trapped in a particular activity.

The best computer programs for preschoolers also provide nothing but positive feedback. Try to avoid programs that display sad faces or toss off "humorous insults" when your child gets something wrong. These messages discourage your child and may even eat away at her self-esteem. The best programs respond to your child's errors by providing more clues that point to the right answer and saying, "Try again!" Good programs for preschoolers also ward off frustration by limiting the number of tries your child can make before the program itself supplies the right answer—and hopefully an age-appropriate explanation of why it's the right answer.

Most of all, software for preschoolers should be fun. Play is, after all, still your child's primary means of learning. And your child won't get anything out of a children's computer program if she doesn't enjoy using it.

Super Software

Computer software enters and leaves the market quickly. Yet the best children's programs have staying power. So chances are, none of the following programs will be obsolete by the time you read this. Any list of the best programs for preschoolers includes:

For young preschoolers (and toddlers):

➤ Alphabet Blocks (letter skills)

➤ My Paint (art skills)

➤ SnapDragon (sorting skills)

For all preschoolers:

➤ Allie's Playhouse (multiple skills): available only on CD-ROM

➤ The Backyard (multiple skills)

➤ Bailey's Book House (reading skills)

➤ Math Rabbit (math skills)

➤ Millie's Math House (math skills)

➤ The Playroom (multiple skills)

➤ Word Tales (letter and reading skills): available only on CD-ROM

For advanced preschoolers:

➤ KidPix 2 (creative art skills)

➤ MetroGnomes' Music (music skills)

➤ Scooter's Magic Castle (multiple skills)

➤ Yearn 2 Learn: Peanuts (multiple skills)

Q-Tip
Many computer magazines now print regular reviews of software for children. These reviews can steer you toward the latest, greatest children's software packages.

Of course, new and exciting programs for preschoolers are introduced every month. So ask your software dealer, other parents of preschoolers, and your preschool teacher for their recommendations.

No matter how good the software, remember that your computer is just one way—and not the only way—for your preschooler to learn numbers, the alphabet, and other skills. You can help your child get the most out of the computer by following up on concepts learned through software during the rest of your day together.

Letting your child move his own piece in a board game will give him practice in counting out spaces. Or prompt your child to use his peas, macaroni, or other foods on his plate to practice addition or subtraction. You can help in letter recognition by pointing out various letters and sounds when you read to your child. The computer should complement or reinforce the concepts and skills learned through these day-to-day interactions. But nothing should take their place.

Going Off Line

Using a computer requires a certain degree of sophistication. But even when your preschooler goes off line, her play will become increasingly sophisticated and complex. Rather than building things with simple blocks, for instance, your child will now be interested in much more elaborate building toys, such as Tinker Toys, Legos, and even Erector sets. If she enjoys jigsaw puzzles, your child will want increasingly difficult puzzles with more and more pieces. Both of these activities will help your child hone her fine motor skills.

Budding Artist

Your four-year-old's artwork also will become increasingly sophisticated. Throughout the year, he will add more and more detail to his drawings and paintings. What's more, your child will probably no longer be satisfied simply with art for art's sake. Now, he'll want his artwork to represent something. Rather than drawing some lines and then seeing what he can create out of them, your child may begin to have a set idea in his head even before he touches crayon or paintbrush to paper. Unless he asks you for ideas, let your preschooler come up with his own ideas of what to draw or paint.

At four, your child also can use scissors with a fair degree of skill. So give him plenty of cutting projects. You can ask your child to cut out and arrange a variety of shapes. Or you might want to encourage him to cut pictures out of old magazines—just the old ones—and make a collage.

> **Childproofing**
> Even though your child has gotten much better at using scissors, stick with safety scissors that have fairly blunt ends.

Music, Maestro!

The preschool years are a great time to teach music to your child. No matter how tone-deaf she may seem, any child with normal hearing can be taught to carry a tune. It's just a matter of how much time you're willing to put into it.

At two and three, your child was probably content just to hum along with the melodies and perhaps join in to sing on the refrain. But at four, your child will want to know all the words (or a close enough approximation of the words) to her favorite songs. By the end of the year, she will know the words and tunes to dozens of different songs, especially silly songs. And she will have more and more fun singing.

Your child also may enjoy learning a simple tune that she can play on a xylophone or a piano. And she will still have fun just banging out a rhythm on a drum or with castanets, or shaking to the beat with a tambourine or maracas. Remember, the more music your preschooler hears, the more she'll learn about it and the more music will mean to her.

The Land of Make-Believe

Dramatic play will remain a favorite activity for your child. If given the opportunity and not discouraged from participating, preschool boys love make-believe as much as girls. So your child, boy or girl, will probably enjoy playing dress-up, acting out scenarios in toy kitchens or workshops, and creating and dramatizing stories with dolls or puppets. Your preschool magician may also transform simple furniture, cardboard boxes and a variety of props into restaurants, airplanes, rocket ships, post offices, beauty salons, construction sites, burning buildings, or cages in the zoo.

Don't discourage your four-year-old or push him away from fantasy play because you think it's for younger children. Knowing that kindergarten is fast approaching, you may understandably want to focus your child's play on improving skills he will need in school: numbers, the alphabet, colors and shapes, and the computer. But creating worlds of make-believe is just as important as these skills to your preschooler's:

➤ **Intellectual development** Fantasy play exercises your child's imagination and creativity and helps him to develop cognitive flexibility.

➤ **Emotional development** Playing at various adult roles, pretending to be grown up and capable and skilled, is actually a kind of self-fulfilling prophecy. Through this kind of play, your child feels—and increasingly becomes—grown up and capable and skilled. Make-believe, if it involves a "rehearsal" of various emotions, also may increase your child's ability to deal with stress, change, and fears.

➤ **Social development** When playing make-believe with other children, free of adult supervision or guidance, your child will create worlds in which he practices different ways of getting along with other people. This kind of pretend play allows a rehearsal of different social roles and experiences.

Extra! Extra! Read All About It!

Your child will grow much more adventurous in her "reading" this year. She will probably love hearing exciting stories with monsters and dinosaurs and lots of adventure.

Children's poetry, especially poems with a sense of humor, will probably appeal to your child. She may even develop a taste for the macabre (Shel Silverstein comes to mind).

With her more sophisticated understanding, your four-year-old will prefer books with more and more words and less and less pictures. But the illustrations that will appeal to your preschooler most will be those that are intricately detailed. She may enjoy, for example, searching for a particular object or character in a complex scene. (*Where's Waldo?* may be a little much for her, but she will still probably enjoy looking for him.)

> **Q-Tip**
> Later in the year, your child may begin to show interest in books that can't be finished at one sitting (unless it's a very long sitting). So you might want to introduce her to her first children's novels. Your child will especially enjoy novels with whimsical elements and those that focus on children.

Favorite Authors

Your four-year-old will continue to love books by the same authors he's loved for the past two years. But in addition, he will probably develop an appreciation for:

➤ Graeme Base

➤ Martin Handford (Waldo)

➤ Robert McCloskey

➤ Peggy Parish (Amelia Bedelia)

➤ Shel Silverstein

➤ William Steig

➤ Chris Van Allsberg

If you want to try some children's novels to see how he likes longer, episodic stories, here are some good ones:

➤ Richard and Florence Atwater (*Mr. Popper's Penguins*)

➤ Roald Dahl (*Charlie and the Chocolate Factory, Matilda*)

➤ Astrid Lindgren (*Pippi Longstocking*)

➤ Hugh Lofting (*Dr. Doolittle*)

➤ P.L. Travers (*Mary Poppins*)

➤ E.B. White (*Stuart Little, Charlotte's Web, Trumpeter of the Swan*)

Tell Me a Story!

Storytelling without books may have even greater appeal at four than earlier in your child's life. You can start by telling familiar stories about children, perhaps ones that feature your child as the main character. You can relate a real-life tale or something you make up. Your preschooler also will enjoy hearing stories about you when you were a child. (Relax—you don't necessarily have to stick to the truth, the whole truth, and nothing but the truth. Take poetic license to make the story more interesting or exciting.)

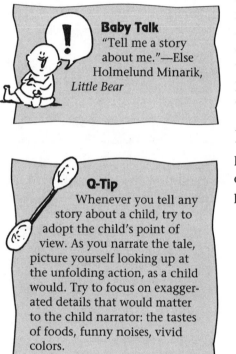

Baby Talk
"Tell me a story about me."—Else Holmelund Minarik, *Little Bear*

Q-Tip
Whenever you tell any story about a child, try to adopt the child's point of view. As you narrate the tale, picture yourself looking up at the unfolding action, as a child would. Try to focus on exaggerated details that would matter to the child narrator: the tastes of foods, funny noises, vivid colors.

After listening to you do all the work of making up and telling stories for several months, your four-year-old might have fun helping you create a new story. You can take one of three different roads in creating stories with your preschooler:

➤ Ask your child to tell you a story. Your preschooler might balk at the idea, but she also might love the opportunity to have your undivided attention. If—and only if—your child seems to need some prompting along the way, ask some questions: "Then what happened?" "Was she sad?" "What did he see there?" (Don't be surprised if your child comes up with much more violent imagery and action in her stories than you would ever include in yours. Your child is merely exploring the power of words.)

➤ Ask your child to supply a few story elements: characters, setting (time and place), or something that happens. (Three to five story elements will work best. Two is too few, while six is too many.) Then, try to tell a story off the top of your head that interweaves these story elements. This kind of cooperative storytelling will not only exercise your child's imagination in making suggestions, but will really exercise your imagination in weaving these elements together into a coherent story.

➤ Start to tell a story and pause near the end of every sentence or two. Encourage your child to fill in the blanks. Your child will in this way take a very active part in inventing the story and in determining in what direction the story will go. This is a great exercise for your child's imagination. It also will help your child improve her listening skills and better understand the context of language. Finally, it also will improve her understanding of logic—or nonsense (which is essentially an inversion of logic).

A typical story of this kind might start something like this:

Once upon a time, a long, long, time ago, there was a…

Fox!

And this fox lived in…

A henhouse!

A henhouse? Hmm. Of course, there were no hens who dared to live with the fox in the henhouse. The hens had all…

Moved to Florida!

Where they worked on their tans and laid brown eggs. One day the fox walked…

Around the henhouse!

Looking for hens, but of course the fox couldn't find any…

Who knows? By working (and playing) with language together, you and your preschooler may make up a story that your child loves more than most children's books.

Q-Tip
Writing down or taping any of the stories you and your child create will lend them extra importance—and provide your child with the opportunity to hear (and admire) her own stories again and again. You no doubt put your child's artwork up on the refrigerator. So why not put her "storywork" on tape?

Baby Talk
"The real menace in dealing with a five-year-old is that in no time at all you begin to sound like a five-year-old."—Jean Kerr

The Least You Need to Know

➤ The computer is not a substitute for other types of play and learning. But it can be a valuable addition as a learning tool.

➤ Choose computer software that features clear sound and colorful, entertaining graphics.

➤ Four-year-olds are not too old for make-believe play. Playing "let's pretend" can contribute to your child's intellectual, emotional, and social growth.

➤ Continue to transport your child to other worlds through reading and storytelling.

Getting Ready for School

Okay, you've almost made it through five years of diapers, toilet training, feeding, caring, nursing through illness, chauffeuring, teaching, and playing. You've kept your child safe and taught her to keep herself safe. You've soothed and placated her worst fears and nightmares. You've struggled to survive (and correct) her sleep problems, misbehavior, and tantrums. You've nurtured a love for learning, a facility for language, and a degree of social grace. You've done your best to raise an independent, friendly, curious, well-rounded, and responsible child.

Congratulations. Your job is almost done. Soon it will be time to turn your child over to the pros. Not really, of course. But that's the way it may feel as your child's fifth birthday—and kindergarten—approaches.

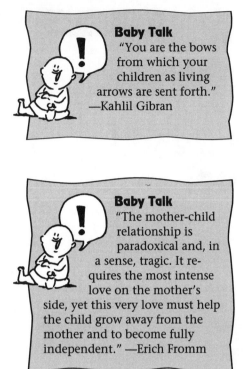

Baby Talk
"You are the bows from which your children as living arrows are sent forth."
—Kahlil Gibran

Baby Talk
"The mother-child relationship is paradoxical and, in a sense, tragic. It requires the most intense love on the mother's side, yet this very love must help the child grow away from the mother and to become fully independent." —Erich Fromm

Starting school will represent a huge milestone for your child—and for you. Even if she attends a full-time day care or preschool program now, your child will look on kindergarten as something completely new and different. You may still drop your child off, as you do at day care, but it will be an entirely new building with many more children (and fewer adults). And you may only need to take her to a bus stop and put her on a bus. Everything will be different. In entering kindergarten, your child will finally be striking out into the world on her own. She will probably find it very exciting—and more than a little scary.

Although you will need to reconcile yourself to your five-year-old's new independence, you won't become entirely obsolete. Indeed, far from it. You will continue to be the kind hands that nurse your child through illness. You will still offer the loving heart that cares for your child and makes sure that she gets enough food, drink, and sleep. You will be the warm chest that comforts your child when she's frightened. And you will be the attentive ear that listens to your child's tales of her day.

Has Preschool Prepared Your Child for Kindergarten?

Preschool can provide an important introduction to the notion of schooling. For many children, preschool provides a "head start" in learning certain academic skills that they will be expected to learn in kindergarten and first grade.

If your child has attended a good preschool program, he will already have some rudimentary knowledge of such concepts as colors, shapes, numbers, and letter recognition (as well as the sounds that different letters produce).

Although the introduction to academic skills can give preschoolers a head start on kindergarten learning, preschool can have an even more important role in preparing kids for school. If your child has been attending preschool, the experience has given him the opportunity to develop social skills in group situations.

Day care or preschool also gave your child the opportunity to develop strong friendships. Preschool provided day-to-day (or every other day, depending on how often your child attended) contact with the same children. Hopefully, this regular contact has allowed certain friendships to build. And his ability to form friendships will go a long way toward making your child's kindergarten experience easier.

Does this mean that if your child hasn't attended a preschool program that he will be socially backward when he first enters kindergarten? Of course not. A child who has had little or no contact with other children his own age may have a more difficult time adjusting to kindergarten. But classes for pre-schoolers (in swimming, gymnastics, dance, crafts, and so on), library reading groups, informal play at local parks, and plenty of playdates—in other words, a preschool program that you've designed and supervised yourself—can offer similar opportunities to practice social skills both in groups and one-on-one.

So if you have made sure that your child has had opportunities to play and learn with other children his age, he will have had plenty of practice at getting along and cooperating with others. And if you've made sure that your preschooler had the opportunity to make close friend-ships by seeing one or two other children on a regular basis, then you can be confident that he will make friends in kindergarten.

> **Q-Tip**
> When you were a child, concepts such as colors, shapes, numbers, and letter recognition were taught in kindergarten. They still are; but today with two-income families and single working parents, children are exposed to these introductory academics in preschool or day-care programs. So if your child hasn't been in a preschool program, he may find himself behind the other children unless you've taken the time to teach him these skills.

Ready or Not, Here I Come: When to Start Kindergarten

School districts around the country vary in their age requirements for starting kindergar-ten. Most suggest that children begin kindergarten in the first autumn after their fifth birthday. Yet your child's age alone is not as important a consideration as her age relative to her other classmates. Because children at this age are still maturing so rapidly, the youngest kid in the class is seldom as socially or emotionally mature as the older kids.

If your child turns five in the late spring or summer, she may have more difficulty adjusting to the changes of kindergarten than someone who will turn six in the late fall or winter. If your child then responds to this difficulty with negative behavior and poor social responses, her classmates may shun her and her self-esteem will plummet.

If you suspect that your child is a "young five" (in terms of maturity, not necessarily age), then you may decide it's best to hold her back a year. If you believe that regardless of her

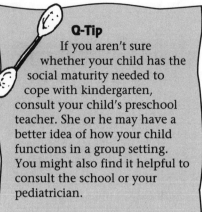

Q-Tip

If you aren't sure whether your child has the social maturity needed to cope with kindergarten, consult your child's preschool teacher. She or he may have a better idea of how your child functions in a group setting. You might also find it helpful to consult the school or your pediatrician.

age relative to her classmates, your child has the social maturity to deal with kindergarten, then by all means enroll her.

Still not sure? You may want to take your child's social, cognitive, and motor skills into account. The following table provides a checklist in each of these three areas. Though your child certainly need not have mastered all of these skills by the time she enters kindergarten, she should have developed at least some of them. You might want to consider waiting a year unless you answer yes to at least a couple of questions in each area.

Table 26.1 Is Your Child Ready for Kindergarten?

Motor Skills

Can your child jump? Hop? Skip?

Can your child handle snaps, buttons, and zippers?

Can your child tie her own shoes?

Can your child use the toilet by herself?

Can—and does—your child wash her own hands?

Social Skills

Does your child help do simple tasks, jobs, or chores around the house?

Can your child participate in group activities?

Will your child (at least sometimes) share with others?

Does your child have one or two close friends?

Does your child make friends easily?

Can your child express her needs clearly to adults other than you?

Can your child control her own behavior much of the time?

Can your child function in a social setting without constant supervision?

Cognitive Skills

Does your child know the names of at least eight colors (red, orange, yellow, green, blue, purple, black, and white) and five shapes (circle, oval, triangle, rectangle, and square)?

Can your child distinguish among different sounds? Can she recognize similar sounds?

Does your child know some simple songs by heart? Can she join in when you teach her a new song?

Can your child listen and follow a story line and then retell it in her own words?

Can your child follow instructions when she's learning a new game or you're introducing a new activity?

In evaluating whether your child is ready for school, remember to take into account all three areas covered in the table above. If your child is very bright, for instance, you may feel tempted to push her into kindergarten early to spare her from the risk of academic boredom. Yet you should also consider her social and physical maturity before making your decision. If your child is not ready socially or unable to keep up physically, then no matter how advanced her cognitive skills are, starting kindergarten early is probably not a good idea.

Is School Ready for Your Child?

Besides considering your child's needs, abilities, and maturity, you also should take the time to evaluate the kindergarten program in your school district. Finding out about your local kindergarten will give you other factors that may help you determine when to enroll your child. Ask the school's principal about:

➤ Class size

➤ The number of teachers and staff per pupil

➤ The use of aides in the classroom

➤ Whether they operate on a half-day or full-day schedule

➤ How much contact your child is likely to have with older children—in the lunchroom, bathroom, playground, and so on

➤ The nature and objectives of the kindergarten's "academic" and social program

All of this information should help you reach the best decision for your own child.

Getting Ready

If you decide to enroll your five-year-old, try to familiarize your child with both the school and his teacher before the first day of school.

You may find it helpful to begin with a visit to the school in June, just before the school year ends. Even if you don't yet know who your child's teacher will be, a visit while school is in session will give your four- or five-year-old a chance to see what kindergartners do in school. If he has a good time during this visit, your child may get excited about going to school there himself.

Next, find out whether your child's school hosts an open house or visiting day in late August, a week or two before school begins. (Many schools do.) If the school does, take advantage of the opportunity to visit the classrooms and meet your child's teacher and the school principal.

Whether your school has an open house or not, you should make a point of going to the school with your child and meeting the principal and your child's teacher before school begins. When you talk to the teacher, try to find out as much as you can about his or her classroom plans for the coming year and his or her kindergarten teaching philosophy in general.

After introducing your child to his teacher and letting him familiarize himself with the classroom, take your child on a tour of the school. Show him the bathroom he will be using, the water fountains, the principal's office, and the gym. Try to choose a sunny day for your tour. That way, you can end your tour by letting your child play on the playground equipment. If your child becomes familiar with the school and his teacher—and sees that you have confidence in them, too—he will be much more likely to feel safe and comfortable there when school does start.

> **Q-Tip**
> If you don't think your child is ready for kindergarten, ask your local board of education or school superintendent whether your school district offers a pre-kindergarten program. Pre-K classes, organized and staffed separately from the kindergarten or elementary school, provide a preschool experience yet often share the same building, grounds, and equipment as the primary school. They usually operate on a half-day schedule. Participation in pre-K programs can be a great way for your child to get used to the idea of going to school.

Competence and Confidence

During your child's last year of preschool or day care, she was among the oldest children there. In kindergarten she will be among the youngest (unless your school district houses its kindergarten in a separate building from the rest of the elementary school). For this reason, your child may need a little boost in her confidence.

Your child's own sense of competence will do more than anything else to keep her level of confidence up. That's why it's important that your child be able to handle at least some of the skills listed in Table 26.1. When you meet with your child's teacher or principal, find out what the typical kindergarten day will consist of. Make sure your child can deal with most of it on her own. If some of the activities will be entirely foreign to her, you may want to use some of the remaining time before school starts—as well as the first few weeks of school—introducing them to her. (You can also use this time to shore up some of the skills from the checklist.)

You also can build your child's confidence by allaying some of her fears, anxieties, and concerns about kindergarten. Start talking about school months before your five-year-old will enter kindergarten. Try to answer as many of her questions as you can. If you don't know the answer to one of your child's questions, contact the school principal or a member of the school's Parent-Teacher Association (PTA) to find out. The questions your child asks about kindergarten address the issues about which she is most concerned. If you can answer or address these concerns to her satisfaction, your child will feel more comfortable and confident about going to school.

What Your Child May Need to Know

The increasing number of young children in preschool means that many children entering kindergarten today have already acquired knowledge and worked on skills that children of your generation did not learn until kindergarten. So, though your child will certainly learn all of the following skills in the school year, you may want to practice some of them even before he begins kindergarten:

➤ Reciting the alphabet or singing the alphabet song

➤ Knowing the colors of the rainbow

➤ Understanding opposites

➤ Counting to ten

Q-Tip
Your child will be at a distinct disadvantage if she cannot yet attend to her personal needs on her own: dressing, feeding herself, going to the bathroom, blowing her nose, even tying shoes. So plan to make it as easy as possible for her to manage on her own. If your child has trouble with zippers, avoid clothes that have zippers. Prepare lunches that she can eat by herself (and don't forget to cut the sandwich just the way she likes it).

Q-Tip
During the summer before your child enters kindergarten, check out books from your local library that tell stories about the first day of school. Your children's librarian can help you find some good ones.

Childproofing

If your child does not yet know his address or phone number, be sure to write it down and put the paper in his pocket or book bag every day. Or give him his own little wallet and put the information inside it.

Baby Talk

"No one has yet fully realized the wealth of sympathy, kindness and generosity hidden in the soul of a child. The effort of every true education should be to unlock that treasure."
—Emma Goldman

➤ Knowing how to count objects (that is, one number per object in sequence with no repeats)

➤ Drawing simple shapes (circle or oval, square or rectangle, triangle)

➤ Drawing a stick figure

➤ Cutting with scissors

➤ Knowing his full name, address, and phone number

➤ Printing his first name

Certainly, you don't need to put pressure on your child to master all of these skills before kindergarten. He will get plenty of practice at them during the school year. But at the same time, it will help if he has some familiarity and practice with these skills. So work on them with your child in a playful way, stopping whenever you see signs of frustration.

If your child is still in a preschool program, let his preschool teacher know what you'd like your child to know before he enters kindergarten. If you find out what your preschool teacher is planning to teach, then you can coordinate your efforts to make sure that all of these skills are covered.

Some children come home from their first day of kindergarten deeply disappointed that they have not yet learned how to read. So try not to build up your child's expectations too high in the months leading up to kindergarten. Let him know in advance that learning will go on throughout the year and that mastering the art of reading, for example, will take some time and effort.

Social Studies

Kindergarten will present your child with a new kind of social situation: a large group of children with relatively few adults. While your four-year-old's preschool class may have 10 to 15 children in a classroom with two teachers and an aide, her kindergarten class will have, at best, one teacher and one aide in a classroom of 20 to 25 children. The child/adult ratio will probably double.

For this reason, it will help if you can introduce your child to social situations involving large numbers of children and encourage her to practice speaking up so that adults can hear her.

Grown-Up Talk

Your child will need to feel relatively comfortable talking to adults other than you to get the most out of her experience with her kindergarten teacher and teacher's aide. So help your child get used to talking and relating to other adults. When any adults visit in the months (or year) before kindergarten begins, ask your child to greet them (or at least to say hello before returning to whatever she's doing). Suggest (without insisting on it) that your child might want to show the guests her room, a prized possession, or a pet.

In addition, encourage your preschooler to talk to adults that you meet during your day-to-day activities together: the librarian, the pediatrician, grocery store clerks, bank tellers. (For advice on talking to strangers, see Chapter 22.) In the safety of your company, talking to the adults your child meets will not serve just as an exercise intended to overcome shyness. It also will provide valuable practice in communicating with adults who don't know your child as well as you do. It may seem a simple matter to you, but your child needs to discover such nuances as:

➤ How to maintain eye contact so that her words are directed toward her intended listener (rather than toward her shoes or in some other direction)

➤ How loudly to speak

➤ How to repeat herself a little louder and more clearly if an adult doesn't quite understand her

➤ How to maintain eye contact to show that she's listening

➤ How to listen to adults

➤ How to ask adults to repeat themselves when she doesn't understand them

If you encourage your child to practice these skills even before she enters kindergarten, she will be better prepared both to speak up in class and to listen to her teacher.

Crowds of Children

The sheer number of children in a kindergarten classroom can overwhelm or intimidate a five-year-old. In kindergarten, your child will be surrounded by 15 (if you're very lucky) to 25 kids, most or all of them unfamiliar to him. And during lunchtime, recess, and assemblies, that number will be much larger.

Your child may feel more comfortable in the class-room if you can find ways to expose him to crowds

Baby Talk
"I wasn't used to children and they were getting on my nerves. Worse, it appeared that I was a child, too. I hadn't known that before; I thought I was just short."
—Florence King

of children in the months leading up to kindergarten. So take your child to places or events that attract crowds of children his own age. Try places like a reading group at your local library, a preschool or a day-care center (if your child does not already attend one), a swimming pool or a beach, an ice cream parlor on a hot summer's day, a circus, a concert for children, a puppet show, or the zoo.

Your child also will feel more comfortable if he has had practice building friendships, so continue to arrange regular playdates. If your child can go into his kindergarten classroom knowing how to make friends, how to share, and how to play together, he will probably enjoy the coming year from the first moment.

> **Baby Talk**
> "As the youngsters grow attached to their teachers and classmates...they can finally say good-bye to their mothers without reenacting the death scene from *Camille*."—Sue Mittenthal

The Least You Need to Know

➤ If your child is not in preschool, make sure you provide her with plenty of playdates and other opportunities to play with children her age.

➤ Make it a point to get to know your child's school and kindergarten teacher before the school year begins.

➤ Do everything you can to make sure your child can attend to her personal needs on her own.

➤ Encourage your child to practice speaking to other adults and try to expose her to large groups of children.

Resources for Parents

Medical Information

General Medical Care

American Academy of Pediatrics
141 Northwest Point Boulevard
P.O. Box 927
Elk Grove Village, IL 60009-0927
(800) 433-9016
FAX: (847) 228-1281
Online: http\\www.aap.org
Provides information and publishes brochures on children's health issues

American Podiatric Medical Association
9312 Old Georgetown Road
Bethesda, MD 20814
(800) FOOTCARE
Publishes brochure on caring for children's feet

American Red Cross
431 18th Street NW
Washington, D.C. 20006
(202) 737-8300
Online: http:\\www.redcross.org
Offers courses in CPR (cardiopulmonary resuscitation) for infants and children, as well as other parenting classes. Please contact your local Red Cross chapter.

La Leche League International
9616 Minneapolis Avenue
P.O. Box 1209
Franklin Park, IL 60131
(800) LALECHE
Online: http:\\www.lalecheleague.org
Provides information and support to nursing mothers

The National Association of Children's Hospitals and Related Institutions
401 Wythe Street
Alexandria, VA 21314
(703) 684-1355
FAX: (703) 684-1589
Provides information on children's hospitals

National Health Information Center
P.O. Box 1133
Washington, DC 20013-1133
(800) 336-4797
Online: http:\\nhic-nt.health.org
Provides publications and referrals on health and medical questions

Nursing Mothers Counsel, Inc.
P.O. Box 500063
Palo Alto, CA 94303
(408) 272-1448
Online: http:\\www.nursingmothers.org
Provides information and assistance to nursing mothers

Specific Medical Conditions

American Diabetes Association
P.O. Box 25757
1660 Duke Street
Alexandria, VA 22314
(800) ADA-DISC
In Virginia and Washington, DC: (703) 549-1500
FAX: (703) 549-6995
Online: http:\\www.diabetes.org

Asthma and Allergy Foundation
Consumer Information Line
1125 15th Street NW
Suite 502
Washington, DC 20005
(800) 7-ASTHMA
FAX: (202) 466-8940

Children and Adults with Attention Deficit Disorders (CH.A.D.D.)
499 NW 70th Avenue
Suite 109
Plantation, FL 33317
(800) 233-4050
FAX: (954) 587-4599
Online: http:\\www.chadd.org

Cystic Fibrosis Foundation
6931 Arlington Road #200
Bethesda, MD 20814
(800) FIGHT-CF
FAX: (301) 951-6378
Online: http:\\www.cff.org

Epilepsy Foundation of America
4351 Garden City Drive
Landover, MD 20785
(800) 332-1000
In Maryland: (301) 459-3700
FAX: (301) 577-4941
Online: http:\\www.efa.org

Juvenile Diabetes Association
432 Park Avenue South
New York, NY 10016
(800) 223-1138
In New York City: (212) 889-7575
Online: http:\\www.jdfcure.com

Sickle Cell Disease Association of America
200 Corporate Point
Suite 495
Culver City, CA 90230
(800) 421-8453

Child Safety

Consumer Product Safety Commission
Publication Request
Washington, DC 20207
(800) 638-CPSC
In Maryland: (800) 492-8104
FAX: (301) 504-0051
Online: http:\\www.cpsc.gov
Establishes and monitors safety standards for children's products; provides safety information and lists of recalled products

The National Safe Kids Campaign
111 Michigan Avenue, NW
Washington, DC 20010
(202) 662-0600
Online: http:\\www.safekids.org
Provides publications on child safety and childproofing

Telephone Hotlines

Child Help USA (National Child Abuse Hotline)
(800) 4-A-CHILD
Provides advice and help to end child abuse

National Lead Information Council
(800) LEADFYI
Offers pamphlets on lead and lead poisoning
(800) 424-LEAD
Answers questions about lead and lead poisoning
Online: http://www.hud.gov/lea/leahome.html

Helping with Grief

Children's Hospice International
700 Princess Street, LL
Alexandria, VA 22314
(800) 24-CHILD
FAX: (703) 684-0226
Online: http:\\www.chionline.org
Provides information on hospice care and resources for terminally ill children

The Compassionate Friends
P.O. Box 3696
Oak Brook, IL 60522
(630) 990-0010
Online: http:\\pages.prodigy.com\CA\lycq97a\lycq97tcf.html
Offers support to families who have experienced the death of a child

The Good Grief Program
Boston Medical Center
One Boston Medical Center Place—MAT5
Boston, MA 02118
(617) 534-4005
FAX: (617) 534-7915
Offers publications, resources, and training programs for schools and health-care providers to help children through bereavement

The Rainbow Connection
477 Hannah Branch Road
Burnsville, NC 28714
(704) 675-5909
FAX: (704) 675-9687
Offers publications and resources to help children cope with death

Intellectual Stimulation

The American Reading Council
45 John Street
Suite 811
New York, NY 10038
Provides manuals on how to encourage your children to become readers

Public Media Inc.
5547 North Ravenswood Ave.
Chicago, IL 60640
(800) 343-4312
Offers two titles in the Buy Me That! video series that will help your child become more aware of commercial advertising tricks.

Ambrose Video Publishing
28 West 44th St.
Suite 2100
New York, NY 10036
(800) 526-4663
Offers Buy Me That, Too!, one of a three-video series produced by *Consumer Reports* to increase children's awareness of how commercials work.

Selected Child Mail-Order Companies

Toys

Back to Basics Toys
2707 Pittman Drive
Silver Spring, MD 20910-1807
(800) 356-5360

Childcraft
Box 29149
Mission, KS 66201
(800) 631-5657

Constructive Playthings
1227 East 119th Street
Grandview, MO 64030
(800) 832-0572

F.A.O. Schwarz
3342 Melrose Avenue NW
Roanoke, VA 24017
(800) 426-8697

Just for Kids!
Box 29141
Shawnee, KS 66201-9141
(800) 825-6565

Sensational Beginnings
987 Stewart Road
Box 2009
Monroe, MI 48161
(800) 444-2147

Toys to Grow On
Box 17
Long Beach, CA 90801
(800) 542-8338

Troll Learn & Play
100 Corporate Drive
Mahwah, NJ 07498-1053
(800) 247-6106

Books, Music, and Videos

Chinaberry Book Service
2780 Via Orange Way
Suite B
Spring Valley, CA 91978
(800) 776-2242

Critic's Choice Video
Box 749
Itasca, IL 60143-0749
(800) 367-7765

Gryphon House Early Childhood Book Catalog
Box 207
Beltsville, MD 20704
(800) 638-0928

HearthSong
6519 N. Galena Road
Box 1773
Peoria, IL 61656-1773
(800) 325-2502

The Video Catalog
Box 64267
St. Paul, MN 55164-0267
(800) 733-2232

Clothes

After the Stork
1501 12th Street, NW
Box 26200
Albuquerque, NM 87104-6200

Biobottoms
Box 6009
Petaluma, CA 94955-6009
(800) 766-1254

Hanna Andersson
1010 NW Flanders
Portland, OR 97209
(800) 222-0544

Olsen's Mill Direct
1641 S. Main Street
Box 2266
Oshkosh, WI 54901-6988
(800) 537-4979

Playclothes
Box 29137
Overland Park, KS 66201-9137
(800) 362-7529

Equipment, Paraphernalia, and Other Products

New York Babyproofing
(212) 362-1262
Provides childproofing products

One Step Ahead
Box 517
Lake Bluff, IL 60044
(800) 274-8440
Specializes in baby and toddler safety items

Perfectly Safe
7245 Whipple Avenue, NW
North Canton, OH 44720
(800) 837-5437
Specializes in childproofing products

Right Start
Right Start Plaza
5334 Sterling Center Drive
Westlake Village, CA 91361
(800) 548-8531
Offers everything from health and safety items to toys and clothes

The Safety Zone
Hanover, PA 17333-0019
(800) 999-3030
Specializes in childproofing products

Index